WESTERN MUSIC

TO 1750

KING DAVID PLAYING THE HARP (SEE P. 24)

A SURVEY OF

WESTERN MUSIC

TO 1750

by

S. B. POTTER

GAMUT MUSIC COMPANY
P.O BOX 474, DEDHAM, MA 02026

Printed in the USA
All rights reserved
Copyright © Gamut Music Company 1993
P.O. Box 454, Dedham, MA 02026
ISBN: 910648-05-0

To My Wife

CONTENTS

Greek music - Greek Music Theory: Writers on Theory; Doctrine of ethos. Instruments: Stringed Instruments; Wind Instruments. Forms: Paean; Nome; Dithyramb; The Dirge; Choric Dances; Lighter Songs; Choral Odes. The Later Music. The Notation of Greek Music: Rhythmic Notation; Rhythm and Ethos. Influences.
The Roman legacy - Instruments;Characteristics; Function.
The Hebrew Legacy -   Performance.
Highlights of the chapter -   Check list for review. List of scores. Chronological chart.

Social background - Historical. Division of the Roman Empire; Rise of Christianity; The Papacy.
Beginnings of Christian chant - Early Christian Practices; Early Christian Figures.
Branches of Chant - Syrian Chant; Byzantine Chant; Other Middle Eastern Chant; Russian Chant. Western chant: Ambrosian Chant; Gallican Chant; Mozarabic Chant.
Gregorian chant - General Characteristics; Sources; Relation to Pope Gregory; Terminology; Structure of the Liturgy; Evolution of the Liturgy; Rhythmic Considerations; The Church Modes; Solmisation; Classifications of Chant. Psalmody: Antiphonal Psalmody; Responsorial Psalmody; Direct Psalmody; Performance. Non-psalmodic chants: Ordinary of the Mass; The Hymn.

Highlights of the chapter - Check list for review. List of scores. Chronological chart.

Background of the Baroque - The Age of Reason; The Age of Absolutism; The Age of the Baroque: Emotional Effects; Uniting of the Arts; Space.

Baroque Music - Thoroughbass; Affective Representation; Instrumental Music; Harmonic Styles; Performance Media; Traditional Harmony; Rhythm; Sources of Baroque Music; Divisions of the Baroque; The Baroque Legacy.

Early Baroque vocal music - Accompanied Monody: Prototypes: The First Opera: Collections of Monody: Monody in Sacred Music: Vocal Polyphony: Polychoral Motet.

Claudio Monteverdi - Operas:; Madrigals; Sacred Music.

Summary. Check list for review. List of scores. Chronological chart.

Forms and styles - The Aria; Recitative; Dramatic Forms; Oratorio; Cantata.

Germany - The Chorale: Chorale Motets; The Chorale Concertato. The Free Concertato. Heinrich Schütz: Biography; Music; Schütz's Style.

France - Ballet; Opera; Lully; Church Music: Charpentier.

LIST OF MUSICAL EXAMPLES

LIST OF ILLUSTRATIONS

***

Preface

This book is intended for use as a text book in a one
semester course covering the period indicated. It assumes
some knowledge of music reading. It aims to relate musical
styles and forms to the cultural periods in which they occur
and to explain some characteristics of the music which might
otherwise seem puzzling to the cultural milieu in which they
arise. Thus, the mixture of the sacred and secular in the
Gothic motet relates to the interpenetration of the sacred and
secular in the late Gothic period. The mixture of texts from
different religious denominations (Catholic, High Episcopal
and Puritan) found in English Renaissance music can be
related to the aims of Elizabeth I in mediating between the
various denominations in order to preserve the nation.

Some notes concerning periods: Though the main divisions
between periods is recognized by most musicologists and
historians in general, the internal division of the periods may
differ. It is perfectly legitimate for the student to recognize that
such classifications are not immutable. It is also true that
geographical as well as chronological considerations play a
role in the determination of cultural periods. Thus, when an
editor comments that Huizinga in his book *The Waning of the
Middle Ages* proved that Burckhardt's thesis on the emergence
of the Renaissance is wrong, he neglects the influence of the

geographical on each man's approach. Huizinga was writing about the last vestiges of Medieval culture in Burgundy, while Burckhardt was discussing the emergence of the Renaissance in the Italian City States. The paleo-anthropologist Louis Leakey also makes a valid point in noting that a period is marked by the emergence of new forms rather than the persistence of old. Thus, while we have electric lights we still occasionally light candles.

The sources used in writing the book are those listed in the bibliography, though detailed documentation is not used. Facsimiles are taken from a 15th century Italian ms. in the Hebrew Union College reproduced in Idelsohn's *Jewish Music in its Historical Development;* Sebastian Virdung's *Musica getutscht,* reproduced in *Akademische Druck-u. Verlangsanstalt,* Graz, Austria; the Kyrie from Machault's Mass in the printed version of Johannes Wolf's *Geschichte der Mensural-Notation von 1250-1460;* the Ms. of Hildegarde von Bingen reproduced by Herman Baeten, Peer, Belgium, and facsimiles from *Musica Enchiriadis* and *Codex Calixtinus* reproduced in Apel's *Notation of Polyphonic Music.* Sources are indicated at each illustration. The picture illustrations are all re-drawn by the author.

Music examples are referenced using abbreviations, e.g. HAM1 (Historical Anthology of Music, Vol I) or NAWM1 (Norton Anthology of Western Music, Vol I) to indicate the source. A list of abbreviations is to be found on page 407.

Left: Woman playing the double aulos, from the so-called Ludovisi Throne (Museo delle Terme, Rome), c. 460 B.C., after Pischel, World History of Art. The aulos was characteristically a double reed instrument, like the oboe, and generally played in pairs, as in the illustration.

Right: Singer with kithara, from an Athenian vase in the Museum of Fine Arts, Boston, c. 480 B.C., after The New Oxford History of Music, Vol 1, Ancient and Oriental Music, ed., Egon Wellesz.

וַיֹּאמֶר שְׁמוּאֵל אֶל שָׁאוּל אֹתִי שָׁלַח יְיָ לִמְשָׁחֲךָ לְמֶלֶךְ
עַל עַמּוֹ עַל יִשְׂרָאֵל וְעַתָּה שְׁמַע לְקוֹל דִּבְרֵי יְיָ
כֹּה אָמַר יְיָ צְבָאוֹת פָּקַדְתִּי אֵת אֲשֶׁר עָשָׂה עֲמָלֵק לְיִשְׂרָאֵל
אֲשֶׁר שָׂם לוֹ בַּדֶּרֶךְ בַּעֲלֹתוֹ מִמִּצְרָיִם עַתָּה לֵךְ וְהִכִּיתָה אֶת עֲמָלֵק
וְהַחֲרַמְתֶּם אֶת כָּל אֲשֶׁר לוֹ וְהֵמַתָּה מֵאִישׁ וְעַד אִשָּׁה מֵעֹלֵל וְעַד
יוֹנֵק מִשּׁוֹר וְעַד שֶׂה מִגָּמָל וְעַד חֲמוֹר וַיְשַׁמַּע שָׁאוּל אֶת הָעָם
וַיִּפְקְדֵם בַּטְּלָאִים מָאתַיִם אֶלֶף רַגְלִי וַעֲשֶׂרֶת אֲלָפִים אֶת אִישׁ יְהוּדָה
וַיָּבֹא שָׁאוּל עַד עִיר עֲמָלֵק וַיָּרֶב בַּנָּחַל וַיֹּאמֶר שָׁאוּל אֶל הַקֵּינִי לְכוּ

Text from the Prophets (1 Samuel 15:1-6) from a 15th century Italian MS in the Hebrew Union College Library, after Idelsohn, *Jewish Music in its Historical Development*. Shown are the ta'amim (accents) and vowel signs of the Masoretes.

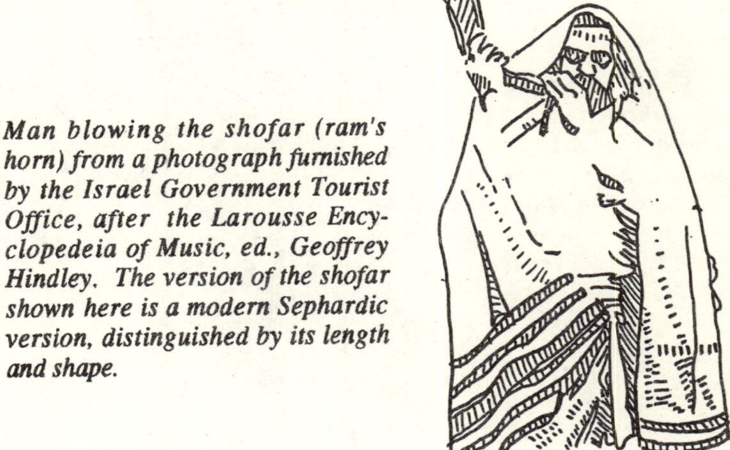

Man blowing the shofar (ram's horn) from a photograph furnished by the Israel Government Tourist Office, after the Larousse Encyclopedeia of Music, ed., Geoffrey Hindley. The version of the shofar shown here is a modern Sephardic version, distinguished by its length and shape.

CHAPTER I

LEGACY OF THE ANCIENT WORLD

ORIGINS OF MUSIC

Our knowledge of ancient music stems from two methods of procedure: (1) historical research and (2) ethno-musicology which looks at the survival of ancient musical practices in societies that are still in existence. The materials of historical research include literary and pictorial references, surviving examples of musical instruments, and the rare instances of ancient musical notation of which the ancient Greeks provide us with the only examples that can be unequivocally deciphered.

Concerning origins, one may speculate that the first undifferentiated sounds made by the human species evolved into speech and music as man organized his sound-world into media of communications and expression. Organization of movement into a form of expression became dance.

Stepwise melodic movement organized in terms of the simplest frequency ratios produce scales such as the anhemitone pentatonic scale (c-d-e-g-a. It can also be obtained by playing the black keys on the piano.) This pentatonic scale is found widely dispersed in almost all ancient cultures as well as surviving folk-song. It is found in China, Polynesia, Africa, Bali, and also among the American Indians, Celts and Scots. Western cowboy songs and Negro spirituals include examples of it.

Instrumental music emerged from the sounds produced by daily activities, such as the chipping of stone tools; the scraping of hides; the twang of a bow; the tapping on an animal skin stretched across a hollow place to dry. Ancient instruments included percussion used as accompaniment to the dance. Stones and stone chimes were the ancestors of bells. In almost all stone age cultures scrapers were found. Convex scrapers were used to prepare skins for clothing. *Homo Erectus,* in spreading around the world, had to deal with varying climatic conditions; thus the preparation of hides for clothing must be among the most basic activities of the hunting-and-gathering cultures. The drying of hides over a hollow became the origin of the drum.

Drums are to be found in all hunting-and-gathering cultures where they are used for communication as well as music. They are among the oldest and most widespread instruments. The bow and arrow made its appearance at the end of the last Ice Age, ca 12,000 years ago. Bone flutes have been found in scattered places associated with farming-and-herding (Neolithic) cultures .

The emergence of music as an art form was preceded by its use in ritual and with magical associations. Rattles and scrapers had magical associations.   Imitation of animal sounds were an ingredient of primitive rites, where they represented mythical ancestors (totems). We can observe man in surviving hunting-and-gathering (Paleolithic) cultures using music and dance in connection with magical rites and incantations. Among the Ancient Greeks music emerged from the worship of Apollo, and significant musical and dramatic forms emerged from the ceremonies of Dionysus. The oldest surviving music with a continuous traceable tradition is the liturgical chant of the Hebrews; and in Western Civilization, the oldest music is the liturgical chant of the Catholic Church.

The Ancient Greeks were the first to study musical sound as a natural phenomenon. They noted the effect on pitch of dividing a string length into halves, thirds, fourths, etc.

With the decline in the power and authority of the Roman Empire the influences of ancient civilization faded from Western Europe, and life reverted to a more primitive state. The removal of the capital of the empire to the East by the emperor Diocletian only underscored an existing situation. At the same time, a new force began to assert itself and establish its authority over the barbarian peoples whose influx into Europe had toppled the empire. That force was the Church, and it laid the groundwork for a new civilization. Christianity was granted official recognition in 313 by the Byzantine Roman Emperor Constantine the Great, Diocletian's successor; and from that time forward its influence spread rapidly throughout Europe. It is with the rise of this power that the history of Western Civilization begins. Because the capital of the Roman Empire had been moved to the East, an administrative void was left in the West that the Roman church came to fill.

GREEK MUSIC

To this new civilization, gradually and painfully emerging from barbarianism, the Ancient World bequeathed a legacy of art, literature, philosophy, and science that have had profound influence on the thinkers of the New World. The *Iliad* and the *Odyssey*, attributed to Homer, (c. 700 B.C.) are tales of the Trojan War and its aftermath and refer to events of the Mycenean period, c. 1200 B.C. Many of the plays of the Classical period were based on legends of the Trojan War, and the influence of these legends extends to the present day in literature and music and play an important role in opera texts from Monteverdi (17th century) to Richard Strauss (20th century).

But what of music? Innumerable literary references attest to the powerful role which this art played in ancient culture. It is the only art whose name is derived directly from the Muses. In his *Republic*, Plato subjected music to strict regulation because of its importance and said that when the modes of music change, the fundamental laws of the state change. Yet, there remain only a few scattered fragments of Greek music, and of Roman music not a single note. The fragments that have been uncovered were unknown in the Middle Ages. In the Late Renaissance two *Hymns to the Muse*, a *Hymn to the Sun*, and a *Hymn to Nemesis* were printed (1583) by Vincenzo Galilei, father of the astronomer Galileo. The Skolion of Seikilos was discovered in 1883, and two *Delphic Hymns to Apollo* were discovered in 1893. All in all some twenty pieces survive.

In classical times music was closely linked to poetry and with the dance as well. Separation of poetry and melody seems not to have taken place until the time of the Romans. The term *music* thus had a broader meaning for the ancient Greeks than for us, since it included text and dance movements as well as melody. Greek music was predominantly vocal and monophonic. Instrumental accompaniment was limited to duplication of the melodic line with occasional dissenting tones - a procedure known as *heterophony* to distinguish it from true polyphony. Music was one of the areas of competition in the great games, such as the Olympic and Pythian games, and it also played a significant role in the drama. The tragedies of the great playwrights, such as Aeschylus, Sophocles, and Euripides, employed both music and speech, as did the comedies of Aristophanes. Originally, the choruses of Greek plays were sung, and there were also parts for solo voice; but, since examples of the music itself were lost to later ages, the influence of the Greeks in music was limited to theory.

Greek Music Theory

Greek theories were of two types: (1) esthetic, involving the emotional and social aspects of music; and (2) technical, involving scale structures and interval ratios. The esthetic theories were embodied in the doctrine of *ethos*. This doctrine, along with the mystical theory of numbers and the music of the spheres, had its roots in Mesopotamia and was introduced into Greece by Pythagoras. It had its most comprehensive treatment in Plato, but it was also treated extensively by Aristotle. These doctrines were also discussed by the Neo-Platonists and were passed on to the medieval world in the writings of Boethius. Some basic contributions to acoustical theory also came to Greece by way of Mesopotamia and the Pythagoreans. As far as we know, the first peoples to develop the concept of a music scale were the ancient Greeks.

Writers on Theory

Our chief source of information on scale structures is Aristoxenus, a disciple of Aristotle and the most important writer on musical practice in the Ancient World. The famous mathematician, Ptolemy of Alexandria, was also an important writer on scale structures. Our knowledge of the notation of Greek music comes from a lesser figure named Alypios (c. 360 A.D.).

Doctrine of ethos

According to the doctrine of *ethos*, music imitates emotional and mental states and can thus evoke these states in the listener. From this it follows that music has the power of forming character and should be studied with a view towards education, catharsis (purification of character), and intellectual enjoyment. The means that music uses to produce its effects are melody, rhythm, and instruments. Melody was organized into a system of scales (*tonoi*) named after various ethnic groups of the Greek world. Rhythm depended largely on text. The chief instruments were the *aulos,* (a double reed instrument like the oboe) and the lyre (a plucked stringed instrument of which there were two main types).

The *ethos* association of the scales depended not upon mode in the modern sense, but upon the location of a main note (the *mese*) as to whether it was high or low in the range of the melody. It must be assumed that the position of the *mese* had influence on the design of the melody. The *mese* could fall on one of seven positions in the scale. The middle position was that of the Dorian *mese*, the mean between the extremes. The Dorian mode was of moderate and settled temper, grave and manly; it was associated with Apollo. The Phrygian, with a *mese* one tone higher, was of quite different character. It inspired enthusiasm and was exciting and emotional. It was the mode of Dionysus, the dithyramb, and the Bacchic revels which were the roots of the drama. The *mese* of the Lydian mode was one tone higher again. The Lydian was gentle and relaxed. The scale with the highest keynote was the Mixolydian, sad and grave, considered suitable for lamentation or wailing. The Dorian and Phrygian were the most important, and the only ones that survived the 5th century B.C. They represented the two esthetic poles: classic (Dorian) and romantic (Phrygian).

The modern concept of mode seems to correspond to the tetrachord (the interval of a fourth) which could be filled in different ways. The diatonic tetrachord used the modern tones and semitones and emerged to dominance in the later stages of Greek culture.

The *aulos* was associated with Dionysus and the lyre-type instruments with Apollo. A corollary of the doctrine of *ethos* was that the various elements must be properly combined to produce their effect. Aristotle reports that when Philoxenus attempted to compose a dithyramb in the Dorian scale,he found it impossible and fell back, by the very nature of things, into the appropriate Phrygian

Ethos treated of the whole universe as being an orderly and harmonious system organized by number, which was common to all things. Music was a microcosm. The seven scales were linked with the planetary system. The Pythagoreans understood the relationship between the ratio of string lengths and the size of musical intervals, and this, also, became part of their numerology.

The two most important types of *ethos* were the Apollonian and the Dionysian. It was these two which to later ages became the prototype of the aesthetic concepts of classicism and romanticism. The Apollonian exalted the qualities of clarity, balance, restraint, simplicity, repose, temperance, and moderation. It enthroned beauty and grace. The sculptors of the Apollonian ethos sought the ideal proportions of the human body by using champion athletes as models for the gods. The Dionysian *ethos* was unrestrained, fantastic, emotional, orgiastic. Dionysus was the god of the vine. The most famous statue embodying this principle was the Laocoön group with its tortured dramatic treatment.

It is interesting to contemplate that the periods usually associated with the Classical, Apollonian spirit have been characterized socially by war, revolution, and upheaval, though not necessarily lacking in commercial prosperity. Thus, the Periclean Age itself saw the Persian wars, followed by the disastrous war with Sparta. During this time the greatest creations of Classical Greece took place. The Italian Renaissance was the time of Macchiavelli, the Borgias, and the rule by *condottieri*. (mercenary soldiers). The creations of Leonardo da Vinci and the great Renaissance composer Josquin des Prez, whose creative career was spent in Italy, took place during this time. The Viennese Classical period, the period of Haydn and Mozart, took place during the time of the American and French revolutions. The neo-Classic works of the 20th century were created during the period of Hitler, Mussolini, and World War II.

Instruments

Stringed Instruments

The two cults had their characteristic instruments. Lyre-type instruments (plucked strings, like a harp) were associated with Apollo. This group included the *phorminx*, the *lyra*, and the *kithara*. The phorminx was the oldest of the lyres and dates back to Homeric times. In Classical times the lyra was the instrument of amateurs while the kithara[1] was a larger and more sturdily constructed form of lyre designed for professional use. These instruments had a sound box from whose sides two arms were extended. Across the ends of the arms was a bar, and the strings stretched across the sound box and were attached to this bar. The sound box of the lyra had a bowl-shaped back and a flat front like the mandolin or lute. The kithara had a sound box that consisted of a flat top and bottom connected by sides in the manner of a guitar or violin.

Wind Instruments

The aulos[2] was the instrument of the Dionysian cult. It was a double reed instrument, and thus of the oboe family. Its sound was much more powerful and penetrating than that of the flute with which it had been identified at one time. Since the drama evolved from the Dionysian rites, the aulos was favored in connection with dramatic performances. It was also the military instrument of ancient Greece. Auloi were frequently used in pairs, played by a single performer. In such cases the cheeks of the performer were supported by a leather band with holes through which the mouthpieces of the auloi were inserted.

An instrument which seems actually to have been of the flute family was the syrinx or panpipes. It was a set of pipes bound together, each of which had a different pitch. The player moved the instrument as he played so that the breath went through the desired holes successively in the manner of a modern harmonica. The syrinx was associated with the shepherd and the pastoral milieu. Plato, though he disapproved of the *aulos* linked as it was with the rites of

---

[1] See illustration, p. xix

[2] See illustration, p. xix

Dionysus, nevertheless permitted the shepherd his pipes in the country.

Forms

Paean

From Homeric times, the form associated with Apollo was the paean. *Paean* was the ancient name for Apollo in his role as healer, and the form with this name was probably derived from a primitive healing rite. It later became a hymn or choral song in praise of Apollo and seems to have included dancing as well.

Nome

The word *nome* was used to distinguish a sung performance from a recitation. Often, the nome was a narrative. *Nome* literally means law, and the term law as applied to it probably referred to a set of melodic formulae or melody types. It was a sectional form, and among its manifestations are found examples of program music (instrumental imitations of sounds connected with a story). Performance was by a soloist, usually with the accompaniment of the kithara (kitharoedic nome) although the aulos was also used. While it could be on any subject, an invocation to Apollo was a required part of every nome. A special genre, the Pythian nome, was on the set subject of Apollo's triumph over the Python, or dragon. The nome was used as a contest piece in some of the great games of antiquity.

The name of the kitharist Terpander of Lesbos (c. 675 B.C.), considered the founder of Greek Classical music, was associated with the nome. In the following century Sakadas won a victor's wreath at the games (586 B.C.) with his *Pythian Nome* for the aulos. A kitharoedic nome by Timotheus of Miletos (c. 400 B. C.), entitled *The Persians,* described the victory of the Greeks at Salamis and used sound effects in the description. Timotheus was known as a musical iconoclast. Kitharoedic nomes were also attributed to as late a figure as Mesomedes of Crete (c. 130 A. D.).

Dithyramb

The dithyramb had its origins around the 6th century B. C. and was the form associated with the worship of Dionysus. It was a choric song accompanied by dancing and performed by men and boys in a circular grouping; the singing was accompanied by the aulos. In the beginning the dithyramb recounted the birth of Dionysus, but later it departed from its original subject matter and became the source from which the drama developed. In structure it made use of strophic organization (repetition of music with changed text), a procedure which influenced the music of the drama as well as the odes of Pindar, and was the prototype of the bar-form (a a b). The bar-form was used by the minnesingers and meistersingers in the Middle Ages. (note: *The Star-spangled Banner* is in bar-form, as is the *Preislied* in Wagner's *Die Meistersinger von Nürnberg*).

The Dirge

The dirge also made use of the aulos and was, in the Greece of Classical times, a genre of violent emotional outpouring. The dirges for Linus (the Linus-song) and Adonis had their origins in Asia. (The word *Adonis* is related to the Hebrew word for The Lord *[Adonai]* and the Adonis story has its counterpart in Sumerian mythology).

Choric Dances

Choric dances were especially cultivated in Sparta. They included the *pyrriche*, a sword dance of rapid tempo; the *gymnopedeia*, ceremonial dances based on the movements of wrestling and danced unclothed by young men; and the *parthenia*, dances of the Spartan virgins.

Lighter Songs

There were also songs of lighter content showing, perhaps, the influence of folk-song. There were work-songs of folk origin, and there were songs for convivial occasions. Among the latter were the *skolia*, sung at a feast after wine to the accompaniment of the aulos. They were sung by guests and sometimes dealt with political subjects. The *Skolion of Seikilos* (the Sicilian) is among the few surviving pieces of ancient Greek music. It dates from c. 200 B. C. and was found engraved on a tombstone in Turkey near Tralles in Asia Minor. The earliest known figure associated with the lighter, more intimate music, was Archilochus of Paros (7th century B. C.), a performer on the lyre. A later school of light lyric song arose in Lesbos in the late 6th century B. C. with Sappho, Alkaios, and Anakreon. Sappho is considered one of the great poets of all time. Anakreon wrote of love and drinking parties in a brilliant if superficial manner.

Choral Odes

Choral odes in honor of the victors at the Panhellenic games (*epinikian odes*) were the productions for which Pindar (522-448 B. C.) was noted. He was a professional musician who made his living by composing choral odes to order. These odes included dancing, singing, and performance on wind and stringed instruments, and were intended for performance at court under an aristocratic patronage. The choral ode was displaced in the 5th century B. C. by the emerging drama.

The Later Music

At the end of the 5th and beginning of the 4th centuries B.C. a new emphasis on virtuosity, sophistication, and exaggerated effects encroached upon the classic serenity of the old melodies. The carefully wrought distinctions between the various types of music began to break down. Instruments, such as the kithara and aulos, which were formerly kept apart by their ethos, were now combined in performance. The aulos superseded the kithara as the most important instrument. All this produced an esthetic revolution which shocked the conservatives and evoked stinging criticism from such playwrights as Aristophanes. A leading figure in the new school was the aforementioned Timotheus of Miletos. His art aroused great controversy with both public acclaim and critical disapproval, but it also marked the emergence of music as an independent art.

The pantomime became the last important form in the declining phases of Hellenistic culture. Music and dancing definitely superseded the words in importance. Music declined from its former place of high esteem to become associated with theatrical shows and banquets where it served to accompany performance of dancing girls. This decline in the status of practical music, in addition to the fact that the only written legacies of the Greeks were their scales and theoretical works, caused the theorist to be held in higher esteem than the musician or composer in the Middle Ages. The composer, indeed, was thought of as a mere craftsman.

The Notation of Greek Music

In spite of the fact that we have knowledge of a music notation, the repertory of Greek music available to us is pitifully small. The notation was used chiefly for theoretical purposes and was applied to practical music only incidentally. Written music was not part of the main corpus of Greek literature. Instrumental performers are never shown reading music in any of the surviving visual representations. There is one example in pictorial art of a singer reading from a scroll, but there is no evidence that the scroll contained music notation and was not simply a text.

Our information about Greek notation comes from late sources (in the 3rd and 4th centuries A. D.), of which the most important is Alypios. Signs which he elucidated are found in musical fragments dating back to 250 B. C. He presented two notations, one of which he called vocal, the other, instrumental. Both use letters of the alphabet and are based on a diatonic series of notes. Each note has a sharped and a double-sharped version, both of which are formed by tilting the original letter to different positions.

Rhythmic Notation

The rhythm of Greek music generally followed the rhythm of the poetic meters quite closely so that rhythmic notation, though available, was hardly necessary. The rhythm of Classical Greek poetry was not accentual, as ours is, but rather quantitative. That is, long syllables were actually sustained for a longer period of time instead of being accented. Some of the most important verse meters were:

iambic (Short,Long)	dactylic (L,S,S)
anapestic (S,S,L)	spondaic (L,L)
pyrrhic (S,S)	paion or cretic
trochaic (L,S)	(quintuple)

Rhythm and Ethos

The various rhythms were embodied in the doctrine of *ethos*. Plato writes of the properties of meanness, insolence, fury, or noble feelings that could be ascribed to these rhythms. He says that both the rhythm and the scale (*harmonia*) are governed by the words. He praises simplicity in rhythm and mentions the Cretic rhythm as being complex.

Influences

Quantitative poetry survived in Greek and Roman usage until about the 3rd century A. D. when it gave way to the accentual. However, the quantitative principle was revived later in the Middle Ages (c. the 12th century) with the Goliards, and some of the earliest measured music seems to have gotten its rhythm from poetry. Knowledge of Greek sources came to Western Europe in the 12th century through Moslem Spain, in Arabic translations. It is possible that the Arabs had a rhythmic system that anticipated that of the Europeans. The knowledge of the Greek language had faded from Europe, not to be revived until the fall of Byzantium (1453) brought Greek scholars to the West. Interest in quantitative poetry revived again in the 16th century when it was applied to settings of the Horatian odes in a rhythm governed by poetic meter. The practice, initiated by Konrad Celtis, a professor at the University of Ingolstadt, was applied by the French to their own language later in the century in the *vers mesuré a l'antique* and then to music in the *chanson mesurée*.

THE ROMAN LEGACY

The dividing line between Greek and Roman art is not always clearly drawn, and the same applies to music. No examples of Roman music have come down to us, though literary references point to lively musical activity around the 1st century A. D.

Instruments

Most of our information about Roman music concerns instruments. The Romans had instruments of the brass family, most of which came to them by way of the Etruscans.

These were military instruments. From the Greek world came the *aulos* (called *tibia* by the Romans); and a special form of it, the *Phrygian pipes* (called by Horace *tibia Berecynthia*), came to Rome with the cult of the Great Mother (Magna Mater) from Phrygia in the late 3rd century B. C. A type of organ, the *hydraulis* , became important in Imperial times and was used in the arena with gladiatorial shows. The lyra was less important among the Romans than it had been among the Greeks, and the kithara became heavier in construction. It was still the instrument of the soloist. There were other instruments as well; among them bagpipes and percussion instruments such as cymbals, bells, and tambourines.

Characteristics

Rhythm seems to have developed new aspects in the Roman era, and it is possible that Roman music had regularly recurring accents like our own traditional music. As for melody, it was recognized as an entity in itself, separate from the words. Virtuosity in solo performance was much admired. The emperor Nero aspired to recognition as a professional musician though such aspirations by a monarch were frowned upon as being socially unacceptable. Amateurs also cultivated music. As among the Greeks, musicians are always depicted in the visual arts as playing without reading music.

Function

Besides military use, music was used also at entertainments, funerals, ceremonial and state occasions, as accompaniment to stage plays, and in the pantomime, where dancing was the dominant art. There was much ensemble performance, but it was the virtuoso soloist who was most admired, and who could command high fees. Persons of high social position could become accomplished amateurs.

THE HEBREW LEGACY

The Hebrew legacy was of a different order than that of the Greco-Roman world. It was the music itself, and the performance practices of that music that were taken over by the Christian Church in the earliest days. Early Christian congregations developed within the Synagogue and took the music with them.. The functions of the Jewish cantor were retained in the office of the *psalmista*, and the psalms themselves occupied a most prominent place in the early Liturgy, as they still do in the Liturgy of the Office. The *Sanctus* of the Ordinary of the Mass also contains a text from the Old Testament. Gregorian psalm-tones show close relationships to the melodies used in the performance of psalms by the Jews of the Middle East. Other similarities can be found between Gregorian melodies and melodies sung in synagogues of the Middle East whose peoples had never had contact with Christian communities of Western Europe. A similar structural principle is found in both. This principle consists of the combining of short melodic formulas in various ways and modifying them to fit different texts. Such a method of structure is implied by the Biblical chant notation developed by the *Masoretes* (traditionalists). They were a group of scholars who established the official biblical texts for Jewish purposes and added punctuation signs and vowel signs as directions for the oral reading of the Scriptures. Their notation (the *ta'amim*, accents) consisted of single signs representing groups of notes. This type of notation is known as *ekphonetic*. notation.

Performance

In the matter of performance, the prohibition of instrumental music in the church was common to both Christians and

Jews in the early Christian era. Though instrumental music had been used in the Temple before its destruction, there had been a growing prejudice, resulting from contact with the Hellenistic world, against using instruments in conjunction with sacred music. Instruments were prohibited in the early Synagogue, and Gregorian chant was purely vocal.

Antiphonal and responsorial singing were also common to the two liturgies. Responsorial singing, the alternation between a soloist and the congregation, was characteristic of the performance of many psalms in the Synagogue and evolved into the responsorial psalmody of the Catholic Liturgy. Antiphonal singing, the alternation between two groups of singers, was a type of performance common throughout the Ancient World, but it came into the Christian Church from the Jewish practice. Both antiphonal and responsorial performance are implied in the structure of many of the psalms whose verses fall into two-part divisions. In some, the second part develops the idea set forth in the first part, e.g.:

First part: Let all the earth fear the Lord
Second part: Let all the inhabitants of the world stand in awe
          of Him

First part: For He spoke and it was
Second part: He commanded and it stood. (Ps. xxxiii. 8,9)

In other psalms we find recurrent responses, such as "For his mercy endureth forever."

O give thanks unto the Lord for He is good
For His mercy endureth forever

O give thanks unto the Lord of Lords

For His mercy endureth forever (Ps. cvii, 1,2)

There are also evidences of strophic structure, especially in some of the prophetic songs. Strophic structure is that in which different verses are sung to the same melody.

A further influence may be in the matter of rhythm. It is probable that the performance of Jewish chant was accentual and non-metrical, and this free rhythm is characteristic of most performance of Gregorian chant. The free rhythm superseded the quantitative performance of Greek poetry and music, and measured rhythm was not revived for some 900 years.

The office of the cantor (Chazzan) was introduced into the synagogue in post-Biblical times in connection with the introduction of religious poetry into the original liturgy. Along with the poetry came improvised music which opened up Hebrew music to the influence of peoples among whom they lived.

HIGHLIGHTS OF THE CHAPTER

Greek

The legacy of Ancient Greece consists of:

1. An acoustical theory

2. The organization of musical material into scales

3. A rhythmic structure based on the quantitative (durational) concept of poetic meter which may well have served as a starting point for the development of rhythmic notation in the Middle Ages. Knowledge of ancient Greek literature spread from Moslem sources in Arabic translation.

4. The doctrine of ethos and the Apollonian and Dionysian (classic and romantic) concepts of esthetics, which have had widespread influence on Western European artistic thought.

5. Attempts to revive Greek drama in the early 17th century led to the emergence of opera. Subject matter based on Greek

mythology dominated opera plots during the Baroque period (1600-1750) and have never ceased to be a fertile source of inspiration for opera librettists. The idealization of the Dionysian spirit, which had given birth to the drama in Ancient Greece, also had its counterpart in the esthetics of Baroque art and music.

Roman

Although our information on Roman music is very limited, we may mention:
1. Brass instruments and their use in the military
2. The possible existence of a divisive rhythmic structure with regularly recurring accents, as in our traditional music
3. The recognition of melody as a distinct entity

Hebrew

1. Specific melodic contributions to the chant repertory
2. Antiphonal and responsorial methods of performance
3. The free rhythm and syllabic accents characteristic of Gregorian chant performance
4. A method of melodic structure based on the combining of short melodic motives and adapting them to various texts

CHECK LIST FOR REVIEW

heterophony	syrinx (Panpipes)	parthenia
ethos	paean	skolion
kalokagathia	nome	epinikian ode
phorminx	dithyramb	pantomime
lyra	dirge	iambic
kithara	pyrriche	anapestic
aulos	gymnopedeia	pyrrhic

trochaic	quantitative verse	cantor
spondaic	tibia	ekphonetic
paion (Cretic)	Phrygian pipes	antiphonal
chronos protos	tibia Berecynthia	responsive
harmonia	hydraulis	

Aristoxenos	Seikilos
Ptolemy of Alexandria	Archilochus of Paros
Alypios	Sappho of Lesbos
Terpander	Alkaios
Mesomedes of Crete	Nero
Pindar	

LIST OF SCORES

Ancient Greek

Euripides, "Stasimon Chorus", fragment from *Orestes*,
        (NAWM1,1[1])
Seikilos, *Skolion* , (NAWM1,2; GMB, 1; HAM1, 7c)
First Delphic Hymn (HAM1,7a)
Hymn to the Sun (HAM1, 7b)

Jewish

Accents (Ta'amim), Syrian (HAM1, 6a)
Pentateuch, intonation, Syrian (HAM1, 6b)
Psalm 144, intonation (4 versions) (HAM1, 6c)

---

[1] See List of Abbreviations, p. 407

CHRONOLOGICAL CHART

Music	Political History	Intellectual History	Art
675 B.C. Terpander, founder of Greek Classical music 650 B.C. Archilochus of Paros (early lyric poetry) 586 B.C. Sakadas of Argos wins Pythian games with *Nomos Pythicos* 600-500 B.C. Origins of the dithyramb 522-488 B.C. Pindar, choral odes 500 B.C. Sappho, Alkaios, Anakreon - lyric poetry Main Greek musical instruments: aulos & lyre-type instruments	800-461 B.C. Rise of city states in Greece c. 600 B.C. Babylonian exile c. 600-501 Mayan civilization in Mexico c. 581 Nebuchadnezzar burns Jerusalem 500-451 B.C. Persian Wars 461-429 B.C. Age of Pericles	800-400 B.C. Minor prophets Apollo is worshipped at Delphi First laws at Athens by Draco 700-601 Solon, Athenian law-giver & statesman c. 551-479 Confucius, Chinese philosopher 497 B.C. Death of Pythagoras 460-400 B.C. Aeschylus, Sophocles, Euripides - Greek tragedy c. 450 B.C. Ezra the Scribe-Redaction of Pentateuch	800-701 B.C. Construction of royal palace at Nineveh is begun 700-601 Acropolis in Athens is begun Marduk Temple in Babylon (tower of Babel) is begun after 600 Romans adopt arch from the Etruscans c. 515 B.C. 2nd Temple in Jerusalem
400 B.C. Timotheus of Miletos. kitharoedic nome, *The Persians*	431-404 B.C. Peloponnesian War 400 B.C. Defeat of Athens by Sparta	401 B.C. Xenophon, *Anabasis* 380 B.C. Plato, *The Republic* 350 B.C. Aristotle, *Politics*	432 B.C. Parthenon completed 350 B.C. Praxiteles, *Hermes*

Music	Political History	Intellectual History	Art
	338 B.C. Macedonian conquest of Greece		
330 B.C. Aristoxenus, *Harmonic Elements*	336-323 B.C. Conquests of Alexander the Great	335 Aristotle founds Peripatetic school of philosophy	after 320 Hellenistic period
325 B.C. Timotheus of Miletos, *Persae*	323 B.C.-200 A.D. Division of Alexander's empire, Hellenistic period	286 B.C. Founding of library at Alexandria	306 B.C. Nike of Samothrace
250 B.C. Earliest known examples of Greek musical notation	264 B.C. First Punic War		c. 241 B.C. Dying Gaul
200 B.C.-100 A.D. Period within which the Skolion of Seikilos could have been written	238 B.C. Carthage begins conquest of Spain	200 B.C. Final form of the Hebrew Psalter Inscription engraved on Rosetta stone	175 B.C. Frieze from the altar of Zeus at Pergamon
150 B.C. Delphic Hymn to Apollo	165 B.C. Judas Maccabaeus rededicates Temple at Jerusalem	165 B.C. Book of Daniel	140 B.C. Venus of Milo
	146 B.C. Greece comes under Roman rule	60 B.C. Lucretius, *De rerum natura*	
	58-51 B.C. Caesar invades Gaul	44 B.C. Caesar's *Commentaries*	
c. 10 A.D. Philo Judaeus of Alexandria describes singing of the Therapeutae, probably in octaves		c. 10 B.C. Vergil, Horace, Ovid (Latin poets)	
	50-300 A.D. Rise of the Papacy		
	54 A.D. Nero becomes Emperor of Rome		

Music	Political History	Intellectual History	Art
	70 A.D. 2nd Temple destroyed in Jerusalem	77 A.D. Pliny the Elder - *Natural History*	75-82 A.D. Colosseum, Rome
100 A.D. Plutarch, *On Music*	100-600 A.D. Germanic invasions		82 A.D. Arch of Titus (Rome)
112 A.D. Pliny the Yonger reports hymn singing by Christians			118-126 A.D. Pantheon (Rome)
130 A.D. Mesomedes of Crete		c. 130 Apuleius, Roman satirist	
150 A.D. Ptolemy, Harmonics	212 Roman citizenship granted to all free-men in the Empire	200-300 A.D. Decline of Quantitative poetry	211-217 A.D. Baths of Caracalla (Rome)
285 A.D. Oxyrhynchos Hymn (fragment)	284-476 A.D. Late Roman Empire (Diocletian, 284-305, moves his capital to the East)		

ROMAN BRASS INSTRUMENTS

Left: tuba, Right: buccina, from a mosaic at Zliten (late first century, A. D. after The New Oxford History of Music, Vol 1, Ancient and Oriental Music, ed., Egon Wellesz.)

Left: King David playing the harp under the inspiration of the Holy Spirit. In the upper left hand corner an attendant juggles balls and knives. In the upper right hand corner another attendant plays the rebec, while below attendants play a trumpet which rests on a fork (left) and a ram's horn on the right. (original in British Museum, Cotton MS Tiberius C VI. English, 11th century, after Reese, Music in the Middle Ages)

Guido of Arezzo and Bishop Theobald of Arezzo with monochord (Vienna, Nat. Bib. 51, South German, 12th century, after Reese, Music in the Middle Ages).

Cymbals, Zither-type instruments, and plucked viol from the De musica section of Hrabanus Maurus, De universo (Monte Cassino, 11th century), after Reese, Op. Cit.

CHAPTER II

THE EARLY MIDDLE AGES

SOCIAL BACKGROUND

The culture of Western Europe in the Middle Ages stemmed from the Catholic Church which was the dominant force in Western Europe from the 5th to the 15th centuries. It preserved what was left of the old civilization after the collapse of the Roman Empire and cradled a new civilization. The removal of the capital of the Empire to the East by Diocletian (245-313) left an administrative vacuum in Rome and began the process which resulted in the schism between the Roman and Byzantine Empires. The Roman Church as an administrative force developed rapidly after the Edict of Milan (313) which, under the sponsorship of Constantine the Great, established the toleration of Christianity throughout the Empire. In the East the Emperors became heads of both church and state. In the west, the Church developed as a state within the Empire. The centralization which its position represented made for a unity of culture during the Middle Ages. Latin was the language of the educated man - not the Latin of Caesar and Cicero, but a very serviceable if less polished tongue which served as a means of communication throughout Western Europe. Education, philosophy, science, political and economic concepts, all emanated from the

25

Church. The Church was the symbol of authority, and authority was the guiding principle of Medieval intellectualism. The intellectual atmosphere stressed the interpretation of what was handed down by *auctoritas* (authority) rather than reliance upon observation; it stressed classification rather than invention. The necessity for authoritative sources and the necessity for official interpretations of these sources were both present, the second considered as a necessary intermediary to understanding the first. The Scriptures were interpreted symbolically.

The authority of the Church with its threat of eternal damnation for the wrongdoer was a force for peace in a violent world- a means for controlling the actions of the barbarian invaders. The disasters which overtook Western Europe in the wake of these invasions and the collapse of secular government made the contemplation of man's fate in the hereafter the means by which his behavior on earth could be controlled. Thus, a preoccupation with death *(memento mori)* dominated the artistic and cultural expression of the Middle Ages. Visigoths, Vandals, Huns and Lombards invaded and destroyed what remained of the Roman system, and their conversion to Christianity was the only unifying force. From the north came the Danes, Swedes, and Norwegians, establishing colonies around the coast of Europe. The growing uncertainties of life turned people's eyes more and more to the hereafter, and their faith was the source of the Church's power and its ability to establish order. Though the Eastern Christian empire long outlasted the West, it finally succumbed to the spread of Islam and the rise of Arab power. In the West, no other authority was able to assert itself until the 15th century, except during the reign of Charlemagne - a reign in which authority issued from the personality of one man. A social order derived from barbarian society, the feudal system, founded upon a rural slave economy, wove a tangled web of interrelationships transcending all other political boundaries.

Medieval art existed to serve the Church. The architectural monuments were houses of worship, and sculpture existed only within, and as part of, the cathedral with each statue in its niche serving to glorify the whole. Painting, likewise, was in the service of the Church. A painting did not exist as a separate entity but was found either decorating religious buildings, or illustrating religious books. Music also found its place in the hierarchy where, united with sacred texts, it served the Liturgy. Philosophy, too, occupied itself with proving the existence of God and mediated between faith and reason in this quest. Boethius, the last of the great Classical thinkers, was executed, and his death symbolized the end of an era. Pope Gregory the Great rejected classical studies maintaining that the only worthy studies for a Christian were the sacred texts.

In this all-embracing scheme the individual was of little importance. Lack of literary records gave the period the name "Dark Ages". The creators of Medieval art remain anonymous. The artists, sculptors, musicians and writers of Classical Greece are known to us by their names, but scarcely a name comes down to us from the creative arts of Medieval Europe.

HISTORICAL

Division of the Roman Empire

There was no sharp dividing line between the world of antiquity and the Medieval world. In the year 283 A.D. the Roman Emperor Diocletian divided the Empire into four administrative sections in order to repel the Germanic tribes. Two sections were in the West and two in the East. After Diocletian's abdication, the emperor Constantine moved his capital to Byzantium (renamed by him Constantinople), temporarily reuniting the Empire. Upon Constantine's death, in 337, the division between East and West that had been initiated by Diocletian was renewed. Theodosius again reunited the Empire briefly, but after his death in 395, it remained permanently divided.

Rise of Christianity

Persecution of the Christians had one of its periodic flare-ups towards the end of Diocletian's reign but came to an end with Constantine's Edict of Milan (313), which legalized Christianity. The Council of Nicea, which also convened under Constantine, established one of the basic tenets of Christianity, i.e. the dual nature of Christ (Deity and man), by deciding the doctrinal dispute between the bishops Athanasius and Arias in favor of Athanasius. The Goths, however, were converted to Arian Christianity by the Bishop Ulfilas, who translated the Bible into Gothic. Theodoric was an Ostrogoth and an Arian Christian. The rest of what is known as the Nicene Creed was actually contributed during the reign of Theodosius at the council of Constantinople in 381, namely the divinity of the Holy Spirit. Under Theodosius Christianity became the state religion and at last gained ascendancy over the various pagan religions. The tenure of St. Ambrose as bishop of Milan also took place during the reign of Theodosius.

The Papacy

Rome now lost its political importance, and the West sank into anarchy. The Popes of Rome (originally bishops) filled the void left by the loss of political administrators. It was a Pope (Leo I) who purportedly persuaded Attila not to sack Rome (452). The capital of the Western Empire was moved to Ravenna, and it was there that the German chieftain Odoacer deposed the last Western Emperor (476). The administration was kept intact by Odoacer and by Theodoric the Great (454-526). Boethius, known as "the last of the

Romans" was Theodoric's minister. In 552, Narses conquered Italy for the Byzantine Empire, and Byzantine Exarchs ruled Rome from Ravenna. Pope Gregory I (St. Gregory the Great, 590-604) was an administrator of the highest skill. Because of his dual role as priest and monk, he was able to bring a unity to the Church that it had not had before. He began to emancipate Rome from the exarchs and gained popular support. The popes became the most powerful authorities in Rome, and the coronation of Charlemagne (800) ended any pretense of Byzantine authority over Rome.

BEGINNINGS OF CHRISTIAN CHANT

Figures of Musical Antiquity in the Christian Era

Several figures significant in the music of antiquity lived in the Christian era. Among them were Ptolemy of Alexandria (2nd century) who wrote on Greek scale structures; Mesomedes of Crete (2nd century) whose hymns sought to revive the long dead style of Greek Classical music; and Alypios (4th century) whose *Introduction to Music* is our chief source of information on Greek notation. Neo-Platonists and neo-Pythagoreans were writing in the 3rd century, expounding ideas on music which stemmed from Plato, Aristotle, and Pythagoras. The Roman Boethius (475-525) was a neo-Pythagorean whose views had great influence on Medieval theorists. At the very beginning of the Christian era, Hellenistic Judaism was represented in the writings of Philo of Alexandria (born c 20 A.D.). Both Plato and the Bible influenced his work. His description of the religious practices of the Therapeutae (thought to be a Jewish sect) is of interest in that it refers to singing in octaves - with men and women singing- and singing in alternation between two groups (antiphony).

Early Christian Practices

There was no uniformity of musical practice among Christian communities in the first two centuries. At an early time singing was applied to the Gospels, psalms, hymns and alleluia; and music was one means of attracting converts. The 3rd century was one of great growth, and we find references to the need for guarding against the influences of non-Christian music that might have undesirable associations - music such as was used at the banquets and theatrical performances of the Hellenistic world. It was these pagan associations that, from the very beginning, led to the exclusion of instrumental music from the Christian ritual.

Early Christian Figures

Clement of Alexandria (ca 150-220) and Eusebius (ca. 260-340) both referred to the undesirability of instruments in the church. St. Augustine wrote of the powerful influence music had on him. He also tells how St. Ambrose, Bishop of Milan, in his efforts to bring encouragement to his people in their struggle against the Arians, introduced the Syrian custom of hymn singing. Augustine's *De musica* discusses rhythm according to the classical principles of quantitative poetic meter.

Branches of Chant

Separate branches of chant developed in various parts of the Christian world. In the East, more or less distinct repertories arose in Syria; in the Byzantine Empire; among the native Egyptian Christians (Copts); and also among the Ethiopians, Russians, Bulgarians, and Greeks. In the West, the important branches of chant were the Ambrosian, Gallican, Mozarabic, and Gregorian.

Syrian Chant

Because of its proximity to Palestine, Syria came under the influence of Christianity at an early date. It was on the road to the city of Damascus in Syria that St. Paul was converted to Christianity. At different times Syria was dominated by Alexander the Great, by Rome, and by Byzantium. Although there is no written repertory of ancient Syrian chant, ancient Syrian melodies are believed to have survived in the modern chant. The chant was influenced by the Hebrew, but also showed some Hellenistic traits. The *oktoechoi (okto,* eight;*echoi,* sounds) were a pre-scalar method of organizing melodic materials. They consisted of stock melodies, classified at first in accordance with their symbolic function in worship. Gradually, the material came to have a specific musical significance and finally evolved, in Medieval Byzantine music, into a modal system which influenced the development of modes in the West. Among the Syrians there developed the custom of singing hymns(devotional songs with verse texts). This custom attained wide influence, being introduced into Western Europe by St. Ambrose, Bishop of Milan. Unlike the ancient Greek quantitative poetry, the hymn texts were based on accentual verse. St. Ephraim (d. 373) was the most important of the Syrian writers of Hymn texts.

Byzantine Chant

The Byzantine Empire centered around the Balkan Peninsula and Asia Minor. The Emperor Constantine made it Orthodox Christian, and with him began the Middle Eastern influence that characterized its culture. It survived invasions and changes of boundary for more than eleven centuries of ebb and flow in fortune. Though its government was the epitome of despotism and cruelty, it became the repository for much of the intellectual legacy of the ancient world. During the Middle Ages its culture was much more polished and sophisticated than that of the West. Beginning with the 7th century, the Church under the leadership of the Patriarch of Constantinople, gained increasing political influence. In 800, with the crowning of Charlemagne, the schism between East and West was complete. Weakened by the inroads of the Turks, Western Europeans, and the new Balkan kingdoms of Serbia and Bulgaria, the power of Byzantium began to decline in the 11th century. Constantinople fell to the Ottoman Turks in 1453 despite vain pleas of the last of the ruling Paleologi, Manuel II and John VIII, for aid from the West. The Byzantine Empire left its mark on Eastern Europe; Russia became the chief outpost of Byzantine culture. In Western Europe Venetian art and architecture, as exemplified by the Cathedral of St. Mark's, shows Byzantine influences. Many synagogues likewise show Byzantine influences in their architecture.

Byzantine music, once considered as being a direct development from ancient Greek practice, is now recognized as being basically Middle Eastern and having Syrian and Hebrew elements. It made use of the kithara and the aulos, but its chief instrument was the organ. It is not known how the instruments were used. The surviving music, almost all sacred, is monophonic and in free rhythm. Its chief contribution was, as with Syria, its hymns. The most important writer of hymns was John of Damascus (8th century). Byzantine music has left its mark on both Russian chant and modern Greek Orthodox chant.

Other Middle Eastern Chant

A branch of chant also developed in Armenia, the first country to adopt Christianity as a state religion. (Catholic Christianity was adopted there in the 3rd century). Armenian chant used an oktoechos system, as seen in its great hymn collection, the Sharakan. Native Egyptian Christians, the Copts, used a liturgical language related to ancient Egyptian and also used an oktoechos system. Closely related to the Coptic rites is the Ethiopian ritual. Ethiopian chant is performed in a loud and ecstatic manner and is accompanied by dancing.

Russian Chant

Russian Christianity and its chant was an outgrowth of Byzantine culture, as we have seen. The Byzantine ritual was translated into the Slavonic language in the 9th century by the monk Cyril and his followers, using an alphabet designed by them (called *Cyrillic*). Russian chant developed individual characteristics and, in later centuries, its own notation (Znammeny notation, 11th century). From the 12th to the 14th centuries the chant became specifically Russian, and within the compass of Russian chant, Greek and Bulgarian types developed.

WESTERN CHANT

Ambrosian Chant

Ambrosian chant (fr. St. Ambrose) is used in Milan to the present day. Milan developed a liturgy distinct from the Roman, though it is questionable how much of it can be attributed to St. Ambrose himself. Ambrosian chant influenced and was influenced by Gregorian chant. Ornate Ambrosian melodies tend to be more ornate than the Gregorian, and the simple melodies tend to be simpler.

Gallican Chant

Gallican chant was used by the Franks in Gaul, the territory corresponding roughly to modern France, which the Franks occupied late in the 5th century. When the Frankish king Charlemagne was crowned emperor by the Pope of Rome (800), the new emperor decreed that the Roman rite (Gregorian chant) replace the Gallican chant. Since this decree came before the advent of staff notation, Gallican chant virtually disappeared except for some parts that were absorbed into the Roman liturgy for Good Friday, e g the *Improperia* (Reproaches, imputed to Jesus).

Mozarabic Chant

The Visigoths (West Goths) occupied Spain towards the end of the 5th century. A Visigothic liturgy developed here and was used over most of the country, except for the northern part held by the sturdily independent Basques. After the occupation of Spain by the Moors in the 8th century, the Visigothic Christians came to be known as Mozarabs and their liturgy, Mozarabic. The Mozarabic liturgy continued in use by the Christians in Moorish Spain and its environs. During the more open environment of the 12th century Mozarabic liturgy began to be replaced by the Roman. Manuscripts of the Mozarabic rite date from as early as 900, the best preserved of these being the Antiphonary of Leon (1066). The music notation of these Spanish manuscripts is almost entirely undecipherable except for 16 melodies transcribed in the 12th century in a manuscript from the monastery of St. Millan de la Cogolla. There are some similarities between Mozarabic and Ambrosian chant. In fact, the four branches of Western chant, Ambrosian, Gallican, Mozarabic, and Gregorian, may have a common ancestry.

GREGORIAN CHANT

General Characteristics

The first enduring body of music created by Western European civilization was the ritual chant of the Roman

Catholic Church, known as Gregorian Chant. Chant depends for its expressiveness purely on melody; there is no accompaniment of any kind, either expressed or implied. Furthermore, even rhythmic articulation - the use of measured rhythm or recurrent accent - plays a very small role in its means of expression. This austere simplicity is, of course, a severe challenge to the modern ear, accustomed as it is to richer fare. Rhythmic patterns play an important role in the music we ordinarily hear; and the melodies, even when the accompaniment is not played, are built on a harmonic structure that makes itself felt. Nevertheless, the greatness of the chant is attested by the fact of its survival in a continuous tradition through the centuries, and it stands as the highest peak of pure melodic expression in the West.

Sources

Some of the melodies in the Gregorian repertory are of great antiquity, survivals of the early days of Christianity when they were taken over from the Synagogue. Some must have come from the Hellenistic world . Other influences must have played their part, emanating from the various lands and peoples through which Christianity spread.

Relation to Pope Gregory

The chant of the Roman Catholic Church is known collectively as Gregorian Chant after Pope Gregory the Great (c. 540-604). Though his name is firmly affixed to the chant, historical attempts to determine his exact relationship to the chant are much less conclusive. One of the chief documents supporting his role is John the Deacon's *Life of Gregory the Great*, written c. 870, some three centuries after his death. Most writers seem to believe that some sort of organization took place in Gregory's time and that it probably involved the assignment of specific melodies to specific places in the

Liturgy. Music manuscripts date from the 9th century from such Carolingian (fr. Charlemagne, Carolus Magnus) cultural centers as the abbeys of St. Gall and Metz. These manuscripts show that a liturgical tradition continuing to the present day had already been established. Other evidences, such as textual evidences, point to the fact that this tradition also extends far back into pre-Carolingian times.

Terminology

Gregorian Chant is also known as plain chant or plainsong *(cantus planus)*. The adjective plain refers to its unmeasured rhythm as opposed to music with measured rhythm *(cantus mensurabilis)*. This use of the term plain chant dates from about the 13th century.

Structure of the Liturgy

Since Gregorian Chant is inseparably bound up with the liturgy, no consideration of the chant is feasible without some understanding of the structure of the liturgy. Broadly, the structure is as follows:

1. There is a yearly calendar of feast days. These fall into two main groups: one centering around Christmas; the other centering around Easter. Interspersed are certain feast days belonging to the saints.

2. On any given day there is an order of worship which consists of two divisions. One, recited daily in the monasteries, is known as the Office Hours, the Canonic Hours, or the Divine Office *(Officium divinum)*. It consists of services held eight times during the day for the offering of prayers. The other is the Mass which is the core of the ritual of the secular clergy and is performed in churches with the participation of the congregation. The Mass centers around a symbolic or mystic repetition of the Last Supper. The term

Mass is derived from the words of the priest in dismissing the congregation after its celebration, *ite, missa est [congregatio]* (Go, [the congregation] is dismissed).

3. Both the Office and the Mass consist of parts that fall into two categories: those that are repeated each day and those which change in accordance with the liturgical calendar. The unchanging parts are called the Ordinary *(Ordinarium)* , and the parts that change are called the Proper *(Proprium)*.

The Ordinary of the Mass is of special interest musically since its text has been set by many of the major composers from the 14th century to the present. The Mass in B-minor by J.S. Bach and the *Missa Solemnis* by Beethoven are two of the most famous. It will therefore be of interest to list the five parts here:

Kyrie (Lord have mercy . . .)
Gloria (Glory to God in the Highest . . .)
Credo (I believe in one God . . .[the Nicene Creed])
Sanctus (Holy, Holy, Holy . . .)
Agnus dei (Lamb of God . . .)

There are also famous Masses by Haydn, Mozart, and Schubert. The text for the Requiem Mass, or Mass for the dead, has received numerous settings. In settings of the Requiem Mass, the joyful parts of the Ordinary are omitted, and the Proper for the memorial service is included. There are well-known requiems by Mozart, Berlioz, and Guiseppe Verdi. (Note: the text of the Brahms Requiem [*Ein Deutsches Requiem*] is not based on the Catholic liturgical text.)

Evolution of the Liturgy

Early Christianity developed along two separate lines. One, the secular clergy, served the laity and consisted of the hierarchy of deacon, priest, bishop, and archbishop. The other, the regular clergy who devoted themselves to a life of prayer and asceticism, began with hermits who often left civilization behind to live in the desert. The second group, under such leaders as St. Anthony in Egypt, St. Basil in Greece, and St. benedict in the West, formed communities governed by order or rule (Latin *regula)* and lived together in monasteries and convents. The Mass was the main ceremony of the secular clergy, while the Office (*Officium divinum*), the observation of prayers at appointed times during the day, was the main religious observance of the regular clergy. During much of the Middle Ages the monastery was the dominant form of Christianity and preserver of culture. Monastic reform groups played an important role throughout the Middle Ages. With the growth of towns and cities and construction of cathedrals the emphasis veered toward the secular. Thus, Mass composition was a phenomenon of the Renaissance. Friction sometimes arose between the two divisions; and Pope Gregory the Great, because of his dual role as monk and priest, was able to bridge the gap and bring unity to the Church.

The Book of Psalms was the sole source of early Christian worship, and the psalms still form the basis of the Office. Later there were added to the Office a series of Canticles which are similar in character to the psalms and which come from the Old and New Testaments. The psalm or canticle is almost always preceded and followed by its antiphon, a short chant with its own melody and text. Readings from the Scriptures were also introduced, each of which was followed by a chanted Responsory. Lastly were added the four Marian Antiphons (c. 1000) which have lost all connection with psalms and are independent chants of much greater elaboration than the true antiphons.

The Mass achieved its present form c. 1000 to 1100. Its musical items include, in addition to the Ordinary which is on non-psalmodic texts, five psalms which accompany ritual actions. The sequences, of which five have become accepted as parts of the Mass, stem from the later Middle Ages.

Rhythmic Considerations

As we have seen, Gregorian Chant consists of a single melodic line without accompaniment of any kind. This kind of music is called <u>monophonic</u>, the antithesis of polyphonic in which harmonic intervals are used. Furthermore, the rhythm of the chant is unmeasured and lacks the pulse or beat that characterizes later music. Accents of words tend to be marked rather by high points in the melodic line. That is, the accented syllable in each word tends to be higher in pitch than the syllable preceding.

There exists, however, much controversy over the rhythm of the chant. Briefly, there are three schools: (1) the accentualist school which believes that all the notes of the chant should be of equal duration but that the accented syllables of the text should be stressed in singing; (2) the Solesmes school which rejects the idea of stress on accented syllables. Instead, it substitutes the concept of grouping the notes into twos and threes, freely admixed. Some of these groups have an upbeat and some a downbeat character. In teaching this method wavy lines are drawn to indicate the rhythmic structure of the chant. (3) The mensuralist school which believes that the notes are of different durations but differs within itself as to what these durations are. This group believes also in stressing accented syllables, as the accentualists do. The method that has been adopted by the churches is that of the Solesmes school.

It should be noted that any of the above methods would result in an absence of regularly recurring rhythmic pulse. Medieval sources are vague and often contradictory. We may conclude that at different times and in different places the manner of rhythmic performance varied. It may also be concluded that matters of accent and duration were of much less concern to the Medieval musician than to us, at least until the emergence of polyphony forced the problem of measured duration to his attention.

The Church Modes

The scale system of Gregorian melodies has been classified in accordance with a system of eight modes based on the distribution of tones and semitones within the octave. The earliest writer to refer in any detail to melodic formulas of modal significance was the French monk, Aurelian of Réomé (mid 8th century). A 10th century work, the *Alia musica,* which contained passages by several authors, was the first source to present the church modes as they are known today. Mistaking the Greek *tonoi* for modes, the *Alia musica* applied Greek names to the various modes. This modal classification was applied to a body of music already in existence. The medieval modal system was presented in its definitive form (not to be modified until the 16th century) in the *Opuscula musica* of Hermannus (1013-1054), called Contractus because of his crippled limbs. Hermannus Contractus was a Benedictine monk in the Abbey of Reichenau located at the northern tip of what is now Switzerland. He was the composer of several Marian Antiphons including the *Alma Redemptoris Mater* which was immensely popular during Medieval times.

Natural and inevitable though the octave may seem to the modern student, its recognition by theorists as a basis for scales represents a long and arduous evolution. Octave scales were recognized by Greek theorists of Late Antiquity, but after Boethius (c. 500) there is no clear mention of them before the 10th century. The system of church modes stemming from Hermannus is as follows: Each mode has two important notes: the *finalis* and the *tenor*. Four modes begin with the *finalis* and are called <u>authentic</u>. There are four other modes where the *finalis* comes near the middle of the range; these are called <u>plagal.</u> Each authentic mode has a corresponding plagal mode; what the two have in common is the *finalis*. These modes can be played using only the white keys of the piano. In the chart below the *finalis* is indicated by parentheses around the letter, while the *tenor* is indicated by brackets:

Authentic Modes   *Plagal Modes*

Dorian   Hypodorian
(D) E F G [a] b c d   A B C (D) E [F] G a

Phrygian   Hypophrygian
(E) F G a b [c] d e   B C D (E) F G [a] b

Lydian   Hypolydian
(F) G a b [c] d e f   C D E (F) G [a] b c

Mixolydian   Hypomixolydian
(G) a b c [d] e f g   D E F (G) a b [c] d

In addition, the B-flat was known, so that chromatic alteration was available from earliest times. For the modern listener one of the chief differences between the church modes and the major and minor scales is the absence of the *ti-do* ending.

Solmisation

Solmisation (the use of syllables for singing) was rediscovered in Western Europe in the 11th century in a system developed by Guido d'Arezzo (c. 990-1050). By taking the first syllable of each line of a hymn to St. John by Paul the Deacon, Guido of Arezzo derived the syllable names for the first six tones of what is now the diatonic major scale *(ut, re, mi, fa, sol, la)* . The 7th degree was not added until the 17th century at which time the Italians changed the *ut* to *do*. Guido d'Arezzo also perfected the staff system of notation. He adopted a four-line staff so that the system of pitch notation became essentially as it is today. The Greeks had had a system of solmisation based on the tetrachord, but Guido's system was probably an independent creation of the Middle Ages.

Classification of Chant

In accordance with the research of such scholars as Peter Wagner and Paolo Ferretti, it has become customary to classify chants in accordance with the way their texts are set to the melodies. By this classification three types are distinguished:

(1) <u>Syllabic</u>, in which there is one note to each syllable of text (or occasionally two or three). This class also includes psalmodic chants that have a reciting tone in which many syllables are sung to one pitch.

(2) <u>Neumatic</u>, in which 2, 3, 4, or perhaps more notes are sung to one syllable.

(3) <u>Melismatic</u>, in which are included melismas (vocalizations) of 10, 20, 30, or even more notes sung to one syllable of text.

Based upon the above classification, the style of a chant is determined by its use or purpose. More ornate, (melismatic) chants are used for more important liturgical occasions, or more important texts. Melismas might be used to emphasize certain words, such as the alleluia. Portions sung by trained singers would be more ornate than those sung by untrained singers. Thus, the Mass sung by a trained choir is more ornate than the office sung by monks. Soloist portions of the chant tend to be more ornate than choral portions.

PSALMODY

The oldest and most numerous body of chants are those sung to psalm texts: the psalmody. Three types of psalmody are distinguished: (1) direct, (2) responsorial, and (3) antiphonal. Direct psalmody without interpolations is rare. The terms *antiphony* and *responsory* as they were used originally in Medieval Europe referred to methods of performance,- antiphony being alternation between two groups of singers, and responsory being alternation between a soloist and a group of singers. In the course of time, however, the chants to which these methods of performance gave rise gained independent status; and in the modern Gregorian repertory, the antiphon and responsory are simply types of chant used along with the psalms.

Antiphonal Psalmody

In antiphonal psalmody the psalm texts are chanted to formulas which show rather clearly the gradual emergence of musical expression from a kind of glorified speech associated with the recitation of sacred words. Models for these formulas exist in the chant of the synagogue. The formulas consist of the following parts (repeated for each verse of the psalm):

1. An <u>intonation</u> or *initium* (beginning). A series of a few notes that ascends to the tenor.

2. <u>Tenor </u>(from the Latin *tenere*, to hold). A single pitch to which most of the words of the psalm are recited.

3. <u>Mediant</u> <u>cadence</u>. An intermediate pause consisting of a melodic fragment at the end of the first part of the verse.

4. <u>Tenor.</u> Usually the same sustained tone used again for most of the text of the second part of the verse.

5. <u>Final</u> <u>cadence</u>. A melodic fragment that brings the verse to a close.

The psalm is preceded and followed by an antiphon. This is a chant with more melodic character than the psalmodic chant itself. The antiphon is usually syllabic, but it may be neumatic for more important occasions. For less important occasions the antiphon may be abbreviated at its first appearance. Antiphonal psalmody is found both in the Office and in the Mass. The antiphonal psalmody of the Mass is more elaborate than that of the Office, but it is similar structurally.

Responsorial Psalmody

Responsorial psalmody consisted originally of a series of psalm verses chanted by a soloist. The chanting of the soloist alternated with a repeated refrain, or response, sung by the choir. The response might be a single word such as *alleluia* or or *amen* , or it might be a phrase from the psalm itself, or it might even be a phrase taken from some other part of the Scriptures. This type of performance is implied by the structure of some of the psalms, such as Ps. 136 in which each verse ends with the phrase "for His mercy endureth forever". In the course of time, the influence of soloist performance led to greater elaboration of the verse and the introduction of melismas, so that the number of verses came to be reduced. In the established repertory responsorial psalmody is highly melismatic and usually uses only one psalm verse. Responsories tend to be less melodic than antiphons. A typical responsorial form would be: Response (in shortened form)-Verse-Response. Responses make use of melody-types which are stereotyped melodic formulas that recur over again throughout the repertory of responses. This method of musical structure is characteristic of many ancient musical systems and includes the Hebrew accents (*ta'amim*) and the Syrian and Byzantine *echoi*. Responsorial chants are found in both the Mass and the Office.

Direct Psalmody

Direct psalmody is, as we have seen, comparatively rare. In it no refrain is interpolated between verses. There is only one example in the Mass, and it is set to a florid melody. Some simple, unadorned examples are found in the Office for use on feasts of somber character.

Performance

Responsorial chants are performed using a soloist and choir. In some cases the soloist still sings the verse and the choir sings the refrain in true responsive manner. It is customary, however, since the 12th century, for the soloist to begin each chant- if for no other reason than the purely practical one of establishing the pitch. Thus, the beginning of the response is sung by the soloist, after which the choir joins in. Then the soloist begins the verse, and the choir joins in near the close, so as to be singing when the chant ends. If the chant ends with a response instead of a verse, the verse may be sung entirely by the soloist.

The soloist also begins the chant, to set the pitch in antiphonal psalmody. In some monasteries, especially in Germany, antiphonal performance is used for the verses; the first half of each verse is sung by one group, the second by the other. Except for the solo beginning, both groups sing the antiphon. Often, however, each verse is begun by the soloist and continued by the choir, and today, true antiphonal performance is rare.

NON-PSALMODIC CHANTS

Ordinary of the Mass

The chants of the Ordinary of the Mass are of later origin than the psalmody though some parts of the Ordinary, such as the Sanctus (which stems from the thrice repeated *Kodosh, kodosh, kodosh* -Holy, holy, holy-from the Book of Isaiah [Isa. 6,3]) are of ancient origin. The Ordinary attained its present completed form in the 11th century.

The Kyrie tends to be melismatic and to employ various repetition schemes in its musical material. The simplest and earliest of the schemes follows quite literally the scheme of the text which consists of Kyrie eleison (3 times), Christe eleison (3 times), and Kyrie eleison (3 times). Glorias tend to be syllabic and are largely free compositions. Credos are generally similar to psalm tones. The Sanctus is predominantly neumatic but often has a melisma on the first Sanctus. The Agnus dei is usually neumatic and in <u>a</u> <u>b</u> <u>a</u> form.

The Hymn

The hymn is defined as being a song in praise of God on a non-Scriptural text in poetic meter. Its musical setting is strophic (that is, with each stanza sung to the same melody). In some hymns musical rhyme is used, and in others we find the more modern devices of repetition and recapitulation of melodic phrases. The hymns have been sung since the earliest days of Christianity. They were the occasion for much controversy in official Roman circles and were not introduced into the Roman Liturgy until the 10th century. Early Ambrosian hymn-chants were syllabic and in quantitative rhythm based on the meter of the text. Later, accentual poetic meters replaced the quantitative, and settings became more ornate. The earliest examples of accentual verse were found in Syrian hymns of the 4th century. In the Gregorian repertory the hymn is found chiefly in the Office. Hymns, like other chants, differ in style in accordance with their use. Simple, syllabic hymns are used for ordinary days, and extended melodies are used for feast days.

HIGHLIGHTS OF THE CHAPTER

1. The various branches of Eastern and Western Christianity developed their own chant repertories. Among the most important groups of chant in the East were the Syrian, Byzantine, Armenian, Coptic, Ethiopian, and Russian. In the West there were the Ambrosian, Gallican, Mozarabic (Visigothic), and Gregorian (Roman) chants.

2. The culture of the Western European Middle Ages stemmed from the Roman Catholic Church. Thus, the most important music of the period was the Roman liturgical chant. Ambrosian chant survived in Milan.

3. General characteristics of the chant are: (a) a single melodic line with no harmony stated or implied; (b) freely flowing rhythm without regular rhythmic pulse or articulated rhythmic patterns; (c) modal scales (not major or minor).

4. The structure of the Roman liturgy is as follows: (a) There is a yearly calendar of feast days. (b) There are two orders of daily worship: The Office in the monasteries and the Mass in the churches. (c) In daily worship the unchanging parts are the Ordinary; the parts which change in accordance with the Church calendar are the Proper.

The Ordinary of the Mass is of particular importance. It consists of five parts: Kyrie, Gloria, Credo, Sanctus, and Agnus Dei.

5. Chant, classified in accordance with the setting of the text, may be syllabic, neumatic, or melismatic.

6. The most numerous chants are psalm settings. Psalmody may be direct, antiphonal, or responsorial.

7. Non-psalmodic chants include the Ordinary of the Mass and the hymns.

CHECK LIST FOR REVIEW

Oktoechoi	Office Hours	Marian Antiphon
hymn	Canonic Hours	antiphon
Improperia	Divine Office	responsory
Mozarabic	Mass	accentualist
plain chant	Ordinary	mensuralist
(cantus planus)	Proper	monophony
cantus	canticles	Requiem

Diocletian	St. Augustine
Constantine	St. Ambrose
St. Athanasius	Charlemagne
Arius	John of Damascus
Theodosius	St. Gall
Boethius	Metz
Pope Gregory the Great	Solesmes
Philo of Alexandria	Hermannus Contractus
Eusebius	Guido of Arezzo
Clement of Alexandria	

LIST OF SCORES

Ambrosian Chant

Aeterne rerum conditor (3 melodies): HAM1, 9a
Aeterna Christi munera: (2 melodies): HAM1, 9b
Verse *Eructavit,* from the Gradual *Speciosus Forma:* HAM1, 10
Psalmellus (Gradual), *Redde mihi,* for Quadragesima:TEM,1

Byzantine Chant
Ode for Christmas: HAM1, 8a
Hymn from *Oktoechos*:: HAM1, 8b

Gallican Chant
Popule meus, Improperia of the Mass for Good Friday:
TEM, 2

Mozarabic Chant
Gaudete populi, Antiphon [independent] from Mass for
   Easter: TEM, 3

GREGORIAN CHANT

Office of Second Vespers, Nativity of Our Lord:
   NAWM1,4

Antiphonal Psalmody of the Office:
Antiphon,*Laudabo* ; Psalm 146, *Lauda anima mea* :
   HAM1, 11
Antiphon, *Laus Deo Patri* ; Psalm 113, *Laudate pueri*:
   MM, 1
Antiphon, *Tecum principium*; Psalm 109, *Dixit Dominus*:
   NAWM1, 4b,c
Antiphon, *Redempionem misit Dominus* ; Psalm 110,
   Confitebor tibi Domine : NAWM1, 4d, 4e
Antiphon, *Exortum est in tenebris* ; Psalm 111,*Beatus vir
   qui timet Dominum* : NAWM1, 4f, 4g
Antiphon, *Apud Dominum* ; Psalm 129, *De profundis* :
   NAWM1, 4h, 4i

Responsorial Psalmody of the Office:
Long response, *Libera me* : HAM1, 14
Short response, *Verbum caro* : NAWM1, 4j, 4k

Hymn:

Veni Creator Spiritus, office, second Vespers of
   Whitsunday: TEM, 4

Mass:

Mass for Septuagesima Sunday: NAWM1, 3

Kyrie IV, *Cunctipotens*, (Ordinary) : HAM1, 15a

Hec dies, Gradual(Proper): HAM1, 12

Alleluia, Angelus Domini (Proper): HAM1, 13

Alleluia, Vidimus stellam (Proper): MM, 2

HILDEGARDE VON BINGEN MS

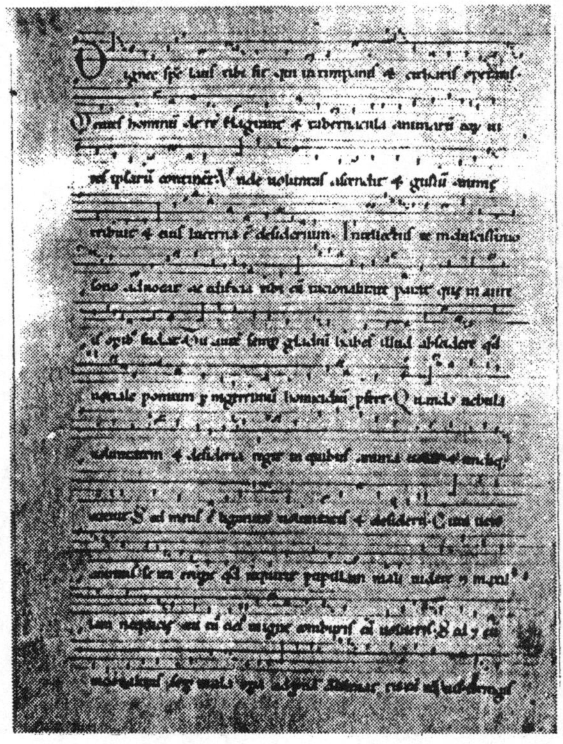

*From a facsimile edition published by Herman Baeten, Peer Belgium.
The ms. was written at the Rupertsberg scriptorium, c. 1175 and contains
a liturgical cycle. Original is in Dendermonde, Belgium.*

CHRONOLOGICAL CHART

Music	Political History	Intellectual History	Art
2nd c Mesomedes of Crete 360 Alypios, Introduction to Music late 4th c. St. Augustine, *De musica* 500 Boethius, *De institutione musica* 485-580 Cassiodorus 622 Isidore of Seville	100-600 Germanic migrations 330 Constantinople capital of the Roman Empire 410 Sack of Rome by Alaric. Angles and Saxons invade Britain 452 Attila the Hun invades Italy. Founding of Venice 455 Vandals sack Rome 476 End of Roman Empire (Romulus Augustulus deposed) 568 Lombards invade Italy	313 Edict of Milan 325 Council of Nicea 374 S. Ambrose Bishop of Milan 413-425 St. Augustine, *City of God* 450 Seven Liberal Arts, Trivium and Quadrivium 529 Benedictine order founded 590 Election of Pope Gregory the Great 622 Hegira of Mohammed 650-700 Rise of monasteries 700 Irish and Anglo-Saxon missionaries in Europe 673-735 Venerable Bede	315 Arch of Constantine 532-562 Hagia Sophia

Below: Bagpipe Player (Miniature from the Escorial MS j b 2 pf the Cantigas da Sancta Maria. after Rokseth, Polyphonies du 13e siècle, fr. Reese, op. cit.)

Above: *Musicians with rebec and lute. The rebec, on the left, is held in a vertical position, resting on the knee of the musician, who is seated. Note that the bow is actually bow-shaped, not having been altered before the 15th century./*
(Miniature from the Escorial MS j b 2 pf the Cantigas da Sancta Maria. after Rokseth, Polyphonies du XIIIe siècle, from ReMMA.)

Musicians playing the tabor (drum) and transverse flute, with dancers. Dance was increasingly important in court life from the 12 c. on.
(Detail after the Bibliothèque du musée des arts decoratif, Paris, from the Larousse Encyclopedia of Music, ed. Hindley).

/Above: Frauenlob (a minnesinger, d. 1318) playing the vielle (fidel). The vielle was the most important stringed instrument from c. 1200-1400.
(Detail from Heidelberg, Man-essische Handschrift. After Besseler, Die Musik des Mittelalters und der Renaissance, from ReMMA).

CHAPTER III

THE LATER MIDDLE AGES

CHARLEMAGNE

The Franks, unlike the Visigoths (who were followers of the non-orthodox Christianity of Bishop Arias), had been converted to orthodox Catholicism and thus were able to gain support of the Western European clergy. The greatest of the Frankish kings was Charlemagne (768-814). A great conqueror as well as a powerful personality, he was able to consolidate under his rule the Western provinces of the old Roman Empire except for Britain, and even extend his control to areas of central and eastern Europe which the Romans had never been able to control.   His crowning as Emperor by Pope Leo III drove a significant wedge between the Byzantine Empire and the West.   The administration of this empire, however, depended entirely on the personal force of this one man and could not long survive his death.

Charlemagne vigorously promoted the adoption of the Roman rite and Roman chant. The first substantial evidence of the practice of adding musical and textual additions to the chant (troping) had its beginnings in the period shortly after his death.

ROMANESQUE AND GOTHIC

No centralized political power arose to succeed the empire of Charlemagne after its dissolution at the end of the 9th century.

Feudalism, a system arising partly from barbarian society and partly from Roman customs, now became the basis of social organization. At its base was an agrarian society with serfs bound to the land exchanging freedom for the protection of militaristic upper classes. In a rising hierarchy of rank each noble owed service to the next higher noble in return for protection. This resulted in a complex web of interrelationships spreading over Europe. Before the mid-12th century the main centers of religious and intellectual life were the monasteries. The Cluniac and later the Cistercian orders wielded vast influence with the Cistercians leading in the development of agriculture. In the Gothic 13th century, the emergence of specialization in occupations and of trade guilds was accompanied by a migration to the towns and cities, and the parish church and the cathedral became the main religious centers. The skills and techniques of the guild of freemasons made possible the building of cathedrals.

12th Century Humanism- The Romanesque Period

From the period of Charlemagne on there was a resurgence of cultural activity. The 12th century was an "open" century, a century of "a thousand flowers". The Crusades, beginning at the end of the 11th century, brought contacts with the more advanced cultures of the Middle East. Plato and Boethius were rediscovered together with other Greek writers, some in translation from Greek into Latin. Many of these writers were made known through translations from the Arabic, reaching northern Europe through Moslem Spain. Friedrich Heer[1] writes:

In this expanding Europe of the twelfth century there was such curiosity and so great a thirst for knowledge that the intellectual

---

[1]Friedrich Heer, *The Medieval World*, trans Janet Sondheimer (New York, World Publishing Co., 1962), p. 19

and cultural treasure Islam had to offer exerted an immense attraction. This treasure was nothing less than the intellectual wealth of Greek antiquity, augmented by the glosses and commentaries of Islamic scholars from the Near East and Mediterranean, masters in a vast and flourishing "empire of learning" which stretched from Persia and Samarkand by way of Baghdad and Salerno to Toledo. Arab (and Jewish) translators and commentators helped to make the heritage of philosophical and scientific writings left by Plato and Aristotle and their disciples and successors available to the West. Not only in Spain, but also in Southern France, Sicily, and southern Italy, there were men who welcomed these contacts and kept the lines of communication with Islam open.

The spirit of tolerance allowed the growth, in Southern France, of a cult of Christianity known as the Cathari, or Albigenses. It allowed groups of wandering students, the goliards, to beg for a night's shelter in a monastery, even while they sang their irreverent drinking songs in Latin and parodied the Liturgy. Their more serious lyrics showed the humanistic influence of Roman poetry. Roman gods and goddesses, Diana, Venus, and Bacchus rear their Classic heads in their poems. The chief seat of humanist thought in the first half of the 12th century was at Chartres. Classical Latin was taught in the cloisters, though here the emphasis was rather on the historians than the poets.

The architectural style of the monastery was the Romanesque, a style which dominated the monastery churches. It was the influence of Roman thought and Roman forms that gave the Romanesque its name. It revived the Roman arch and barrel vault and contained something of the grandiose ideal that dominated Roman structures with their large, massive, monumental forms. Monumental statuary reappeared in the mid-twelfth century, first at St. Denis, then at Chartres. This statuary, too, was representational.

The resurgence of artistic creation brought with it a new era of sacred monophony - the so-called "silver age" of Gregorian chant - with the creation of musical and textual additions to the Gregorian repertory, the tropes and sequences. The first manuscripts of polyphony also appeared. The first phase of rhythmic organization in music was dominated by texts applying the quantitative (durational) principle of Classical poetry.

Likewise the new openness led to the influence of Gregorian chant on Mozarabic chant which had developed in relative isolation from the 6th to the 11th centuries.

The Gothic Period

A reaction against humanism and tolerance followed in the 13th century known as the Gothic period. The goliards were outlawed and the humanists lost out; the Albigensian crusade destroyed this religious cult, and along with it the culture of Southern France. The Moslems were gradually driven out of Spain, a process completed by the end of the 15th century. But there resulted in the 13th century the emergence of a new indigenous European culture.

A striving for height in architectural effects, aided by the pointed arch and the flying buttress began to manifest itself, using techniques developed by the guild of Freemasons working with calipers, T-squares, and plumb-lines . This constituted a characteristically Western European style.

The troubadours and trouvères were the musical representatives of the institution of chivalry. They created new musical forms and used the Western European dialects. We know the names of such troubadours as Marcabru of Gascony (d. c. 1147), Jaufre Rudel (fl. 1130-41), Bernart da Ventadorn (d. 1195). Characteristic cultures began to make themselves distinguishable in Western Europe, each with a dialect that grew out of the Ecclesiastical Latin. These dialects became the media of the texts of the secular music of the time. The troubadours sang in the *langue d'oc,* the tongue of what is now southern France while the trouvères used the *langue d'oil,* the ancestor of the modern French language.

The Gothic period thus marks the first mature, perfected, expression of the new peoples of Europe. Polyphony emerged as the most important medium of musical creation. Note-groups (the rhythmic modes) were the first means of showing rhythmic notation independently of text. It was this method of notating rhythm to which a later age applied the term *Ars antiqua.* French art dominates the Gothic period, and the musicians of the Cathedral of Notre Dame in Paris constitute the most important school of the time. Daily life was saturated with religion - one religion that admitted of no deviation - and nowhere is this fact more evident than in the way that sacred and profane melodies were combined in a single musical composition. The Gothic motet of the Paris school employed troubadour and trouvère songs with their original words to sound simultaneously above a cantus firmus of Gregorian chant. This motet was thus both a sacred and a secular form. A serious religious note was introduced into the tradition handed down by the troubadours. In Germany Walther von der Vogelweide sang his famous *Palestine Song*; in Spain the *Cantigas da Sancta Maria* sang of the miracles of the Virgin Mary; the *laudi spirituali* were musical representatives of the popular religious revival inspired by St. Francis of Assisi.

TROPES AND SEQUENCES

The musical and textural additions to the chant were known as *tropes* and *sequences*, and the practice of creating them flourished chiefly from 800 to 1200. In the early part of the period, which began with the reign of Charlemagne, it became customary to add melismas to parts of the liturgy which, because of their importance, seemed to call for elaboration. A more highly developed and extended kind of elaboration included the composition of new texts as well as new melodies. These new texts, many of them poetic, would enlarge on the ideas expressed in the original liturgy. These new additions were called *tropes* . The most important of the tropes, and the one that crystallized into a distinct form, was the trope to the *jubilus* on the last syllable of the Alleluia. This trope was given the name of *sequence*. The usual sequence form is: *a b b c c d d . . . y y z*. Thus, each melodic phrase is repeated except the first and last. The practice of troping proliferated to such an extent that the Council of Trent (1545-63) banned all but four sequences. Masses had been named by the beginnings of the texts of their Kyrie tropes (e.g. *Missa Lux et Origo*), and these names have been retained even though the tropes that gave rise to them have been eliminated.

The creators of these additions are also known to us by name. Among them were Tutilo (d. 915), a monk of the monastery of St. Gall in Switzerland; Wipo of Burgundy (d. c. 1048); Hermannus Contractus (1013-1054) of the monastery of Reichenau; and Adam (d. 1192), a monk of the Abbey of St. Victoire in France. With these musical creations of the 11th and 12th centuries we have before us the first incontrovertible examples of music created in Western Europe.

Of the sequences, perhaps the most famous is the *Dies irae* from the Proper of the Mass for the Dead (Requiem Mass). Its text is one of the best examples of the rhymed accentual poetry of medieval Latin. The melody was a favorite of various 19th century composers and was quoted by such composers as Berlioz' (*Fantastic Symphony*), Liszt (*Dance of the Dead [Totentanz]*) and Rachmaninoff.

In the later Middle Ages the sequence, as well as the hymn, became models for secular forms. These forms were used in the music of the troubadours, the trouvères, and the minnesingers; in instrumental dance music; and even in polyphony. The hymn and sequence both owed their influence to their strophic structure, i.e. the use of melodic repetition with changing text. Strophic form itself dates back to the time of the ancient Greek drama.

The Liturgical Drama

Another interesting outgrowth of the practice of troping was the liturgical drama. Note that the term *liturgical* is not strictly accurate since these compositions were not actually part of the Roman Catholic Liturgy. They included chanted dialogue and action and gave opportunity for colorful costumes and processions. Dialogue is inherent in the antiphonal and responsive performance of the chant, and drama is an integral part of some of the ecclesiastical rites. The actual origin of the ecclesiastical drama was a trope which was introduced before the Introit of the Easter Mass, and which consisted of a brief dialogue. The earliest literary references to liturgical dramas date from the 10th century. Music for these dramas was borrowed or adapted with varying degrees of freedom from antiphons, sequences, hymns, and the songs of the troubadours and trouvères.

Marian Antiphons

The Marian Antiphons, chants in praise of the Virgin Mary, also belong to this period of musical composition (11th and 12th centuries). The four which have survived are among the most important and beautiful of the compositions of the later Middle Ages. They are: *Alma redemptoris mater, Ave regina caelorum, Regina caeli laetare,* and *Salve regina.* They are much more elaborate and extended than the typical antiphons which are used with psalms, though at one time they seem to have been used with the psalmody. They received frequent polyphonic settings in the Renaissance. One, and possibly two of these antiphons were composed by Hermannus Contractus.

SECULAR MONOPHONY

Goliards

Secular monophony, called *Cantilenae* by writers of the period, had its beginnings in Latin verse. Medieval Latin verse (e.g. the *Dies irae*) was accentual in its rhythm, like modern English verse, not quantitative (i.e. durational, with rhythmic note values) like Classical Latin or Greek. There was, as we have noted, a revival of Classical Latin in the humanistic movement of the first half of the 12th century. Secular Latin verse was written at the court of Charlemagne. Another body of Latin lyrics came from a group of wandering scholars and clerics of minor orders of the 10th to 12th centuries. The group included runaway clergymen and clergymen who had completed their studies but could not buy benefices (positions). This movement, in spite of its unsavory aspects, produced some brilliant secular song. The self-styled Archipoeta (King of the Poets) in the 12th century wrote of the *Ordo vagorum* (Order of Wanderers) and of the mythical Bishop Golias (*Golias* is the Ashkenazic Hebrew variant of the name *Goliath*), their patron. The founding of universities in the 12th century swelled the number of wanderers by leading to a great migration of young theological students who took to the road in the process of coming to the universities. There was also much movement from one university to another. The wanderers led a merry life, drinking, gambling, and singing outrageous parodies on the Liturgy. Yet they included among their writings some moving and serious secular verse based on a knowledge of the Classics and dealing with their favorite subjects of Spring and love. They were known as *vagantes* (wanderers), *falsi fratres* (false brothers), or more commonly goliards (after Bishop Golias).

The budding secular art, in a culture dominated by the Church, characteristically sought its expression in parody of sacred texts. Translations of goliardic verse into the vernacular are believed to have played a part in the creation of early troubadour songs. Perhaps the best known source of goliardic verse is the 13th century manuscript found in the early 19th century in a secularized Benedictine monastery at Beuren in Bavaria. Its verse was published under the title of *Carmina Burana* (Songs of Beuren) in 1847. A modern (1937) setting of some of the poetry, for chorus and orchestra, was made by the German composer Carl Orff. Most of the verse of the Beuren collection was in Latin, but some was in the vernacular. What little of its music survives is notated in staffless neumes which cannot be deciphered as to pitch. However, there are a group of some 40 melodies that can be deciphered with the help of other sources, such as the St. Martial manuscripts where the notation is decipherable. Their knowledge of Classical Latin verse suggests that the rhythm of their music was determined by the scansion of the text, at least where the texts were in Latin.

Peter Abelard

A towering figure of the early 12th century was that of Peter Abelard (1079-1142), philosopher, teacher, poet, and composer. His disputatious temperament, skill at dialectic, and contempt of their other teachers endeared him to his young students. His skill at disputation won him the sobriquet of "Goliath with the club of Hercules" - an interesting combination of biblical and Classical figures.   When he became the lover of his young pupil Héloïse, her uncle, Canon Fulbert had him castrated. The songs he composed for her became famous all over France. She wrote of his gifts in making poetry and singing "both *in the classic metres* and the new rhyming."

Jongleurs, Gaukler

Other groups of wanderers, not of the educated class, were the *jongleurs* in France and their German counterparts, the *Gaukler*. They were poor and lived by doing tricks and singing songs (though not original) to provide entertainment, usually for the common people. Sometimes they assisted the troubadours and trouvères for whom they were expected to perform on instruments. Some of the more fortunate might become attached to a noble household where they were known as *ministrelli* (the diminutive of *ministri,* household help) or minstrels.

Chanson de geste

A type of composition later cultivated by the trouvères was the *chanson de geste* (lit. song of deeds). It was probably created some time after the year 1,000 by the joint efforts of clerks and jongleurs and performed by the jongleurs. The *chanson de geste* was perhaps meant to attract pilgrims to the shrines where its heroes were supposed to be buried. The most famous of the genre was the *Chanson de Roland* (c 1100). An incident occurring during the withdrawal of Charlemagne's armies from Spain gave rise to this important literary source. The army was attacked by Basques at Roncevalles and Roland, the leader of Charlemagne's forces, was killed. The incident was recounted in a *chanson de geste,* entitled *Chanson de Roland* and received its most important literary manifestation at the hands of the great Italian poet of the Renaissance, Ludovico Ariosto, in his poem *Orlando furioso* (Roland driven mad,1532). It became the source of many opera libretti including one by Handel (*Orlando*, 1733).

Another *Chanson de geste* tells of Huon de Bordeaux, the hero of von Weber's opera *Oberon*. (1826). These epics were possibly sung to a single snatch of melody repeated for each line of the poem with a modification for the last line.

Chivalry

The troubadours and trouvères flourished in the Age of Chivalry which arose in the Gothic period with the emergence of a specifically Western European culture. They developed new and complex musical and poetic forms and used the vernacular languages. Chivalry represented an idealized concept of the military man which grew among the nobility of feudal society. It developed a complex code of behavior stressing the virtues of piety, bravery, honor and loyalty. Loyalty was owed to God, to the suzerain (temporal superior) and to the mistress of the heart. Honor meant individual dignity; and the existence of the concept of honor interjects a personal note into the other-worldly anonymity of medieval culture. Courtly love has had a deep influence on Western culture. It had an ascetic flavor and placed the object of its desire on a pedestal of unattainability. It was influenced by the cult of the Virgin as developed by St. Bernard of the monastery of Clairvaux. The concept of romantic love was a creation of this culture.

Troubadours

Courtly love was first set forth in the songs of the troubadours in 12th century Provence. The troubadours, as well as their French successors from the north, the trouvères, were members of the chivalric aristocracy, and their activity centered around a court. The names *troubadour* and *trouvère* meant that these men were composers. Both terms were derived from the verbs meaning 'to find', since their concept of musical composition was to find a melody.

It is believed that the troubadour movement was begun by Guillaume, Count of Poitier and Duke of Aquitaine, a nobleman of the southwestern part of France. He and his followers wrote songs using the langue d'oc, a tongue of southern France related to the modern Provencal. The troubadour movement declined after the beginning of the 13th century because most of the people of the region were members of the Cathari, or Albigenses; and the Albigensian crusade, beginning in 1209, destroyed their culture. The surviving troubadours were scattered throughout the courts of northern France, England, Italy, Spain, and Sicily in the 13th century.

Trouvères

The northern counterpart of the troubadour was the trouvère who sang in the langue d'oil, the ancestor of modern French. The troubadour movement spread to northern France partly through the influence of the crusaders whose travels had a unifying effect on European culture. Not to be underestimated was the personal influence of Eleanor of Aquitaine. An ardent admirer of the troubadour art, she was the granddaughter of Guillaume of Poitier and the only woman in history to be queen of both France and England. She married the King of France in 1137 and divorced him to marry the Duke of Anjou who later became Henry II of England. The famous troubadour Bernart da Ventadorn was in her retinue and her own son Richard I, the Lionhearted, was himself a trouvère.

The trouvère art, originally the province of the aristocracy, came, in the second half of the 13th century, to be practiced by the bourgeois poets from a class created by the institution of craft guilds. The most important of these, gifted as both poet and musician, was Adam de la Halle (1240-1287), the Hunchback of Arras. Among his works are both monophonic and polyphonic pieces, and he wrote the oldest extant secular play with music, the *Jeu de Robin et Marion* (the Play of Robin and Marion).

Texts

The formalism of chivalric codes is reflected both in the music with its complex forms and in the various categories into which the poetic texts fall. These text categories include: the *canso*, or love song; *partimen*, a dialogue usually discussing a question of love; the *tenso*, more general in subject matter, often a debate and sometimes a satire, such as a song criticizing King Rudolph I for his parsimony; dance songs; and dramatic songs. The dramatic songs include the *pastourell* in which the poet-knight makes love to a shepherdess usually (though not always) unsuccessfully (in its later, bourgeois phase, it frequently told of a rape followed by a beating given by the outraged peasantry. *Robin m'aime* of Adam de la Halle is somewhat in the vein of the later pastourell.); the *chanson de toile*, or spinning song, in which an unhappy wife pines for her lover, or a young girl bewails her lover's absence or decries the social barriers between her and her beloved; the *alba* (Fr. *aubade*),or dawn song in which the singer, a friend of two lovers, stands watch to warn them of the coming of daylight; the *sirventes* (song of service) which treated of political or moral matters; the *planh* (Fr. *plaint*), a song of mourning; and the *eneug,* a satire. The bourgeois phase of trouvère song is reflected in the work of Adam de la Halle. The end of the period also saw the entrance into the trouvère repertory of the religious song -

another reflection of the intermixture of the sacred and secular in the late Gothic period.

Various devices of text repetition, such as the use of a refrain, are found in the poetry. The troubadour Arnaut Daniel (d. 1199) was particularly noted for the virtuosity of his poetic forms, one of which (the sestina) was employed by Dante 100 years later and was made the basis of a serial composition by Ernst Krenek in the 20th century.

Troubadour and trouvère melodies

Troubadour and trouvère melodies often show the influence of Gregorian chant and may be in one of the church modes; but there is a tendency to use the major and minor modes. The rhythm of the songs is believed to have been governed by the principles of modal rhythm (a system somewhat related to Greek poetic meters), and it has become customary, in modern editions, to transcribe them in accordance with one or the other of the rhythmic modes. The notation itself gives no clue in most cases. The languages of troubadour and trouvère texts were much more strongly accented than is modern French, and the accent is used to give clues as to the rhythm.

The forms of troubadour and trouvère melodies exhibit great variety and ingenuity and anticipate almost all of the later song forms. Because of their organization, these melodic forms have been termed *formes fixes* (fixed forms), and their direct influence extended well into the 15th century. Church sequences and hymns may have been a starting point for the development of troubadour forms, but the high degree of organization was a creation of the troubadours and trouvères. Schemes of repetition and recapitulation are many and varied and range from adaptations of the simple litany-type (the repetition of a single melodic phrase for all lines of text as seen in the *chanson de geste*) to types of great complexity. Most of the troubadour and trouvère melodies fall into balanced phrases of four measures and periods of eight measures, and the repetitions are based on these symmetrical phrases and periods. Strophic structure also plays a significant role. The text settings were mostly syllabic with occasional neumatic passages. The following example is a *rondeau,* one of the fixed forms of which examples are found (in polyphonic versions) through the first half of the 15th century. The repetition and recapitulation scheme of the music and text is as follows:

Example 1 (See HAM1, 19d)

Music: (a) (b (a) (a) (a) (b) (a) (b)
Text: [a] [b] [c] [a] [d] [e] [a] [b]

[a] *On my lady dwells my heart,* [b] *and my thought.*
[c] *From her I will never part,* [d] *I was conquered by her gray eyes* [e] *lively and clear*

(a)*En ma dame ai mis mon coeur,* (b) *et mon penser*
(a)*N'en partiroi e nul fuer* (a)*En ma dame ai mis mon coeur.*
(a)*Si m'ont sorpris si vair oeil,* (b) *viant et clair*
(a)*En ma dame ai mis mon coeur* (b) *et mon penser.*
[Note: the letters in parentheses refer to the melodic scheme.]

The Minnesinger

The Minnesingers, who flourished in the 12th and 13th centuries, were the German counterpart of the troubadour and trouvère. *Minne* was the German word for courtly love. Their relationship to the trouvères is revealed by the fact that some German poems were written to go with French melodies. The troubadour influence reached Germany in various ways. Chief among these was by way of the royal household. When Frederick Barbarossa, the Holy Roman emperor, married Beatrix of Burgundy in 1156, she brought a troubadour in her retinue. The Minnesingers came mostly from Southern Germany and Austria, and though they stemmed from the troubadours, they made their own individual contributions. The expression of the Minnesingers tends to be more serious than that of their French counterparts. Moreover, the Minnesinger tends to make more frequent use of the church modes. The best period of the Minnesingers was the last decade of the 12th century and the beginning of the 13th.

A favorite form of the Minnesingers was the bar-form: *a a b* . This form was subject to various modifications, such as melodic links between the *a* and *b* sections. The ending of the *b* section might resemble the ending of the *a* section.

As to rhythm, it is customary to transcribe Minnesinger melodies in measured rhythm. However, because of the nature of the accentuation of German poetry, the rhythmic modes are not used, and the meter is often duple.

Two important sources of materials for both French and German courtly lyrics were the Celtic legends of Tristram and Iseult, and King Arthur and his knights. The story of one of Arthur's knights, Sir Percival, under the name of *Parzival*, became a literary classic in the hands of the Minnesinger Wolfram von Eschenbach. From *Parzival*, Wagner took the theme of his last music drama *Parsifal*. The Tristram story, in its version by the Minnesinger Gottfried von Strassburg, became the source of Wagner's music drama *Tristan und Isolde*. Tannhaüser, the subject of another work by Wagner, was a historical figure, a Minnesinger; and the competition at the Wartburg between him and Wolfram von Eschenbach, described by Wagner, actually took place. Teutonic legends also furnished material for the Minnesingers. The *Nibelungenlied* (Song of the Nibelungs), a Christianized version of a Teutonic legend, was another Minnelied that became one of the sources of a work by Wagner (*Götterdämmerung*). One of the most celebrated of the Minnesingers was Walther von der Vogelweide whose *Palestine Song* describes his spiritual and religious feelings on visiting the Holy Land during the Crusades. He also appears as a character in Wagner's opera *Tannhaüser*.

In the area of musical production, England appears to reflect a rather unsettled state of affairs at this time. The Catholic community in Moslem Spain, however, left a musical legacy in the *Cantigas da Sancta Maria* dating from late in the trouvère period. At about the same time, the *laudi spirituali* (spiritual praises) appeared in Italy. Both the *Cantigas* and the *laudi spirituali* are in the vernacular tongues and use the forms of troubadour and trouvère art but imbue them with a strong religious flavor, thus reflecting the previously mentioned trend toward the fusion of the sacred and secular in the Late Gothic period.

The Use of Instruments in Secular Monophony

Organs were constructed in Germany in the 9th century and by the 10th century they were being built in England also. Stringed instruments were used, including the lyra and kithara - the plucked stringed instruments of Classical Antiquity - which are known to have survived as late as the 6th century and possibly later. The jongleur was expected to accompany himself on such instruments as the small portable organ, the harp, the guitar, the lute (introduced by the Moors), the psaltery (a plucked stringed instrument with a flat sound board), and the vièle (a bowed stringed instrument).

We do not know how instruments were used in the accompaniment of troubadour and trouvère music since all the surviving notation is monophonic. The absence of text under the refrain of a piece by the trouvère Thibaut of Navarre may indicate that this refrain was to be performed instrumentally.

EARLY POLYPHONY

During the Carolingian period (9th century) we come upon the first clear accounts of a new type of music which was to determine the future course of the art in the West. This was *polyphony*, the music of simultaneously sounding tones. Like tropes, sequences, and the liturgical drama, polyphony served as an addition to the chant. Thus, like most important cultural developments in the Middle Ages, polyphony stemmed from the Church. In medieval polyphony the notes of the chant were always present to serve as the controlling and organizing force. The polyphony consisted of nothing more than the addition of harmonic intervals to the ecclesiastical melodies. The evolution of medieval polyphony was toward greater melodic independence of the added parts- a trend which reached an apex in the Gothic period.

Early History

Though the contribution of the Ancient Greeks to the science of acoustics was a great one, it is believed that their studies of musical intervals were limited to melodic succession and not harmonic combination. Certain passages in the writings of the early Christian era, notably those of Boethius and St. Augustine, seem to refer to the simultaneous sounding of tones of different pitch, but the meaning of these passages is obscure. Philo of Alexandria, in the first century A.D. describes the simultaneous singing of men and women with the clear implication that they must have been singing in octaves. The first known unequivocal reference to part singing occurs in 7th century England in the writings of Bishop Aldhelm. The earliest clear description of polyphony stems from the 9th century *Musica enchiriadis* (Handbook of Music), a work of unknown authorship. The passages describing polyphonic practice, however, indicated that what was being described was the culmination of a practice that had gone through a long period of evolution. According to the author of this treatise, the purpose of polyphony was to decorate the chant.

Parallel organum

Musica enchiriadis describes two kinds of polyphony or *organum* (*organum* was a medieval term for polyphony constructed on plainsong). The first kind is a very simple kind in which to each note of the plainsong is added a harmonic interval a fifth below. This is called strict organum at the fifth. If the voices were doubled at the octave, a strict composite organum at the fifth would result. The same procedure could be carried out using the fourth. Only intervals of the simplest ratios are used: 2/1, 3/2, 4/3. In this type of polyphony the harmonic intervals are the sole determinants of the harmonic style. The chordal emphasis of the music is underscored by the slow, solemn tempo of the performance, minimizing the melodic flow.

EXAMPLE 2

The second type of organum described in *Musica enchiriadis* is of a freer type. It embraces, though in rudimentary fashion, the principle that melodic movement can itself play a role in the determination of harmonic intervals. It thus contains the seeds of a further evolution clearly lacking in the first type. In this freer type of organum the two voices begin on the same note. The lower (added) voice sustains its note while the upper voice (the chant) moves diatonically until the two voices are a fourth apart, whereupon both voices continue in perfect fourths. The passage ends with unisons. Occasionally, a fifth may be substituted for a fourth to avoid the *fa-ti* sound. Guido d'Arezzo's *Micrologus* (c. 1100) shows leanings toward the free type of parallel organum just described - a type which now gains preference over the older strict parallel organum.

EXAMPLE 3

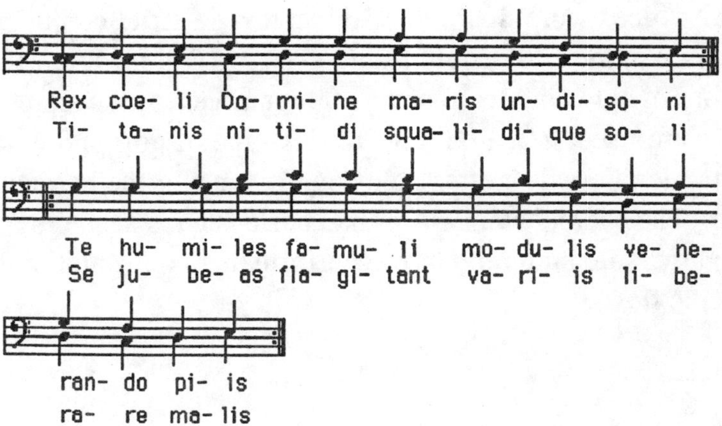

Another stage in the evolution of polyphony is recognizable in an 11th century treatise of apparently French origin, *Ad organum faciendum* (On the Making of Organum). The organum of this treatise is known as free organum. In it there are two factors which point to increased importance of the added voice: (1) The recognized consonances of the medieval period, the octave, fourth, and fifth are used in free alternation so that the added voice has a degree of melodic independence and (2) the added voice is above the chant so that it is given more prominence.

In free organum the added voice begins to move in melodic directions of its own, frequently in contrary motion to the original chant melody. The voices also cross occasionally, and an occasional dissonance is to be found. Note that at this time the third was considered dissonant.

EXAMPLE 4

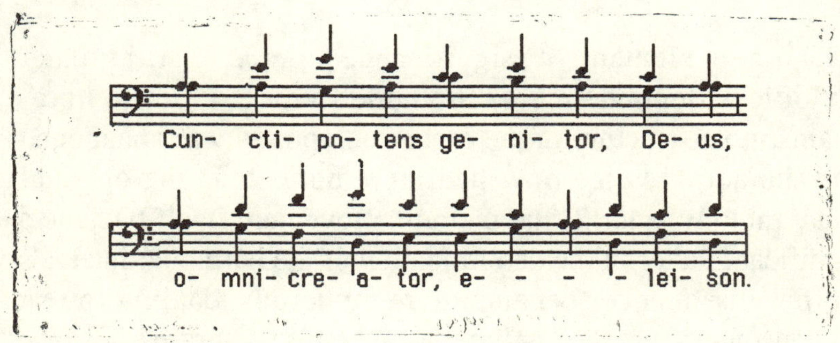

Melismatic Organum

The added voice gains still more independence - rhythmic independence - in the style known as melismatic organum. This style is found in several manuscripts of French origin dating from the early 12th century. Four of them come from the monastery of St. Martial in Limoges; and one comes from the cathedral of Santiago da Compostela in Northwest Spain, a section which escaped the Moorish conquest and became a shrine to which large numbers of French pilgrims journeyed. It was believed that the body of St. James the Apostle was buried here.

EXAMPLE 5

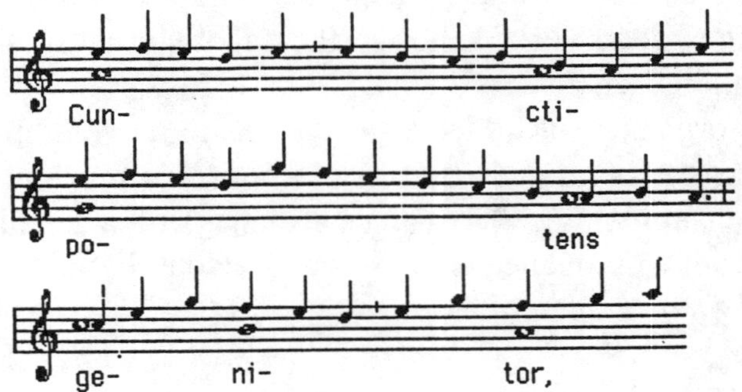

Two new elements of significance pointed to still greater melodic independence of the added voice: (1) The note-against-note structure of the earlier polyphony was abandoned and the added voice now had more notes than the original chant melody, and (2) the melodic movement itself became a significant factor in the determination of the harmonic intervals so that dissonances became more numerous, coming to rest on consonances at the beginnings and ends of phrases.

Rhythmically Measured Music

With the emergence of polyphony in which the added voice moved at a pace different from the original, the problem of rhythmic notation became an increasingly pressing one. Rhythmic notation became necessary to correlate the notes of the chant with the added voices. Eventually, the name *discant* came to be associated with rhythmically measured music. Meanwhile, the writing of parts in *score* i.e. one above the other, helped to show how the voices fitted together. All the polyphony to which the term organum is applied is notated in score form. The score form was discarded in the first quarter of the 13th century, not to be revived until the rise of orchestral music c. 1600.

As compared with pitch notation for which the basic solution was worked out in the time of Guido of Arezzo, the development of a system of rhythmic notation was painfully slow. The expression of time values by means of filled and unfilled note-heads and by stems and tails, came about very gradually. The appearance of notes (called *neumes)* used for plainsong notation varied so much from region to region in the Romanesque period that this circumstance alone would have made impossible a rhythmic notation such as we use today. Rhythmic notation remained in a fluid state, constantly changing, from the 12th to the 14th centuries.

Rhythmic Modes

Rhythmically measured music (mensural music) came into existence before a notation for it existed. As we have seen, measured rhythm had existed in the quantitative meter of Classical poetry. There is evidence that some poetic texts gave their meter to the music, a circumstance which may indicate the influence of Classical quantitative meter though the extent of the influence is questioned by some writers. A possible influence on rhythmic thought in the humanistic revival of the 12th century was the *De Musica* of St Augustine (late 4th century). This work treated largely of rhythm and meter in six volumes and had reference to Classical poetic meter.

The first system of mensural notation was based on rhythmic patterns indicated by groupings of notes rather than note-shapes in the modern manner. These groupings correspond to the meters used in Latin (and French) verse. These patterns when used in music were called *rhythmic modes*, and they first appeared in the late 12th century. The system was refined during the 13th century. The medieval musicians, however, modified the system by converting all poetic feet into compound meter (triple division of the beat). Medieval writers, with a kind of Neo-Pythagorean mysticism, rationalized that the triple division was adopted in honor of the Trinity.

The standardization of note-shapes was an important factor in the emergence of a rhythmic notation. Notes which differed in appearance could become associated with different durational values, but there were intermediate steps in this direction. The system of rhythmic modes was just such a step. In poetry there were two possible values for a syllable, viz., long and short, and these were the first rhythmic values to be used in music. With the melismatic text settings to which the rhythmic modes were applied the notes were written in group characters, called ligatures. They first appeared in the late 12th century. In this modal notation the time values (long and short) were not shown by means of note-shapes but by standardized combinations of notes. Walter Odington, writing c. 1300, discusses the system retrospectively and is the first source to use names derived from Greek poetry for these rhythmic modes. Frequent ambiguities characterized the system. There were six rhythmic modes, as shown below. Note in the illustration that the time-values are expressed in modern notation. The poetic symbols for long and short are shown above the notes:

EXAMPLE 6

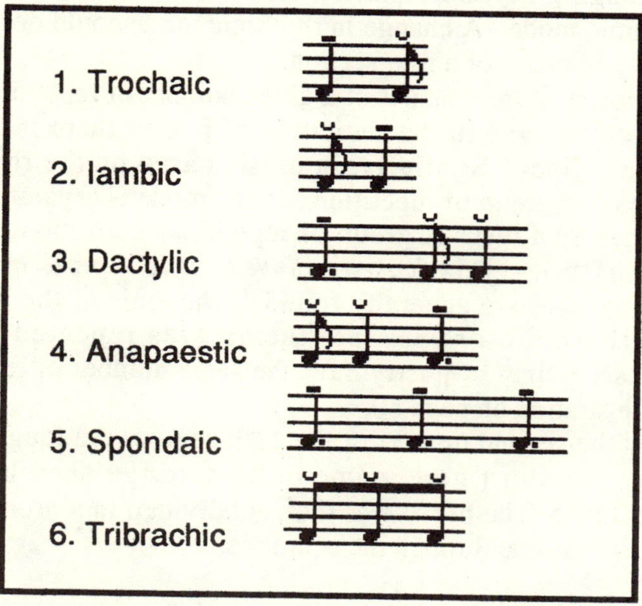

The system of poetic feet, which was perfectly satisfactory for poetry, broke down when applied to polyphonic music. As illustrated above, the following inconsistencies are immediately apparent. Firstly there are two different longs: (1) the long of the trochee (the quarter note) and (2) the long of the dactyl, its first note (the dotted quarter note). Secondly, there are two different shorts: viz., the two shorts of the dactyl (1) an eighth note and (2) a quarter note. Thirdly, the second short of the dactyl and the long of the trochee must both be transcribed as quarter notes. Thus, in order to read modal notation, it is necessary to be able to decide beforehand what rhythmic mode is intended.

Music based on the rhythmic modes is characterized by a strongly marked, repetitive rhythmic pulse as well as an unchanging rhythmic pattern associated with the particular rhythmic mode. A change in rhythmic mode could occur only at the beginning of a new section.

In poetry a line consists of a given number of repetitions of a poetic foot, and in the recitation of poetry there is a pause between lines. Similarly, in music based on the rhythmic modes one group of repetitions of the mode is separated from another by a rest. A group of repetitions corresponding to a line of poetry is known as an *ordo* (pl. *ordines*). Consonances are generally found at the ends of the *ordines*. The rhythmic *ordines* are themselves repeated just as successive lines of poetry have the same number of feet. See the illustration on page 80.

By the second quarter of the 13th century the long and the breve, or short note, came to be distinguished by their appearance. The breve was then subdivided in a process that was to continue through the centuries.

The Notre Dame School

The earliest music using measured rhythm is found in the Notre Dame school of composers who were writing at about the time when the Cathedral of Notre Dame, Paris was being constructed (ca. late 12th and early 13th centuries). In addition to the anonymous compositions of the school there appear the names of two composers: the earliest known composers of polyphony, Léoninus (Léonin) and his successor Pérotinus (Pérotin). These composers were both choir-masters at the earlier church, the Church of Beatae Mariae Virginis. Pérotinus, the younger of the two, may have even been associated with the new and subsequently famed Cathedral of Notre Dame.

Léoninus

The polyphony of Léoninus, called *organa* (the plural of *organum*) is found in a collection called *Magnus liber organi* (Great Book of Organa). It was written to be used at important feasts where it replaced the chants of the soloist in the responsorial psalmody. The choral portion was still sung in plainsong.

The organa of Léoninus fall into sections written in two different styles. In one style the chant is set in long sustained tones against a faster moving added voice in measured rhythm. In the other style, applied where the chant is melismatic, both voices move in largely note-against-note procedure and both voices use rhythmic modes. In actual performance plainsong passages by the choir constitute another style.

Melodic Sequences

An interesting feature of the Notre Dame school is the use of melodic sequences (not to be confused with the sequence form previously mentioned). A melodic sequence consists of the repetition of a melodic fragment at different pitch levels, and it was to become an important device in later centuries:

EXAMPLE 7

Pérotinus

Léoninus's successor was Magister Pérotinus whose activity in Paris began about 1183. He substituted new sections, or *clausulae*, in note-against-note (discant) style for various sections written by Léoninus. Pérotinus tended to abandon the style in which the chant was set in sustained tones. Note: when chant is used as the basis of a polyphonic composition, it is frequently called *tenor*. Since Pérotinus's tenor moved in faster note values it often had to be repeated several times. If the tenor and the rhythmic pattern coincide in the repetitions, a ground bass or *basso ostinato* (repeated bass melody) will result. However, the number of tones in the tenor may be such that the repetition of the tenor does not coincide with a repetition of the rhythmic mode. In such a case, the tones of the tenor will fall in different places in the rhythmic pattern with each repetition.The shifting relationship between a pitch pattern and a rhythmic pattern played an important role in tenors well into the 15th century.

The following example from a French motet of the 13th century illustrates the rhythmic shift of the tenor tones. In the illustration below the numbers below the notes refer to the sequence of tones in the pitch pattern:

EXAMPLE 8

Some of Pérotinus's organa are in three voices, and there are examples of four-voiced organa. Upper voices sometimes show the influence of folk-song. There is occasional exchange of melodic material between the added voices of a composition. This exchange foreshadows the deliberate imitation of one voice by another, a device that achieved structural significance in the Renaissance. As to harmonic intervals, Pérotinus's style makes abundant use of dissonance resulting from the movement of the melodic lines. Frequent use of the same rhythmic mode in all voices builds up a feeling of tremendous power by its insistent reiteration. Pérotinus's work consisted essentially in modifying parts of the *Magnus liber organi* left by Léoninus. Pérotinus did not seek to create an independent artistic work in the sense that a 19th century composer might. He left much of Léoninus's work unaltered or only slightly modified.

Terminology of the Notre Dame school

Following are some terms which apply to the form and style of the music of the Notre Dame school: (1) **Form**. The whole polyphonic composition of a responsory is called an *organum*. The individual sections are called *clausulae* or *puncta*. (2) **Style**. When the tenor has long sustained tones, the style is called *organum*. If the tenor is in modal rhythm, the style is called *discant* or, by some writers, *clausula* . Note that the terms *clausula* and *organum* may be used for both a form and a style. The discant clausulae (sections with tenors in modal rhythm) are based on melismatic portions of the chant. Organum style (with sustained tones in the tenor) tends to be based on chant which is syllabic or neumatic. Discant clausulae are more frequent in Pérotinus's version than in that of Léoninus.

The Paris Motet

Ever since the time of the emergence of the melismatic organum of the school of St. Martial, the creation of polyphony resulted in long sections of music without text. In the music of the later Middle Ages there was a tendency to add syllabic settings to untexted music. Tropes and sequences were given syllabic and neumatic settings, and in Pérotinus's time the same process took place in the discant clausulae. In the discant clausulae even the tenor had very few syllables of text. Where the text was so sparse, the upper voice might abandon the Word (Fr. *mot*) of the Liturgy and substitute a little text (motet) of its own. Eventually, the whole composition with added text came to be called a motet. There are pieces which appear in one source as discant clausulae and in another (with text added), as motets. The motet came to be the most important form of the 13th century. It is usually called the Paris motet or 13th century motet in modern terminology to distinguish it from compositions of later periods which use the name motet.

Originally, the upper voices of the motet, usually two, were in the same rhythmic mode and used the same text, which paraphrased the text of the tenor and thus produced a simultaneous troping. Incidentally, one voice above the tenor was called *motetus* while another was called triplum from which we get the modern word *treble*. In later years, however, the two upper voices came to have different texts and different rhythmic modes; and with the advent of French texts in the second half of the 13th century their connection with the sacred words of the tenor completely disappeared. These French texts were often taken from secular trouvère songs (to be discussed in the following section) and included love songs and drinking songs. The motets now became secular as well as sacred and are thus the earliest examples of secular polyphony. The nature of the intermixture of the sacred and secular in the later phases of the Gothic period has been noted by Jan Huizinga[2] who speaks of "the astonishing ingenuousness with which, before the Council of Trent, worldly occupations were mixed up with words of the Faith." He adds:

> All life was saturated with religion to such an extent that the people were in constant danger of losing sight of the distinction between things spiritual and things temporal. If, on the one hand, all details of ordinary life may be raised to the sacred level, on the other hand, all that is holy sinks into the commonplace, by the fact of being blended with everyday life . . .the demarcation of the sphere of religious thought and that of worldly concerns was nearly obliterated. It occasionally happened that indulgences figured among the prizes of a lottery . . . There was a constant interchange of religious and profane terms. No one felt offended by hearing the Day of Judgement compared to a settling of accounts. "Then to the sound of the trumpet God shall open his general and grand audit office."

In the field of literature we find a writer such as Dante in his *Inferno* combining Christian theology with figures from Classical history.

Harmonic Style

The harmonic idiom of the motet continued the style characteristic of the Gothic period. Melody even more than

---

[2]Jan Huizinga, *The Waning of the Middle Ages* (New York: Doubleday, 1954), p. 156

ever became the determinant of the harmonic intervals. Johannes de Garlandia (c. 1200-1250), English-born author of several tracts on music, wrote that "a dissonance is excused, for instance, in ornamented motets, namely, when above a fixed tenor some portion of a melody is repeated." Repetition could consist of a portion of the motet melody itself, or a quotation of some well-known troubadour or trouvère song.

Voice Ranges

The voices in Gothic polyphony all lay in the same general range. The classification of voice ranges and their separation into different levels came in the Renaissance.

Notre Dame Conductus

Another class of polyphony in the Notre Dame school was the *conductus*. The term conductus seems to have referred originally to processionals. It was used by writers of the later Middle Ages to apply to Latin songs of the period from 1000-1300 and included both monophonic and polyphonic compositions. The texts of these songs were metrical and the melodies non-liturgical. One of the first uses of the term conductus occurred in the liturgical drama *The Play of Daniel,* mentioned earlier. Music sung to accompany the entrances and exits of the characters of this play are called conducti; the play contains numerous processions. The name conductus is also applied to processional songs in the manuscript from Santiago da Compostela. These early conducti were monophonic.

In the polyphonic conducti of Notre Dame the tenor is not borrowed from plain chant but is of original composition. This tenor is the main voice and is usually the lowest part.

The texts are metrical as in the monophonic kind. There is only one text for all voices, and all voices move in the same rhythm. The text settings are normally syllabic; but some types of conductus have simultaneous melismas in all voices at the beginning and end of the piece and in other places of structural emphasis. The texts of conducti whether monophonic or polyphonic varied in character. Many texts were on religious subjects, but there were some of a secular though serious character. Many conducti appear to have been composed for state occasions of especial importance.

Use of Instruments, General Considerations

Though medieval music notation itself does not give any clues as to how instruments were employed, numerous literary and pictorial references attest to the fact that they were employed. Instruments were to be found in a great variety of shapes, sizes and kinds during the medieval period. Bagpipes of various kinds existed and were much admired. There were percussion instruments of many kinds, such as triangles, castanets, tambourines, drums, and bells. The bell achieved its modern shape in the Gothic period. Huizinga wrote[3]: "One sound rose ceaselessly above the noises of busy life and lifted all things into a sphere of order and serenity: the sound of bells." Wind instruments in all their varieties were also in existence. Processions and street pageants included not only choristers, but also instrumentalists with trumpets, drums, and pipes. The retinue of a noble included trumpeters who were his official representatives. Horns were also used though only for signalling purposes. A notable advance in instrumental construction was made in the 13th century with the invention of the keyboard.

---

[3] op. cit., p. 10

Dances

The earliest purely instrumental music of the Middle Ages consisted of dances. These dances were performed by jongleurs on vièles, and their name, *estampie,* seems to indicate that the dance steps involved stamping. The form of the dances is based on the form of the ecclesiastical sequence (*a b b c c ...*) except that the repeated sections have what we would now call first and second endings. The first ending of each repeated section is a half close (*ouvert*), and the second ending is a full close (*clos*). Usually, the same first and second endings are used for all sections of an *estampie.* Open and closed endings are also to be found in courtly monophony.

SUMMARY

It is convenient to treat the Later Middle Ages in terms of two phases: the Romanesque and the Gothic. (1) The Romanesque period is characterized by a resurgence of creativity based on models of the past, such as Roman architecture, Roman and Greek literature, and liturgical chant. (2) The Gothic period finds European civilization striking out in new directions of its own and seeking models from within the tribal cultures of the peoples of Europe.

The monasteries, preservers of culture during the Early Middle Ages, gained new impetus in the Romanesque period, and the abbey became a familiar landmark on the countryside. The economy was agrarian and the social organization, feudal. In the Gothic period the most important architectural creation was the cathedral, while the parish church gained in importance, and religion entered more intimately into the daily lives of the people. Towns and cities arose and the Mass, the chief ceremony of the secular clergy and the one in which the people participated, achieved its fully established structure by the 11th century. Some monastic groups abandoned the enclosure and entered into the mainstream of town life. The spirit of tribal cultures infused Gothic architecture, combining it with the skills of the craftsmen to create soaring pinnacles. Celtic and Teutonic mythology entered into the subject matter of courtly monophony, and the first significant polyphonic forms were created, using note-shapes and groupings to indicate rhythm.

Musical Forms

Charlemagne and after
    1. Chansons de geste
    2. Sacred monophony: tropes, sequences
    3. Parallel organum, strict and free
    4. Free organum

Romanesque
    1. Songs and poetry of the Goliards, influence of Classical Latin quantitative poetry with allusions to the Roman gods
    2. Rhymed sequence with medieval Latin texts and accentual meter. Marian antiphons
    3. Whatever rhythmic measurement existed depended on poetic texts
    4. Melismatic organum-the style of St. Martial

Gothic
    1. Secular music, using vernacular tongues: troubadour, trouvère, and minnesinger songs
    2. The organum of Léonin, measured rhythm determined by the rhythmic modes. Léonin and Pérotin
    3. Polyphonic conductus, non-liturgical polyphony

4. The motet, a form both sacred and secular. Beginnings of freedom from rhythmic modes (late 13th century).

CHECK LIST FOR REVIEW

Romanesque	sequence	*Carmina Burana*
Gothic	*Dies irae*	jongleur
troubadour	minnesinger	gaukler
trouvère	hymn	minstrel
laudi spirituali	liturgical drama	Council of Trent
Cantigas da Sancta Maria	Marian Antiphon	*chanson de geste*
	cantilena	*Chanson de Roland*
trope	goliard	*formes fixes*

rondeau	melismatic organum
bar-form	school of St. Martial
Musica enchiriadis	discant
organum	score
strict parallel organum	neume
free parallel organum	mensural music

free organum	*Magnus liber organi*	Paris motet
rhythmic modes	melodic sequence	triplum
Ad organum faciendum	*clausula*	conductus
ligatures	tenor	vièle
ordo	basso ostinato	psaltery
School of Notre Dame	puncta	

Archipoeta	Bernart da Ventadorn
Tutilo	Adam de la Halle
Wipo	Arnaut Daniel
Adam de St. Victoire	Léoninus
Walther von der Vogelweide	Pérotinus

Tropes

Tuotilo (d. c. 915)Kyrie trope, Omnipotens: HAM1, 15b

Quem quaeritis in praesepe, trope (dramatic dialogue, 10th c.):NAWM1, 6. Note: this trope is the origin of the ecclesiastical drama

Sequences

Notker Balbulus (d. c. 912): *Alleluia, Dominus in Sina*, with sequence,*Christus hunc diem:* HAM1, 16a

Wipo (c. 1000-1050), *Victimae paschali laudes*, sequence: HAM1, 16b; MM, 3; NAWM1, 5

Adam de St. Victoire(12th c.), *Jubilemus salvatori*, sequence: HAM1, 16c

Troubadours

Bernart da Ventadorn (d. c. 1195), *Be m'an perdut* (canzo): HAM1, 18b; TEM, 6; *Can vei la lauzeta mover*: NAWM1, 7

Comtessa de Dia (d. c. 1212), *A chantar m'er de so queu no voiria* (canzo):NAWM1, 8

Guiraut de Bornelh (d. c. 1220), *Reis glorios* (canzo): HAM1, 18c

Marcabru (d. c. 1150), *Pax in nomine* (vers): HAM1, 18a

Rambault de Vaqueiras, (d. 1207) *Kalenda Maya* (estampie): HAM1, 18d

Trouvères

anon, *C'est la fin* (virelai): HAM1, 19f

anon, *Douce dame* (ballade): HAM1, 19c

anon, *E, dame jolie* (virelai): HAM1, 19g

anon, *En ma dame* (rondeau): HAM1, 19d

anon, *Or la truix* (virelai): MM, 4

anon, *Pour mon cuer* (rotrouenge): HAM1, 19h

Richard Coeur de Lion (1157-1199), *Ja nuns hons pris* (ballade): HAM1, 19a

Guillaume d'Amiens, *Vos n'aler* (rondeau): HAM1,19e

Guillaume le Vinier, *Espris d'ire* (lai): HAM1, 19i

Perrin d'Agincourt, *Quant voi* (ballade): HAM1, 19b

Adam de la Halle (1240-1287), *Robins m'aime* (rondeau from *Jeu de Robin et Marion)*: NAWM1, 9; *Li maus d'amer* (ballade): HAM1, 36a; *Tant con je vivrai* (rondeau): HAM1, 36b

Minnesinger

Spervogel (12th c), *Swa eyn vriund* : HAM1, 20a

Walther von der Vogelweide (d. 1230), *Nu al'erst* ("Palestine Song", barform): HAM1, 20b

Neithart von Reuenthal (d. c. 1240), *Der May*: HAM1, 20c;*Winder wie ist* (barform): HAM1, 20d; *Willekommen Mayenschein*: MM, 5

Wizlau von Rügen (c. 1268-1325), *We ich han gedacht* : NAWM1,10

Conductus   (Latin lyrics, single-voiced): HAM1, 17

Cantigas da Sancta Maria

anon, *A Madre* (villancico): HAM1, 22a

anon, *Mais non faz* (villancico): HAM1, 22b

anon, *Aque serven* (villancico): HAM1, 22c

Alfonso el Sabio, *Gran Dereit'* : TEM, 7

Laudi Spirituali

Gloria in cielo : HAM1, 21a

A tutta gente (ballata): HAM1, 21b

Santo Lorenzo (ballata, modified): HAM1, 21c

Ogne Homo : TEM, 8

Liturgical Drama
>   *Infantem vidimus* (Play of the Three Kings): TEM, 5

Early Polyphony
>   <u>Parallel</u> <u>organum</u> <u>(strict)</u> (c. 850): *Nos qui vivimus* fr *Scholia enchiriadis*:, HAM1,25a; *Tu patris sempiternus et filius* fr *Musica enchiriadis* (2 voices), NAWM1, 13a (4 voices), NAWM1, 13b;

>   <u>Parallel</u> <u>organum</u> <u>(free)</u>: *Te humiles famuli modulis venerando piis* from *Musica enchiriadis*, organum: NAWM1, 13c*Sit gloria Domini* fr *Musica enchiriadis*: HAM1, 25b; *Rex caeli Domine* (sequence) fr *Musica enchiriadis*: HAM1, 25b, MM,2

>   <u>Free</u> <u>organum</u> (note against note) (11th c.): *Cunctipotens genitor* (fr *Ad organum faciendum*) HAM1,26a; *Ut tuo propitiatus*: HAM1, 26b

>   <u>School</u> <u>of</u> <u>Chartres</u>: *Alleluia angelus Domini* : HAM1, 26c;*Alleluia justus et palma* (fr *Ad Organum faciendum*): NAWM1, 14;Versus: *Senescente mundano filio* (Paris, Bibl.Nat. MS lat 3549) (partially melismatic): NAWM1, 15

>   Trope: *Agnus Dei*, organum, (partially melismatic): MM, 7

>   <u>Melismatic</u> <u>organum</u>
>   Note: the chant melody *Benedicamus Domino* , is the tenor in HAM1, 28. The chant melody *Alleluia pascha nostrum* is the tenor in NAWM1, 16. The titles indicate what part of the chant melody is used.

>   <u>School</u> <u>of</u> <u>St.</u> <u>Martial</u>:
> *Viderunt Hemanuel* : HAM1, 27a;
> *Benedicamus Domino* : MM, 8

>   <u>School</u> <u>of</u> <u>Compostela</u>:
> *Cunctipotens genitor* : HAM1, 27b
> *Benedicamus Domino* : HAM1, 28b

Notre Dame School (rhythmic modes, c. 1175-1250)
   Domino (tenor) from chant *Benedicamus Domino*
Domino , clausulae: HAM1, 28de
Domino fidelium-Domino (Latin motet): HAM1, 28f
Dominator-Ecce-Domino (Latin motet): HAM1,28, g
Ave gloriosa Mater-Ave virgo-Domino (Latin motet):
   TEM, 10
Domino, clausula: HAM1, 28h1
Pucelete-Je languis-Domino, (French and Latin motet),
   HAM1, 28h2, NAWM1, 20
Flos filius (tenor) clausula, French & Latin motets:
   HAM1 28i
En non Diu!-Quant voi-Eius in Oriente (tenor), French and
   Latin motet: MM, 10
Léonin's style (c. 1175): *Hec dies* (organum duplum):
   HAM1, 29
Léonin, *Viderunt omnes* (organum duplum): TEM, 9

(*Nostrum* and *latus* (tenors) from chant melody *Alleluia
   Pascha nostrum immolatus*). .
Léonin. organum duplum with clausulae on *nostrum* and
   latus: NAWM1, 16b
Conductus motet (upper voices in nearly the same rhythm
   and with the same text) on *nostrum* clausula:
   NAWM1, 16c
Substitute clausula on *nostrum*: NAWM1, 16d
Latin motet: *Salve, salus hominum-O radians stella-
   nostrum*: on Léonin's clausula on *nostrum*:
   NAWM1, 16e
Latin motet: *Ave Maria, Fons letitie-latus* on Léonin's
   clausula on *latus* : NAWM1, 16f
French and Latin Motet: *Qui d'amors veut bien-qui
   longement porroit-nostrum* on substitute clausula on
   *nostrum:*NAWM1, 16g

French and Latin motets, *Huic main-Hec dies: HAM1*,
    32a;*Quant voi-O mitissima-Hec Dies: HAM1*, 32b
Pérotin, *Alleluia* (tenor) *(Nativitas)*, organum: MM,9
Pérotin's style (13th c.): *Hec dies,* clausulae: HAM1, 30
    Hec dies, organum: HAM1, 31;
Pérotin *Sederunt* Organum quadruplum: NAWM1, 17

<u>Conductus</u>
(polyphonic, 13th c., not based on chant, Latin text)
Roma gaudens jubila (2 voices), HAM1, 38
Hac in anni janua (3 voices) ,HAM1, 39
Ave virgo virginum, Conductus (3-voices): NAWM1, 18
De castitatis thalamo (2 voices), MM, 11

<u>Late 13th c. motets, Petronian</u>
(faster moving triplum, not in modal rhythm)
French and Latin motet , *Aucun vont-Amor qui cor-*
    Kyrie : NAWM1, 19
Latin motet (late 13th c) *Alle,psallite-Alleluya* : HAM1, 33a
Petrus de Cruce, *Aucun-Lonc tans-Annuntiantes*: HAM1, 34
period of Petrus,*Je cuidoie-Se j'ai-Solem*: HAM1, 35

<u>Late 13th c. motets, Franconian</u>
French and Latin motet , *Je n'amerai-In Seculum*, TEM, 12
Latin motet (late 13th c) *Alle,psallite-Alleluya* : HAM1, 33a
French motet (freely invented tenor, common in late 13th c)
    On parole-A Paris-Frèse nouvele:, HAM1, 33b

Instrumental Dances
<u>Monophonic</u>
Istampita Palamento, Estampie: NAWM1, 12
Estampie: MM, 12
ductia (shorter form of estampie), *Danse Royale:*
HAM1,40a

estampie, *Danse Royale*: HAM1, 40b
    <u>Two-voiced dance</u>
ductia: HAM1, 41ab
    "Motet" for instruments
In Seculum longum: *TEM, 11*

Medieval English Music

    <u>Songs</u> <u>(monophonic)</u>:
St. Godric, *Sainte Marie*: HAM1, 23a
Worldes blis: HAM1, 23b
Hymn to St. Magnus (parallel thirds): HAM1, 25c
Rex virginum (13 c.,) trope-2 voices: HAM1, 37

A representation of Pythagoras. Bells achieved their modern form in the Gothic period. (after the Larousse Encyclopedia of Music, ed. Hindley).

Music	Political History	Intellectual History	Art
900 Introduction of Arabic musical instruments Tropes and sequences begin. *Musica enchiriadis* **1025** Guido of Arezzo - the musical staff **Early 11th c.** Wipo of Burgundy, sequence *Victimae paschali laudes* **1066** Antiphonary of Leon **1073** Winchester Troper **12th c.** Peak of Goliardic movement **1100** Beginnings of St. Martial organum	**768-814** Charlemagne **997** St Stephen, King of Hungary **1054** Separation of East and West churches **1066** Battle of Hastings - Norman invasion of England **11th-14th c.** Rise of towns and cities **1096-1099** First crusade	**760** *The Book of Kells* Gospels in Irish **1000** *Beowulf,* heroic poem in Old English **1050** *Chanson de Roland* **1054** Mass achieves its present form **1079** Omar Kayyam - reform of the calendar **1079-1142** Peter Abelard	**796** Charlemagne builds Palatine chapel at Aix-laChappelle **1007-17** Hildesheim doors **1020** Crypt of the Chartres Cathedral **1063** Pisa cathedral **1080** Bayeux tapestry **1094** St. Mark's cathedral, Venice **1145** Chartres facade

Music	Political History	Intellectual History	Art
1150 Troubadours (Provence) Dominance of the Notre Dame school (France) Liturgical drama	1150-1180 Henry II (England) Friedrich Barbarossa (Germany)	1150 Rise of universities High point of Scholasticism 1167 Oxford University founded 1170 University of Paris founded	1163 Cornerstone of Notre Dame Cathedral (Paris)
1175 Leonin at Notre Dame (*Magnus liber organi*) 1183 Perotin at Notre Dame	c. 1180 Philip Augustus (France) 1189 Richard Coeur-de-Lion crowned		
1200- Trouveres in France Minnesingers in Germany	1209 Albigensian Crusade 1215 King John signs *Magna Carta*	1209 St. Francis of Assisi,Francis-can order founded *Canticle of the Sun* attrib. to St. Francis Cambridge University founded	1200 Cathedral at Rheims begun 1213 Alhambra begun
1240 Motet the chief musical form			1240 Chartres cathedral rebuilt
1248 Sequence *Dies irae* attrib. to Thomas a Celano 1250 Sequence *Stabat Mater*, attrib. to Jacapone da Todi	1248 Seventh Crusade, Louis IX of France		
1260 *Ars cantus mensurabilis*, Franco of Cologne			1260 Pisa pulpit (Pisano)

Music	Political History	Intellectual History	Art
1270 *Cantigas da Sancta Maria* Petrus de Cruce Motets of the Bamburg Codex 1284 Adam de la Halle, Jeu de Robin et Marion	1270 Eighth Crusade, Louis IX of France 1297 Marco Polo's account of his travels to Cathay	1270 Roger Bacon, *Opus maius* St. Thomas Aquinas , *Summa theologica*	1288 Amiens Cathedral completed

SCORES OF MEDIEVAL POLYPHONY (ORGANUM)

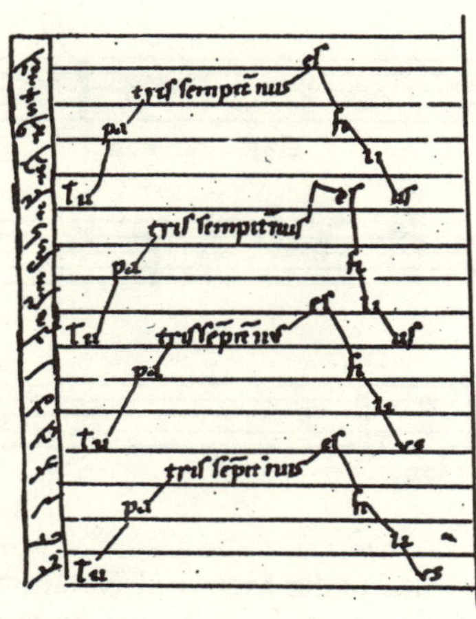

L. from Musica Enchiriadis, c. 9th century, earliest source dealing with polyphony, written in Daseian notation.

R. from Codex Calixtinus, Compostela, Spain, 12th century., (Facsimiles after Apel, Notation of Polyphonic Music).

KYRIE I FROM MACHAULT'S MESSE NOTRE-DAME (14th c.)

The above, from Johannes Wolf, Geschichte der Mensural-Notation von 1250-1460, is a printed version of the notation of the ms. in the Paris, Bibl. Nat. f. fr. 22546. Here the parts are notated separately, rather than in score.

CHAPTER IV

THE ARS NOVA

MIDDLE AGES AND RENAISSANCE

The Renaissance marked the end of religion as the dominant force in men's daily lives. The various kinds of cultural expression all of which served the Church in the Middle Ages began to go their separate ways and soon developed autonomously. Separate political governments grew as the nationalistic ideal took hold. The feudal system which had sprawled over Europe declined, and a free peasantry arose. Natural disasters of famine and plague swept away old institutions. The Hundred Years War between France and England established a new political system with France emerging as an established monarchy by the mid-15th century.

Separate national governments, however, never achieved the cultural dominance of the Medieval Church, and various aspects of culture sought their own goals. The first stage of the reaction against medieval thought was a humanistic stage in which the scholar transferred his interest from the Church to Antiquity. It was this stage that we term the Early Renaissance. It manifested itself culturally in a flowering of art and literature.

The 13th century represents the climax of Gothic culture, a climax in which French art reigned supreme. It is impossible to draw a fine line between the end of one period and the beginning of the next. In fact, Renaissance and Medieval characteristics existed side by side for many years, perhaps for two centuries. Cultural trends evolved differently in different parts of Europe. Italy which had never participated wholeheartedly in medieval artistic expression, became the enthusiastic herald of the dawn of the Renaissance in the 14th century. When Italy's artistic production waned temporarily toward the end of the century, the new cultural leader which emerged was Burgundy. Basically French in orientation, Burgundy was dominated by a resurgence of neo-Gothic ideals. Its power stemmed from the 'bastard feudalism' of a nobility who rebuilt their influence in the confusion arising from the Hundred Years War and organized private armies. Burgundy was England's ally in the Hundred Years War. The transition from the Middle Ages to the Renaissance can be made clear only by observing the emergence of the various concepts and techniques of Renaissance art and society as they make their appearance.

The 13th century synthesis began to disintegrate in the 14th century. At this time, the power of the Papacy declined and with it the unifying influence of the Church. During most of the 14th century the seat of the Popes was at Avignon where the Papacy became the tool of the French monarchy. The last third of the century saw the Great Schism with one Pope at Avignon and another at Rome. The enveloping web of feudalism was rent by the rise of powerful monarchies in England and France and by the appearance of wealthy, independent city-states in Italy and northern Europe. The political concept of a city-state harks back to Ancient Greece. It was in Italy particularly, that a wealthy laity emerged, its wealth derived from commerce with the East. Exotic spices and silks introduced into the West by the Crusades were in great demand. This new secular wealth led to the emergence of secular education particularly in the areas of law and medicine. The collapse of the Byzantine empire and the advance of the Turks brought an influx of learned refugees into Italy. Through these refugees from Byzantium Classical Greek, little known in the Middle Ages, was rediscovered.

Italy also led the way in the emergence of vernacular literatures. At the height of the Gothic period St. Francis of Assisi's lauda *Cantico del sole* (Canticle of the Sun), written in Italian, was vibrant with the joy of nature. Dante, also, influenced by the troubadours as evidenced by various references to them in his poetry, sought expression in the language of the people. He also included reference to figures from Classical Antiquity in his writings. Petrarch (1304-74), master of both Latin and Italian, wrote his famous love-poems to Laura in the vernacular. Boccaccio, a contemporary of Petrarch, one of the world's great story tellers, also wrote in the vernacular. Dante and Boccaccio both hailed from Florence, a great center of 14th century culture. Meanwhile, England, also peripheral in terms of Gothic art, produced Chaucer in the 14th century, writing in Middle English. In the same period a musical composition, the Summer Canon (*Sumer is icomen in*, anon.), also had a text in Middle English.

Humanism

The scholarly side of the Renaissance spirit is reflected in humanism which had had a brief flowering in the first half of the 12th century. The word comes from the Latin *humanitas,* a word which expresses the attitude that was now developing, namely interest in life on earth, in humanity. The humanists delved into the works of that period that came closest to representing their own view of life, the period of Ancient Greece and Rome. In doing so they rebelled against authority which insisted in functioning as an intermediary for the interpretation of ancient works. The humanists believed in reading the original writings, and they resurrected classical, as opposed to medieval Latin. They also had a direct knowledge of ancient Greek. Erasmus made a new translation of the New Testament from original Greek sources, and thus contributed to the Reformation. Humanism thus became associated with both the new thought and the scholarly process itself.

Influence on Music

Direct influence of ancient music itself was, of course, impossible since no actual examples were available. Opera, however, began as an attempt to revive the principles of Ancient Greek drama. Music freed itself from dependence on the liturgical chant. Secular *canti fermi* are to be found in the Mass compositions of the 15th and 16th centuries replacing a religious *auctoritas* with a secular. Whole secular compositions came to be used as the basis for Mass movements in the 16th century, making use of all the voices of a polyphonic model (parody Mass). The *chanson mesurée* of the 16th century attempted to apply the quantitative principles of ancient Greek poetry to the secular chanson.

The Reformation

Reform movements had occurred at various periods of history, and the medieval Church had had periods of reform. The foundations of the Protestant Reformation were laid in the 14th century with the dissident movement of John Wyclif. Humanism played a role by its emphasis in going directly to source writings: Erasmus with his translation of the New Testament into Latin; and Luther with his translation into the vernacular German. Thus the authority of former translations was challenged, and the spirit of individualism asserted the right of individual interpretation.   The rise of secular powers from the decay of feudalism challenged the political power of the Church and was aided directly by Luther's turning to the Princes to support his challenge to the Roman Church. The rise of a wealthy and educated merchant class marked the end of the Church's monopoly on educated men. Meanwhile, reform took place within the Church itself.

The Calvinists Reformation contributed to the secularization of music. Calvinists, in their zeal for simplification of ceremony, destroyed church organs and insisted on plain community singing without accompaniment of any kind. Martin Luther, on the other hand, was an able musician who made contributions to the music of his own Church and laid the groundwork for a tradition of German music that flowered in the 17th and 18th centuries, reaching a climax in the works of J. S. Bach.

Realism

Emerging somewhat later, the Empirical Renaissance, dealing with direct observation of nature, had its first prominent manifestation in the works of Leonardo da Vinci (1452-1519). In the Middle Ages art served the Church, helping to control the violence of the period by emphasizing death and eternal damnation. It sought, not to portray life, but to present religious ideas. Interest in life on earth manifested itself in a new realism which emerged first in art. This was the second phase of the Renaissance, the empirical phase. Leonardo da Vinci, uneducated in humanistic research, emphasized detailed observation of nature to the point of using dissection to study natural forms. The science of biology had its beginnings in the work of the Renaissance artists. Painting now became the most important art replacing architecture which, as applied to the cathedral, dominated late medieval art.

Unity and universality gave way to individualism. The artist was no longer an anonymous craftsman but an individual whose talent demanded recognition. Painting was no longer used merely to illustrate a book or to serve as a medium of religious expression, but became an end in itself as an art form.

In music the empirical side of the Renaissance showed itself in a new preoccupation with beauty of sound. The third became accepted as a consonant interval. There arose a highly developed treatment of consonance and dissonance. Secular polyphony came into existence with new methods of organization, such as imitation. Rhythm freed itself from domination by the rhythmic modes and scansion of text; and rhythmic notation developed autonomously using note-shapes and time signatures. The leading composer of the High Renaissance was Josquin des Prez (1450-1521), whose years coincided almost exactly with those of Leonardo.

Stylistic Balance

Extremes characterized Medieval artistic expression, like the dichotomy of Faith and reason in religious philosophy. Romanesque art emphasized mass or solid form while the perfected linearity of the Gothic facade was its supreme artistic achievement. Realism in painting demanded a balanced consideration of line and mass. A realistic consideration of sound in part-music demanded balanced consideration of line and chord. The balance between melodic movement and chord was governed by rhythm. Franco of Cologne made the earliest known statement of this principle when he said that a consonance should come at the beginning of each perfection (or beat). The search for euphony also led to the acceptance of 3rds and 6ths as consonances.

Independence of Forms

Music became independent of the Church, just as painting did. Even in painting on religious subjects there is an obvious concern for representation of the human form. Music developed polyphonic forms that did not depend on liturgical melodies. The composer of medieval part-music began by taking a Gregorian chant melody as the first part and then simply added other parts above or below it. The Renaissance composer began to write independent melodies for all parts of a polyphonic composition. His part music was organized by a melodic device known as imitation. Imitation in music was considered by Renaissance philosophers to be analogous to imitation of nature in pictorial art. It first came into existence in representation of the chase, or hunt. The familiar folk-song example of the device of imitation is the *round* where a melodic idea presented in one part is repeated a little later in another part. The Renaissance also developed an autonomous polyphonic device to mark the ends of phrases or other subdivisions of a larger piece. This device was the *cadence*, a formal ending corresponding, in language, to the dropping of the voice at the end of a sentence, and marked in written language by a period.

Rhythmic Notation

The years from about 1300-1500 were years of great change in the area of rhythmic notation. In this period the notation of rhythm gradually emancipated itself from the rigid confines of the rhythmic modes. The domination of poetry over music was thus broken, and as a result, the Renaissance composer had a much richer repertory of rhythmic patterns. The solution of the problem lay in the assignment of a definite and unchanging system of rhythmic values to specific note-shapes.

Thus, in our relatively stable system the whole note is divided into two half-notes; the half note into two quarter notes; the quarter note into two eighth notes, etc. The various rhythmic values are indicated by the appearance of the notes which are distinguished from each other by the use of filled or unfilled note-heads and the presence or absence of stems and tails. The evolution of this system of rhythmic notation was a slow process extending over some 200 years; but its importance can hardly be overestimated, not only for the organization of harmonic materials, but also for the furnishing of a new dimension in melodic structure, and hence, in musical form.

Towards the end of the 13th century Franco of Cologne (fl. 1250-1285) devised a notation system that made it possible to mitigate the strict application of rhythmic modes, as was already being done in musical performance. He still used ligatures (groups of connected notes) but assigned unchanging values to the various note combinations so that they could be read the same way every time without reference to the scansion of the text. Another rhythmic innovation was the introduction of shorter note-values. The first steps in this direction were made by the Frenchman Pierre de la Croix (Petrus de Cruce) at the end of the 13th century. He used the form of the semibreve to represent up to nine subdivisions of the breve. Another French writer, Philippe de Vitry (1291-1361) assigned specific note-shapes to subdivisions of the breve and semibreve and also put double division of the note values (such as are used today) on equal footing with triple division. He set forth his ideas in a treatise known as *Ars Nova* (New Art), a name which is commonly applied to the music of the 14th century. He introduced the term *Ars Antiqua* to refer to the older notation, a name now commonly used for the music of the Central Gothic period.

In the ligature the rhythmic value of a note depended partly on its shape and partly on its position within a group of notes.

Thus, it depended for its interpretation on the idea of a predetermined rhythmic pattern, such as the poetic foot. The use of ligatures declined during the 15th century and virtually disappeared in the 16th century. The system of ligatures gave way to an autonomous system of measured durations determined by time-signatures and note-shapes and allowing of unprecedented freedom in the creation of rhythmic patterns.

The division into measures as we know it today did not exist in the Renaissance. Bar-lines, even when used, did not necessarily have their modern significance as to meter even into the 17th century. The basic rhythmic unit in the 15th and 16th centuries was the beat (called *tactus*). It varied little in speed and was meant to serve the same purpose as metronomic indications do today. The duration of the tactus was approximately one second. Beats were not necessarily grouped into units of equal length, and such grouping should not be assumed in modern performance.

Thirds and Sixths

The earliest proven use of thirds in polyphony, treated as consonances, comes from England at c. 1200. There is some evidence that the use of thirds may have come about as a result of Norwegian influences. In English descant the voices sometimes proceed in parallel thirds, but at other times the motion is varied by having the voices cross through a unison to another third. Parallel sixths may also be used, interspersed with octaves. Parallel imperfect consonances (3rds and 6ths) were first found in examples of the conductus form. Thirds and sixths began to be introduced into continental polyphony in the 14th century, but the older sonorities persisted side by side with the new. In the 15th century the new style was given the name *gymel*, (from the Latin *cantus gemellus*, twin-song). With the consonant treatment of thirds and sixths came the discovery of the triad and its spacings, e.g. *do-mi-sol, do-sol-mi, mi-sol-do* . At the same time the voice-parts, all of which moved in the same range in the Middle Ages, came to be separated into their modern classification of soprano, alto, tenor, and bass. This process took place towards the end of the 15th century.

Consonance and Dissonance

The polyphonic styles of the Middle Ages swung from extremes of total dependence on harmonic intervals (12th century) to almost complete disregard of harmonic intervals (13th century). Dependence on harmonic intervals is represented by strict parallel organum where the added voice is obtained by adding the same harmonic interval to each note of the chant. In a polyphonic style which disregards harmonic intervals the harmonic intervals are by-products of melodic movement. Two examples come to mind: (1) the school of St. Martial, where the added voice soars in melodic flight above a series of sustained tones and (2) the Paris school, whose motets introduce well-known trouvère melodies with little regard for the intervals they make with the rest of the texture.

In the Renaissance a balance was achieved between the two extremes by means of measured rhythm. The technique was developed of having consonances at places that were strong rhythmically. e.g. at the beginnings of beats and introducing dissonances by means of melodic movement in places that were weak rhythmically. An important device was the suspension in which a tone introduced as a consonance on one beat became dissonant at the beginning of the next beat. The tone would then move stepwise downwards to a consonance. The suspension was a means of introducing dissonance in a rhythmically strong place.

EXAMPLE 9

The development of the technique for handling consonances and dissonances took place in the late 15th century in the Low Countries where, at the same time, Franco-Flemish painters were developing techniques of realistic representation on their canvases.

The Cadential Formula

As a means of producing independent musical structures in polyphony, the cadential formula played an important part since it was a means of marking the ends of phrases - of bringing music to rest or pause. The use of melodic formulas for endings can perhaps be traced to the device of musical rhyme found in plainchant and also to the open and closed endings of the secular dances of the 13th century. The earliest type of cadence is known, though not with complete justification, as the Landini cadence. It is found in the works of other 14th century composers, such as Guillaume de Machault and was used extensively in the 15th century. The association with Landini's name emphasizes the role of Italy and in particular, Florence, in initiating the Renaissance style.

The Landini cadence is characterized by the melodic formula 7-6-1 (*ti-la-do*) as distinguished from the *ti-do* cadence to which we are accustomed. Incidentally, the *ti,* as used in moving up to *do* at the end of a phrase, is known as the leading tone. In some early cadences a second leading tone using the raised fourth degree (*fi* in the movable *do* system) is used to resolve to *sol*. This cadence, in terms of church modes, belongs to the Lydian mode (beginning on F using the white keys of the piano).

EXAMPLE 10

Imitation

In the emergence of autonomous musical structures independent of the *auctoritas* of the liturgical chant, the Renaissance polyphonist had need of a new structural principle, and this he found in the device of imitation. Unity and variety are the bases of artistic form. Repetition with change (varied repetition) is one means of achieving unity and variety. Imitation is one type of varied repetition. In imitation one voice repeats the melody that another voice has presented but repeats it after a time-lapse, so that the original voice is singing something else at the point where the second voice enters. Examples of imitation, arising from the exchange of melodic material between the upper voices of organa, were found in Perotin, but here the imitation was purely incidental. As the main compositional technique, imitation first occurred in the music of the 14th century. Early examples of imitation were carried out very strictly. Both voices sang the same melody at the same pitch in what we would call imitation at the unison. The 14th century forms based on this device were named after the hunt: *Chace* (Fr.) and *caccia* (It.). The symbolism of the hunt and the following of one voice by the other is obvious. What is less obvious is the relationship between imitation in music and imitation of nature in painting. Chronologically, at least, the two concepts emerged together. Furthermore, their function in each case was to provide a basis for artistic creation which was autonomous and independent of the liturgy. In the paintings of the Florentine Giotto one senses that the artist seeks to represent faithfully what he sees. Even where the subject matter is sacred, the artist strives for realism. Various musical theorists of the High Renaissance drew parallels between the technique of imitation in music and imitation of nature in art.

THE ITALIAN ARS NOVA

Florence, a leading seat of culture (called the first modern state in the world) produced an important school of secular music in the 14th century. The leading composer was the blind organist Francesco Landini (1325-1397) whose surviving works represent more than a third of the surviving music of that school. Now there appeared for the first time a body of secular polyphony of which the music is entirely the creation of the composer without recourse to borrowed material of any kind. The model for this secular polyphony was the conductus, especially the type that included melismas. Unlike the conductus, however, the 14th century secular polyphony had its melody in the upper voice. There were three main forms: the *madrigal*, the *ballata*, and the *caccia*.

The Madrigal

First used in the Florentine school, the term *madrigal* persisted as the name of a secular form, though with changed meanings, through the early 17th century. Two different explanations are given for the origin of the term. According to one, it is derived from the word *matricale* (from *mater*) and refers to a poem in the mother tongue. In this sense the term refers to the use of the vernacular as against the Latin of sacred music. Another explanation links it to the word *mandriale* (sheepfold) which gives the term pastoral connotations. Spellings were subject to many deviations in that period.

The 14th century madrigal was usually strophic with up to four stanzas sung to the same melody. It ended with two lines set to a new melody in contrasting rhythm. The setting might be in either two or three parts. The extreme dissonance of Gothic music was avoided, so that the madrigal had a more mellifluous sound. Where Gothic music used sustained tones in one voice, the voices of the madrigal were rhythmically similar. Imitation was frequent in the madrigal though the form was not based upon imitation.

Ballata

The ballata was derived from one of the fixed forms of the troubadours (the virelai). Like the virelai it was originally a dance form, but during this period it was very likely a dance-derived art form like the Bach keyboard suites of the 18th century. Frequently, the lower parts of the ballata lacked text so that it tended to be solo song with instrumental accompaniment.

Freed of the restrictions of modal rhythm, Italian *trecento* (14th century) music shows great rhythmic variety and richness with syncopations and with triplets and duple divisions intermixed. Rhythmically, the music stems from the reforms of Petrus de Cruce. In this music melismas are frequent at the beginnings and endings of phrases; but they may occur elsewhere also. The music calls for skilled singers such as existed in 14th century Florence.

Caccia

In the caccia, imitation became the dominant feature of the music. The caccia was a form consisting of two sections. The first, the longer of the two, was always imitative; and the second section was imitative for the most part. In the 14th century imitation was exact and literal with both voices at the same pitch; but the second voice entered a comparatively long time after the first. A third voice, the lowest of the three, served to support the imitative voices and fill out the sonority. The texts of the caccia were of the liveliest sort and reflected the new-found expression of the joy of living. The sound of the hunt, the cries of peddlers in the market-place, and the lively confusion of putting out a fire, all found expression here.

Instrumental Music

Methods of performance were not fixed in the 14th century. Literary references and pictorial evidence point to a great variety of instruments, but there is little indication as to how they were used. The Faenza codex of the first quarter of the 15th century contains keyboard pieces based on sections of the Mass and ornamented versions of secular compositions by Machault, Landini, and other 14th century composers. Mass sections substituted organ performance for vocal performance of parts of the Mass. There are also monophonic dance compositions in estampie form.

THE FRENCH ARS NOVA

During the 14th century the organa of Leonin and Perotin were still heard at Notre Dame though the new generation wrote in a different style. Innovations in notation influenced the motet, particularly the top voice (*triplum*) which was the first to be emancipated from the rhythmic modes. Many motets showing these innovations are found interpolated in a poem by Gervais le Bus which attacks abuses within the administration of the Church. The poem is entitled *Roman de Fauvel* (*fauve* =beast in French). The interpolations in this poem included two-and three-part motets as well as sacred and secular monophony. Secular polyphony of the French *Ars nova* included polyphonic adaptations of trouvère forms, such as the ballade, rondeau, and virelai.

Isorhythmic Motet

The motets of the *Roman de Fauvel* were of a type known as *isorhythmic*, a type which continued in favor through the first half of the 15th century. The term *isorhythmic* refers to a repeated scheme of time-values and is applied chiefly to the liturgical tenors, or *canti fermi*, of the motets. The isorhythmic principle was first introduced in the Notre Dame school, but in the 14th century rhythmic patterns were much longer, and the forms were conceived on a much larger scale.

The isorhythmic motet represented a continuation of the Gothic influence and preserved the Gothic harmonic style throughout the 14th century, even after thirds and sixths had been introduced into the more progressive imitative forms. Two important devices were introduced in the 14th century to modify the rhythmic structure of isorhythmic tenors: augmentation and diminution. Augmentation means doubling the note values of a rhythmic pattern, and diminution means halving these note values. These devices were to be used in the latter half of the 15th century to extend resources of the imitative technique: i.e., an imitating part might move twice as rapidly or twice as slowly as the original part.

Mass Settings

With the rise of towns and cities the focus of religious observance shifted from the monasteries to the churches and cathedrals and emphasized the role of the secular clergy. This emphasis brought the Mass into greater prominence. The French Ars Nova produced the earliest polyphonic settings of the Ordinary of the Mass and thus introduced a musical form which has had a continuous history since then. An example earlier than the French examples came from Tournai, Belgium. It was probably not, however, by one composer and seems to have been assembled from various early 14th century sources.

The first unified setting of the Ordinary of the Mass by a single composer, and a particularly famous work, was the *Messe Notre Dame* by Guillaume de Machault. In this work musical unity is attained by the use of an original melodic motive which recurs in all movements and is employed in various contrapuntal combinations. Each movement uses a different Gregorian melody, usually as a cantus firmus in long notes in the tenor. (Note that a polyphonic Mass in which each movement uses a different chant melody is known as a *plainsong Mass*).   The chant melody in the Credo is ornamented and is placed in the upper voice (a technique known as paraphrase), and the Agnus Dei uses the style of the isorhythmic motet. The *Messe Notre Dame* of Machault is a work of great historical importance.

Chace

There are five French compositions based on strict imitation and with secular vernacular texts which date from the early part of the 14th century. The existence of these compositions proves that the caccia (chace) form originated in France though it had its most significant flowering in Italy. The French version of this form is usually in two parts only, without the supporting lowest part found in Italian sources. Though there are other themes also, the hunt is a frequent subject of the texts. One of these imitative compositions uses a technical device that was to be of importance in later times. It is the musical equivalent of the literary palindrome which reads the same backwards as forwards. Proceeding backwards (called *retrograde*) was a device which came to be used in the latter half of the 15th century in the Flemish school. This device, along with augmentation and diminution, served to extend the resources of the imitative technique. Such deviations from strict imitation helped to lay the groundwork for the free imitation of the High Renaissance.

Composers

The most important composers of the French Ars Nova were Philippe de Vitry and Guillaume de Machault. Both are mentioned by the Italian poet Petrarch, and the Papal court at Avignon was the likeliest common meeting ground of the three men. Very little remains of the music of de Vitry (1291-

1361) whom Petrarch considered to be unsurpassed by any other composer of his time. Some of the motets of the *Roman de Fauvel* are attributed to de Vitry. A manuscript in the chapter library at Ivrea in northeastern Italy contains the three motets most clearly ascribable to him. (This is the same manuscript that contains examples of the chace.) These three motets are isorhythmic with a lyrical melody free of modal rhythm.

In view of the small number of surviving works by de Vitry, Guillaume de Machault (1300-1377) must be regarded as the most important composer of the French Ars Nova. Poet, composer, ecclesiastic, secretary to King John of Bohemia (the Duke of Luxembourg), Machault lived a vigorous and widely traveled life. In 1340 he became canon at Rheims and remained there until his death.

Among Machault's surviving compositions are some 40 monophonic pieces in the trouvère tradition. With Machault, however, these works are in the nature of a conscious archaism which expresses nostalgia for the lost Age of Chivalry. His polyphonic compositions include three chaces and also secular pieces which preserve the fixed forms of the trouvères, but which apply such highly sophisticated devices as retrograde. Some of the fixed form compositions are in the character of solo songs with the accompaniment of two instruments. Among Machault's works there are also isorhythmic motets and the *Messe Notre Dame* discussed above. In his polyphony Machault makes use of the 7-6-1 and double leading tone cadential formulas; his rhythmic style is richly varied and uses syncopation.

PERIPHERAL COUNTRIES OF THE 14TH CENTURY

England

A famous composition of the 14th century stemming from England was the rota (or round) *Sumer is icomen in*

(Summer is Coming In). Related to the caccia in its form, it is, however, a much more ambitious and modern-sounding piece. Four parts participate in the imitation though much of the time they are reduced to two by doubling. The supporting part consists of two voices which exchange material and repeat themselves throughout the composition. Thirds and sixths are frequent, and the mode is major. The English represent the most progressive tendencies of the time in their polyphony, as is shown both by their writing for greater numbers of voices and their use of thirds and sixths as well as exchange of material between voices. The forms, however, tend to be conservative and to be written in conductus-like style. The most important sources of English polyphony in the 14th century stem from Worcester (c. 1300).

English Instrumental Music

The Robertsbridge Codex of c. 1325 contains organ arrangements of three motets as well as an organ estampie. This codex is the earliest example of keyboard music that has been preserved. It is generally believed to be of English origin.

Germany

German music, on the other hand, was conservative and still clung to the old monophony. With the decline of the feudal system the aristocratic tradition of the Minnesinger gave way to a bourgeois tradition. Organized into guilds, these tradesman-singers became known as Meistersingers, and their tradition extends through the 15th and 16th centuries. Hans Sachs, portrayed in Wagner's *Die Meistersinger*, was an historical figure. The Minnesinger tradition persisted into the 15th century with such composers as Oswald von Wolkenstein (c. 1377-1445).

HIGHLIGHTS OF THE CHAPTER

Forms

1. <u>Madrigal.</u> A strophic form in two or three voices
2. <u>Caccia. (chace).</u> A form of two sections, the first always based on strict imitation. The *caccia* had a supporting third voice part; the *chace* did not.
3. <u>Ballata.</u> A polyphonic form based on a fixed form of the trouvères
4. <u>Isorhythmic</u> <u>motet.</u> A motet in which the tenor has a scheme of repeated note values- an outgrowth of the Paris motet
5. <u>Ordinary</u> <u>of</u> <u>the</u> <u>Mass.</u> First settings of the ordinary of the Mass in polyphony. Each movement had a separate Gregorian cantus firmus.

Techniques

1. <u>Imitation.</u> Repetition in one voice, after a time lapse, of a melody introduced in another voice
2. <u>Paraphrase.</u> The elaboration (ornamentation) of a borrow- ed melody and placing it in the top voice of a composition
3. <u>Cadential</u> <u>formula.</u> A polyphonic formula used to mark the ends of phrases
4. <u>.Rhythm.</u> Emancipation from the rhythmic modes towards an autonomous system of rhythmic notation
5. <u>Thirds</u> and <u>Sixths.</u> Thirds and Sixths began to be accepted as consonances.

6. <u>Augmentation.</u> Doubling of time values, applied to the tenors of motets

7. <u>Diminution.</u> Halving of time values, also applied to the tenors of motets

8. <u>Retrograde.</u> Having a melody go backwards, a technique first used significantly in the 14th century

The 14th century presents two distinct trends: one Gothic, and one Renaissance. The Gothic trend, as manifested in France, is seen in the isorhythmic motet and in the fixed forms. The isorhythmic motet continues the tradition of the Paris motet in its organization around a pre-existent cantus firmus; and the fixed forms continue the trouvère tradition, though with written-out accompaniments. A late example of Gothic constructivism, the devices of augmentation and diminution, had even more far-reaching influences - in their application to imitative techniques-in succeeding centuries. These devices were first applied to motet tenors. The conservative forms which continued the Gothic tradition maintained a conservative attitude towards harmonic intervals and treated thirds and sixths as dissonances.

The first significant body of secular polyphony was a product of 14th century Italy. It represents the Renaissance trend in its use of imitation; thirds and sixths; and polyphonic cadential formulas. The love of life is reflected in its texts. It was not for another hundred years, however, that forms based on imitation became the established technique of composition that they were in 14th century Italy.

CHECK LIST FOR REVIEW

Renaissance	leading tone	Messe de Tournai
Ars Nova	imitation	Messe Notre Dame
Ars Antiqua	chace	plainsong Mass

Humanism	caccia	paraphrase
Reformation	madrigal	retrograde
ligature	ballata	augmentation
tactus	trecento	diminution
gymel	triplum	rota (round)
suspension	isorhythmic	Meistersinger
cadential formula	cantus firmus	

St. Francis	Landini	Guillaume de Machault
Petrarch	Pierre de la Croix	Phillippe de Vitry
Boccacio	(Petrus de Cruce)	Ivrea (library)
Chaucer	Gervais le Bus	

LIST OF SCORES

Italian Ars Nova
Madrigal

Jacopo da Bologna (c 1350), *Non al suo amante:* HAM1, 49;
Fenice fu: NAWM1, 22, ballata

Giovanni da Florentia (c 1350), *Nel mezzo*: HAM1, 50;
Io son un pellegrin: HAM1, 51

Landini, Francesco (1325-97), *Sy dolce non sono*: HAM1, 54;
Amor c'al tuo soggetto: HAM1, 53; *Chi più le vuol
sapere*: MM, 14; *Non avra ma' pieta:* NAWM1, 23

Caccia

Ghirardello da Firenze (c 1375), *Tosto che l'alba*:
HAM1, 52; *Con brachi assai:* TEM, 16

Dances

Lamento di Tristano w. *Rotta*, (14th c), estampie
(monophonic) : HAM1, 59a

Saltarello, estampie (monophonic): HAM1, 59b (14th c)

Faenza Codex (keyboard)
Kyrie, Paraphrase for organ: TEM, 15

French Ars Nova
Isorhythmic Motet
Roman de Fauvel, *Detractor est*: HAM1, 43
Vitry, Philippe de, *Garrit Gallus-In nova fert-Neuma*:
     NAWM1,21
Machaut, Guillaume de, *S'il estoit nulz*: HAM1, 44
Mass Settings
Machault, Guillaume de, *Agnus Dei*, Mass movement
     (ordinary): MM, 13, NAWM1, 25
Messe de Tournai, Agnus Dei , Mass movement (ordinary)
     (14th c.): TEM, 13
Fronciaco, *Kyrie* Trope (2-voiced): TEM, 14
Ballade
Machaut, Guillaume de, *Je puis trop bien*: HAM1, 45; *Quant
     Theseus-Ne quier veoir*: NAWM1, 24
Jacopin Selesses, *En attendant*: HAM1, 47 (late 14th c)
Anthonello de Caserta, *Notes pour moi:* TEM, 17
Rondeau
Baude Cordier, *Amans ames*, and *Belle bon : HAM1*, 48ab
     (c 1400)
Solage, *Fumeaux fume:* NAWM1, 26 (late 14th c)
Virelai
Machaut, Guillaume de, *Comment qu'a moy* and *Plus dure*:
     HAM1, 46a

England
Sumer is Icomen In, rota (round) c 1310: HAM1, 42
Estampie for organ 2 vc: HAM1, 58 (1325)
Worcester polyphony
Alleluia psallat, motet: HAM1, 57a (14th c)

Gloria in excelsis (fauxbourdon) mass movement (ordinary):
    HAM1, 57b (14th c)
Fulget coelestis, rondellus motet: NAWM1, 27
Salve, sancta parens, Carol: NAWM1, 28

Germany
Oswald von Wolkenstein (1377-1445), *Der May,*
    accompanied song: HAM1, 60

*From a 14th century illustration of an episode in the Roman de Fauvel
(1310, 1314: Fr. fauve=beast), a poem by Gervais de Bus attacking
abuses which harassed the Church .   Pieces were interpolated by
Chaillou de Pestain in 1316 . It includes motets probably written by de
Vitry. (After The Larousse Encyclopedia of Music, ed. Hindley).*

CHRONOLOGICAL CHART

Music	Political History	Intellectual History	Art
1300 French *Ars nova*	1250-1450 Decline of feudalism	1305 Dante, *Divine Comedy*	1304-5 Giotto, Madonna Giotto, Arena Chapel
1316 *Roman de Fauvel*	1309-78 "Babylonian exile" of the Papacy in Avignon	1309 Founding of Orleans University	early 14th c. Exeter cathedral
1318 Marchetto da Padua			
1319 Jean de Muris, *Ars novae musicae*	1327 Aztecs found Mexico city	1327 Petrarch, sonnets	1320 Giotto, *Francis' Death*
1325 Philippe de Vitry, *Ars nova* Robertsbridge Codex	1337-1453 Hundred Years' War between England and France		1334 Erection of Papal Palace at Avignon Giotto begins Campanile at Florence
1330 Italian *Ars nova* Francesco Landini Jacob of Liege, *Speculum musicae* *Messe de Tournai*	1348 The Black Death 1354 Rienzi murdered in Rome	1353 Boccacio, *Decameron*	1351-1412 Gloucester cloister vaults
1360 Machaut, *Messe Notre Dame* Beginnings of development of clavichord & cembalo	1378-1417 Papal schism	1362 Wm Langland, *Piers Plowman*, poem	1366 Completion of *El Transito* Synagogue at Toledo
		1376 Wycliffe's Bible	
		1385 Founding of Heidelberg University	
		1386 Chaucer, *Canterbury Tales*	

CHAPTER V

THE XVth CENTURY

THE BURGUNDIAN SCHOOL

The Burgundian court presents a spectacle of neo-medieval tradition and splendor in its last manifestation. Politically, Burgundy rose to power in the confusion resulting from the havoc of the Hundred Years War between France and England- a war in which it was allied with the English. The upheaval arising from this war gave the Dukes of Burgundy a chance to reassert feudal rights and raise their own private armies. Under this condition of 'bastard feudalism' Burgundy began its rise to power with Philip the Bold who received the Duchy as a fief from his father, John II of France, in 1361. Under him and his successors, John the Fearless, Philip the Good, and Charles the Bold, the territorial possessions grew to include most of what is now Belgium, the Netherlands, and Luxembourg; the then provinces and now regions of northern France, Picardy and Artois; Franche-Comte, in eastern France; Nivernais and Charolais in central France; and the German province of Baden. Its trade and industry became the most important in Europe. Its court at Dijon became a great cultural center attracting the most famous artists and musicians of the day from the various regions under its rule. The sculptor Claus Sluter was at Dijon under Philip the Bold (1390). During the reign of Philip the Good Flemish artists such as Hans Memling and Jan van Eyck flourished at Bruges in

Flanders. At the same time music reached its height with the composers Dufay and Binchois.

A description has come down to us of the Banquet of the Oath of the Pheasant at which Philip the Good and the Knights of the Golden Fleece vowed to undertake a crusade to recapture Constantinople which had fallen to the Turks in 1453. The crusade was never undertaken, but the banquet was the occasion for elaborate costumes; table decorations; masques; and vocal and instrumental music.

MUSICAL INFLUENCES

In the 15th and 16th centuries the center of musical culture lay in the Low Countries, which included the lands controlled by Burgundy until the last quarter of the 15th century when they came, at least nominally, under the sovereignty of the Holy Roman Emperor. At that time the Low countries included what is now Belgium, Holland, and northern France (Artois), and of these Belgium was the most important musically. The term *Franco-Flemish* is applied to those regions that are now Belgium. (The name Belgium came to be applied in the 18th century). These regions contained city-states of considerable autonomy. Among the leading city-states of the north were Antwerp, Brussels, Ghent, Liege, Rotterdam, and Utrecht.

Belgium consists of two main regions, a northern, Flanders, in which a Germanic language is spoken (Flemish), and a southern, in which a French dialect (Walloon) is spoken. The southwestern county, Hainaut, was the birthplace of the 15th century composers Dufay (probably), Binchois and Johannes Ockeghem and the 16th century composers Josquin des Prez and Orlandus Lassus. Just to the west, in Artois, now northern France, Busnois (15th century) was born. Flanders was also the birthplace of Adriaen Willaert (16th century).

Philippe Verdelot (16th century), called Flemish in some sources, has a French name and was probably Walloon. Jacob Arcadelt (16th century), if born in Liége, was born in the heart of Walloon country (though the name seems Flemish). Heinrich Isaac (late 15th century) stems from Brabant which lies just to the east of Hainaut and Flanders. Jacob Obrecht (late 15th century) was the most important composer of Dutch ancestry.

England

In the Hundred Years war (1337-1453) France was the battle ground and as a result its position as a cultural center was greatly weakened. The Burgundians, though nominally vassals of the French king, sided with England; and it was Philip the Good who had Joan of Arc captured and turned over to the English. The English composer John Dunstable (c. 1380-1453) played an important role in shaping the style of Dufay and Binchois. Dunstable was for a time in the service of the Duke of Bedford who was regent of France during the English occupation and who was married to the sister of Philip the Good. His compositions include examples of all the forms extant in his time. An important contemporary of Dunstable was Lyonel Power whose work was similar to Dunstable's in style.

Guillaume Dufay

The Burgundian culture was essentially French, and many of its characteristics sprang from the French Gothic. Sacred music was of much greater importance than it had been in 14th century Italy. The greatest composer of the Burgundian school, Guillaume Dufay (c. 1400-1474), was at his best in his Masses. Compositions of the Ordinary of the Mass now became one of the chief types of sacred music and remained so during the Renaissance. Of the 14th century innovations, the imitative technique had relatively little influence and was rarely used as the main basis of a piece of music. There is a caccia by Dufay, the *Gloria ad modum tubae* (Gloria in the manner of trumpets); but, significantly, Dufay has used this originally secular form for a sacred composition. The lowest parts of this piece, with their reiterated *do-sol* echoed by two different voices, are reminiscent of the Summer Canon; and the whole work shows English influences in its structure, in its tonal feeling, and in its use of the major mode. In the early 15th century each voice in a polyphonic texture had its own individual melodic material with little interchange except for brief imitations. At the same time, the voices tend to be in the same range. The secular music was conservative, but incidental imitation was to be found in some of Dufay's secular works. Some of his imitation was at different pitch levels, and this was a progressive trend. Other Renaissance characteristics are (1) the use of cadential formulas similar to those of the 14th century (e.g. in Machault and Landini, Francesco) and (2) the sonority, which, under English influence, is increasingly permeated with the sound of thirds and sixths. During this period the High Renaissance technique of handling dissonance begins to emerge.

Cantus Firmus Mass

Two kinds of structural technique are found in the Masses of the Burgundian school: *cantus firmus* technique and *paraphrase* technique. The cantus firmus Mass is the more important of the two. Here, a borrowed melody is used in the tenor while the other voices weave polyphony around it. Frequently, moreover, the tenor is of secular origin. The use of a secular tenor in a sacred composition is an example of the intermingling (characteristic of the late Gothic) of the sacred and the secular. By this time the sacred had lost the dominant position represented heretofore by the ubiquitous presence of the ecclesiastical melody. The folk-song *L'Homme armé* (Beware the Armed Man) was used as a cantus firmus in numerous Masses. Modeled after the practice of using borrowed melodies in organa and motets, the cantus firmus Mass was probably of English origin, based on compositions by such composers as Lyonel Power and John Dunstable.

Dufay's Cantus Firmus Masses

The most important of Dufay's compositions were his Masses, predominantly of the cantus firmus type described above. In his hands this structural technique produced works of a scope comparable to that of a symphony. The cantus firmus constitutes a single melody which reappears throughout the five sections of the Ordinary of the Mass and thus unifies the work. A melody borrowed from a sacred or secular source is set in long notes in the tenor with two voices above the tenor and one below. The cantus firmus thus functions as an inaudible unifying device, almost always present throughout the Mass. Machault's Mass, though it had used plainchant melodies in the tenor, was not unified in this manner. There, the chant melody was different in each section since it came from the corresponding section of Gregorian Ordinary. Machault, however, had used a unifying motive in the upper voices, and this procedure influenced Dufay, who used a head-motif, or brief melodic motive, in the upper voices at the beginning of each section. This motive served as an audible unifying device, as opposed to the cantus firmus, which could not have been easy to hear. The cantus firmus, in fact, could be subject to augmentation, diminution, or retrograde; or the direction of the melodic intervals could be reversed, producing inversion. Thus, repetitions of a preëxistent melody (first found occasionally in Perotin's organa and later used as the basis of the isorhythmic motet) emerge on a greatly enlarged scale in the cantus firmus Mass.

Dufay's Paraphrase Masses

The influence of the secular accompanied song is seen in the other type of Mass treatment known as the paraphrase Mass. Here, the preëxistent melody, always of ecclesiastical origin, was placed in the top voice and ornamented. Paraphrase technique is also used by Dufay in his sacred songs.

Dufay and Fauxbourdon

A device which uses thirds and sixths and is found in compositions using the paraphrase technique is known as fauxbourdon (false bass). It may have been introduced by Dufay himself and represents the attempt to make use of the sonorities of English descant in art music. In fauxbourdon the tenor is a sixth below the top voice except at cadences where it moves to the octave. The middle voice is always a fourth below the melody. This device results in chains of parallel first inversion chords (with the root on top, the third on the bottom and the fifth in the middle), hence "false bass'". Fauxbourdon was the model for the consonant sonorities of the High Renaissance. As thirds and sixths come to be more firmly established as consonances, the perfect consonances come to be treated in what might best be termed a "gingerly" fashion. Parallel fifths and octaves are avoided, and fourths between the bass and the higher parts are treated very carefully. Fauxbourdon set the stage for this treatment.

Dufay's Use of the Isorhythmic Motet

During the early 15th century the isorhythmic motet continued in favor, and many examples of it are found in the works of Dufay. Imitation is used between upper voices. Augmentation, diminution inversion, and retrograde are applied to the cantus firmus and also to the relationship between imitating voices. The subject matter of the texts tends more toward the sacred than it had in the 14th century. Many motets use Latin texts in all voices, and even when vernacular texts are used, they tend to be more unified in subject matter.

Secular Music

Many of Dufay's secular pieces have two important voices instead of one, and the third voice fills in. Though he reigned unchallenged in the field of sacred music, his contemporary at Dijon, Gilles Binchois, could rival him in the more modest field of secular composition. Binchois excelled in the writing of chansons. The chanson, like the Italian ballata or French ballade, was a solo song with accompaniment. It reflected the trouvère influence in its use of fixed forms and the conductus in its fondness for long melismas at the ends of phrases. The melismas may have been performed as instrumental interludes. Melancholy treatment of the love theme is characteristic of many of the texts and reflects the troubadour-trouvère tradition.

THE LATE 15th CENTURY

Charles the Bold, in attempting to further his ambitions, met defeat at the hands of the Swiss in 1476-7. Most of his holdings came into the hands of the Hapsburgs, one of whom married his daughter. Burgundy itself reverted to France. As the Renaissance spirit took hold, attention was focused once again on secular music which, in contrast to the conservative and limited treatment it had received in the last generation, flourished and partook of the most advanced techniques. The chanson was the most important form of the late 15th century and appeared in collections called *chansonniers*. The isorhythmic motet declined in importance, and the Mass owes its importance to the work of one towering figure, Johannes Ockeghem. Four-part writing came to be the standard for secular as well as sacred works. Voice ranges began to separate into their modern disposition. Imitation became frequent and began to play a more important part in secular music. There are occasional examples of imitation at the fourth below or fifth above - a practice which became important in the imitative style of the High Renaissance. Earlier imitation, as in the caccia, had been at the unison (as in a round). Imitation now frequently involved all voices of a polyphonic complex. As the voices separated in range, they began to become more homogeneous in musical material. The lowest part (contratenor) began to participate in the imitation instead of being merely a supporting bass. The cadence with the leading tone to tonic (*ti-do*) in one voice while the bass leaps from *sol* to *do,* comes into favor.

Busnois

Of the composers of chansons the most important was Antoine Busnois (d. 1492) who was in the employ of Charles the Bold. Melancholy love themes recur in his work, reminiscent of the chansons of the preceding generation; the name of his beloved appears in many guises in his texts. His chansons exhibit all the technical advances mentioned above. Frequently, the lowest voice of a chanson, after beginning imitatively, leaves off to become a supporting voice. Busnois was at his best in small forms.

Ockeghem

Johannes Ockeghem (c. 1420-1495) was the greatest master of the late 15th century. Born in what is now Belgium, his mature creative period was spent in the employ of the royal chapel of France under three kings. He was at his best in his sacred works whose larger forms gave fuller scope to his creativity. His chansons made more use of imitation than those of the preceding generation.

Style

In his sacred works Ockeghem cultivated a continuous flow of music, avoiding the clear-cut cadences of Dufay. Ockeghem used paraphrase technique freely and tended to avoid chromaticism. He was particularly famous for his skilfull use of canon (in the imitative sense). Examples of canon are not numerous in his works, but they are handled with such consummate skill that their importance is out of proportion to their number. The term *canon* means rule, and it was originally applied to verbal instruction for modifying a cantus firmus by augmentation, diminution, etc. It now came to be applied to the relationship between an original part and an imitating part. Ockeghem used all the canonic devices previously mentioned including imitation at pitches a fourth or fifth above or below the original voice. Even where imitation is not used, each voice in Ockeghem's polyphony has its own melodic individuality and is never mere filling in.

Motets

Ockeghem's motets exhibit great variety. Among them are some examples of the old bilingual motet and some based on paraphrase. Stratification of melodic material, common in the first half of the century, becomes rare now, and melodic material travels from one voice to the other. Ockeghem shows a desire to investigate new possibilities in the treatment of form, and his compositions show great individuality in this respect.

Ockeghem's Masses

Ockeghem's Masses, his most important works, also show individuality of form. There are cantus firmus Masses which use canonic devices, though imitation is not basic to their structure; and there are Masses that appear to be freely composed, though some obscure paraphrase may be lurking somewhere. There is a Mass in an improvisational style, completely free of learned contrapuntal devices; another (*Missa prolationum*) uses a series of double canons (two canons simultaneously). In such works as the *Missa prolationum* imitation again becomes the basic structure-producing device, as it had rarely been since the 14th century. More important, in his restless search for new vistas to explore, Ockeghem succeeded in expanding enormously the resources of the imitative technique by applying to it in an imaginative way the procedures that had previously been applied to the cantus firmus.

Ockeghem's polyphonic setting of the Requiem Mass is the oldest surviving example of the genre, though a lost Requiem by Dufay is probably older. Its text differed from that of the present day Requiem. For example, Thomas a Celano's famous 13th century sequence *Dies irae* was not introduced into the liturgy until the mid-16th century.

In his expressiveness, his contrapuntal skill, and the predominance of religious expression in his music, Ockeghem invites comparison with the great master of the Late Baroque, Sebastian Bach.

German Music in the Late 15th Century

Germany, though not important in the field of vocal polyphony, was a leader in the composition of organ music. The types of organ music include arrangements of vocal compositions, organ-Mass sections, and freely composed preludes. Important sources are: The tablature of Adam Ileborgh (1448), Paumann's *Fundamentum organisandi* (1452, *Manual of Instruction in Organ Composition*) and the *Buxheimer Orgelbuch* (c. 1460). Of these the Buxheim Organ Book is the most extensive with over 200 pieces. Tablatures by Kotter and Kleber date from the second decade of the 16th century. Note: a tablature is a system of notation for instruments, most importantly keyboard and lute. In addition, the Glogauer Liederbuch (c. 1477-1488) includes 61 pieces which seem to have been intended for instrumental performance, including dances.

The styles of organ composition show sustained-tone organum style and conductus style in the Organ-Mass sections. In most of the song settings the melody is preserved in essentially its original form in the tenor while the upper voice has free counterpoint. In some song settings the melody, in free paraphrase, moves from one voice to the other. Preludes for organ are included in these tablatures. These preludes are the earliest examples of independent, idiomatic keyboard compositions. In the *Buxheimer Orgelbuch* some of the compositions that have been arranged have been identified as pieces by Dunstable, Binchois, and Dufay, among others.

English Music in the Late 15th Century

There was decline in the appearance of musical sources during the latter half of the 15th century until the closing years. A ms of c. 1450 includes the earliest known polyphonic settings of the Passion. There are also polyphonic carols of a popular nature, characteristically English, with their roots in the medieval dance. Carol texts came to be of a religious nature because of the use of the genre by the Franciscans in popularizing religion. There are also secular part songs from the latter quarter of the century.

HIGHLIGHTS OF THE CHAPTER

Forms

<u>Mass</u>:   Polyphonic settings of the Ordinary of the Mass were an important form from this time on. Three types appear in the 14th and 15th centuries:

(1) Plainsong Mass. A separate Gregorian melody is used as a cantus firmus in each movement. Usually it comes from a corresponding section of a Gregorian Mass.

(2) Cantus firmus Mass. One preëxistent melody is used as a cantus firmus in each movement of the Mass. In the 15th century secular tunes were frequently used.   A melodic motive (head motif) was also used frequently to unify the work in a way apparent to the hearer. This is also true of the plainsong Mass.

(3) Paraphrase Mass. The liturgical melody is placed in the top voice and ornamented.

<u>Motet.</u> The isorhythmic motet continued during the first half of the 15th century and decreased in use during the second half. It tended to become more purely a sacred form in its later stages.

<u>Chanson.</u> In the early 15th century it was a fixed form- a solo song with instrumental accompaniment. In the second half it became infused with imitation which involved all parts. This was a secular form.

Techniques

<u>Canon</u> Strict imitation, modified in one or more of the following ways:

(1) The imitating voice repeats the melody at a different pitch than the original voice.

(2) The imitating voice doubles the time values of the original voice (augmentation).

(3) The imitating voice halves the time values of the original voice (diminution).

(4) The imitating voice repeats the original voice backwards (retrograde).

(5) The imitating voice repeats the original voice but with the melodic intervals going in the opposite direction (inversion).

CHECK LIST FOR REVIEW

Mass	head motif	canon
cantus firmus	inversion	*chansonnier*
l'Homme armé	chanson	

Claus Sluter	Guillaume Dufay	Antoine Busnois
Hans Memling	Gilles Binchois	Johannes Ockeghem
Jan van Eyck	John Dunstable	

LIST OF SCORES

Early 15th Century

English School

Dunstable, John (1370-1453), *O rosa bella*, accompanied song, HAM1, 61; *Sancta Maria*, hymn (motet), HAM1, 62; *Veni Sancte Spiritus*, Isorhythmic motet, TEM 18

Power, Lionel (d. 1445), *Sanctus*, Mass movement (ordinary), HAM1, 63

Damett (early 15th c.), *Beata Dei genetrix*, hymn (Marian), HAM1, 64

Burgundian School

Dufay, Guillaume (1400-74) sacred: *Alma redemptoris mater*, discant motet, HAM1, 65; Kyrie I, Agnus Dei, *Missa l'homme armé*, HAM1, 66. , 29, Kyrie I, *Missa Se la face ay pale*, MM,15, Gloria, NAWM1, 39a; *Quam pulchra es*, motet, NAWM1; *Conditor alme siderum*, motet (hymn), NAWM1, 30; *Nuper rosarum flores*, motet, NAWM1, 31;

Secular: *Se la face ay pale, Ballade*, NAWM1, 39a; *Mon chier amy*, ballade, HAM1, 67; *Adieu m'amour*, rondeau, HAM1, 68; *Resveilles vous et faites chiere lye*, ballade, NAWM1, 45; *Adieu ces bons vins de Lannoys*, rondeau, NAWM1, 46

Binchois, Gilles (c. 1400-1467), secular: *De plus en plus*, rondeau, HAM1,, 69; *Files à marier*, chanson, HAM1, 70, *Adieu m'amour*, Chanson, MM, 16

de Lantins, Arnold (fl. c. 1450), *Puisque je voy*, rondeau, HAM1, 71

de Lantins, Hugo (fl. c. 1450), *Ce ieusse fait*, rondeau, HAM1, 72

Morton, Robert (b. c. 1440-1475), *l'Homme armé*, chanson for instruments , NAWM1, 63

Late 15th Century

Franco-Flemish School

Ockeghem, Johannes (1430-95), sacred: Kyrie, Agnus Dei III, *Missa l'homme armé*, HAM1, 73; Agnus Dei, *Missa Caput:* , NAWM1, 40.

Secular: *Ma maîtresse*, virelai, HAM1, 74; *Ma bouche rit*, virelai, HAM1, 75; *D'ung aultre amer*, chanson, NAWM1, 48

Obrecht, Jacob (1450-1505, Dutch),sacred: Agnus Dei, NAWM1,41; *O beate Basili (prima pars)*, motet, HAM1, 76a; *O vos omnes*, motet, HAM1, 76b; Kyrie, Agnus Dei II, *Missa sine nomine*, HAM1, 77 ; Sanctus-*Missa prolationum* , MM, 17.

Secular: *Tsaat eén meskin*, instrumental canzona, HAM1, 78

Compère, Loyset (d. 1518), *Royne du ciel*, rondeau, HAM1, 79

German School

Finck, Heinrich (1445-1517), *Veni sancte spiritus-Veni creator spiritus* quodlibet, HAM1, 80

Paumann, Conrad (c. 1450), song from *Lochamer Liederbuch*,HAM1, 81a; (1452), organ setting of above from *Fundamentum organisandi*, HAM1, 81b

Glogauer Liederbuch (c. 1460), songs (quodlibet), HAM1, 82; instrumental piece, HAM1, 83a; *Der Neue Bauernschwanz*, dance, HAM1, 83b; *Nu bitten wir den hiel'gen Geist, Lied*, NAWM1, 50

Ileborgh tablature (1448), organ preludes HAM1, 84ab

Buxheim organ book (c. 1470), organ preludes, HAM1, 84cd

Late 15th Century English School
(Secular Partsongs)

Anon, *Tappster, Drinker (c. 1475)*,HAM1, 85

Cornysh, William (c. 1465-1523), *My love she mourneth*, NAWM1, 47; *A dew, a dew*, HAM1, 86a

Cooper, Robert (?), *I have been a foster*, HAM1, 86b

CHRONOLOGICAL CHART

Music	Political History	Intellectual History	Art
c. 1400-1453 Works of Dunstable	1363-1404 Philip the Bold reigns as Duke of Burgundy		
	1390-1477 Ascendancy of the Duchy of Burgundy	1398 John Hus lectures at Prague University	1395 Claus Sluter, *Moses*
c. 1400 Faenza codex, keyboard arrangements of 14th century secular pieces	1404-1419 John the Fearless, Duke of Burgundy		1400 *Alt-Neu* Synagogue in Prague
			1412 Brunelleschi, *Rules of Perspective*
	1415 Battle of Agincourt, England defeats France	1415 Hus burned at the stake for heresy at Constance	1416 Limbourg Book of Hours
	1417 End of Papal schism at the council of Constance (1414-1418)		
1420 Squarcialupi codex, source for Landini	1419-1467 Philip the Good, Duke of Burgundy		1419 Brunelleschi designs Foundling Hospital
c. 1425-1460 Works of Binchois		1425 Alain Chartier, *La Belle Dame sans merci,* poem	1425-1447 Ghiberti, *Gates of Paradise,* portals of Baptistery in Florence
c. 1425-1474 Works of Dufay			
c. 1425-1600 Meistersingers in Germany			c. 1425-1482 Works of Della Robbia
	1429 Joan of Arc raises the siege of Orleans		

Music	Political History	Intellectual History	Art
1430 Ascendancy of Franco-Flemish school	**1431** Joan of Arc burned at the stake **1434-1494** Ascendancy of Medici in Italy **1438-1445** Church Council of Ferrara-Florence (East and West Churches) **1447-1455** Papacy of Nicholas V	**1430** Emergence of modern English from Middle English	**c. 1430** Donatello, *David* **1432** The van Eycks, *Ghent Altarpiece* **1434** Jan van Eyck, *Arnolfini* **1446** Fra Angelico works at the San Marco Monastery, Florence
c. 1450 Trent Codices, chief source of 15th c. music. White notation introduced	**1452-1493** Reign of Emperor Frederick II, last Holy Roman Emperor crowned in Rome	**1447-1527** Humanist Popes **1447** Vatican library founded **1450** Florence under the Medici becomes center of Renaissance	**1452** Ghiberti completes Gates of Paradise at Florence baptistry
1453 Paumann, *Fundamentum organisandi,* collection of organ pieces, songs, and dances **c. 1454-1495** Works of Ockeghem	**1453** End of Hundred Years War Constantinople falls to the Turks		**1454** Holy Sepulchre at Tonnerre, Burgundy Mantegna, *St. James*
1455 Lochamer Songbook, early German folksong	**1455-1485** Wars of the Roses, England	**1454** Gutenberg invents printing from movable type cast in molds **1456** Gutenberg's "Mazarin" Bible	

Music	Political History	Intellectual History	Art
1460 Buxheim Organ Book: Mass compositions, preludes, arrangements of French and German folksongs First printed music c. 1475-1505 Works of Obrecht	1477 Battle of Nancy, defeat of Burgundy 1492 America discovered by Europeans	1471 Poliziano, *Orfeo*-use of Tuscan vernacular in poetry	1470 Memling, *Madonna* 1476 Van der Goes, *Nativity*

Hieronymus Bosch (c.1460-1518) detail from the 'Garden of Delights'. The instrument at right center is a hurdy-gurdy. Note the crank at the top. The crank turns a wheel which sets against the strings, causing them to vibrate. Popular from the 10th to 14th centuries, it was later considered a street instrument. (After Pischel, A World History of Art).

CHAPTER VI

THE HIGH RENAISSANCE

SOCIAL BACKGROUND

Much that we associate with the Renaissance spirit had an early flowering in 14th century Italy. By the early 15th century the cultural center had shifted to the Burgundian Empire where the upheaval of the Hundred Years War enabled the Dukes to revive feudal rights. This neo-medieval spirit had been reflected in the music. The 16th century saw the emergence of the High Renaissance. The term *high* does not imply any superiority of the 16th century style over the 15th; it simply implies that "practically every feature of Renaissance music that did not already exist made its appearance" This observation can be applied with equal relevance to other aspects of Western European culture. Man's interest in life on earth and his observation of the world around him-opened up by the Crusades- were manifested in a lively outburst of exploration beginning with the discovery of America by Europeans in 1492.

Though they produced few composers during the 15th and early 16th centuries, the Italian city-states were the most important political and economic centers in Europe under merchant families, such as the Medici, in Florence, and *condottieri* (professional soldiers), such as Ludovico Sforza in Milan. These courts attracted the leading artists, musicians, and thinkers of the day including many composers of the Low Countries, Leonardo da Vinci (1452-1519) and Josquin des Prez (c. 1450-1519), the greatest composer of the early 16th century, may have been at Milan at the same time. (Josquin is known to have been there at least as late as 1479, and Leonardo arrived there in 1482.) The presence of so many Low Countries musicians and composers laid the groundwork for a resurgence of native Italian composition in the late 16th century.

During this period man became aware of his own importance as an individual, and with the growing awareness the number of composers began to increase rapidly. Thus the concept of talent and genius came into existence. The famous Italian sculptor, Benvenuto Cellini, is said to have remarked "Ah, what a genius I am." The composer Josquin des Prez would teach composition only to those who had a special gift for writing music.

MUSICAL STYLE

Music Printing

Printing from movable type is considered by some to be the motivating force in the emergence of the Renaissance. It was first introduced into Western Europe in the mid-15th century and became widespread fifty years later. The printing of music conformed to this trend. Printing techniques were applied to music on a large scale in the 16th century, and the first to accomplish this feat was Ottaviano de' Petrucci of Fossombrone and Venice. Previously, printing techniques had been applied to plainchant only, but Petrucci now applied them to polyphony and turned out music in large quantities. His first publication of part music was dated 1501 and included music of Ockeghem and Busnois, as well as light pieces (*frottole*) by native Italian composers. Music printing soon spread to France and the Low Countries.

While score had been used for the notation of medieval organum, the rise of the motet led to the choir book arrangement, in which the voice parts were notated separately on (usually) two facing pages of an open book. The choir books were large manuscript books from which a choir of up to 15 singers could read. About the middle of the 16th century it became customary to put each separate part in its own book (the part book method). The production of multiple copies of each part book is the logical function of music printing, and this method suggests the possibility of larger numbers of singers on each part.

Imitation

Free imitation in which all parts participate is characteristic of the High Renaissance. The forms are sectional, and each section has its own melodic material which is shared by all voices in that section. Cadences between sections tend to be covered up to "hide the seams." Typically, the melodic idea of a new section is introduced immediately at the cadence, so that the flow of the music is continuous. Here the influence of Ockeghem is seen. Furthermore, the influence of the canonic manipulations of 15th century imitation have served to free the imitative technique of the limitations of strict imitation at the unison found in 14th century music. Imitation in the 16th century is usually at the fourth or fifth instead of at the unison, and it is not carried out in a rigid manner.

Harmonic Style

A further modification of imitative technique with tonal implications is the so-called tonal answer. In its simplest terms this means that a leap from *do* to *sol* (I-V) in one voice is answered by a leap from *sol* to *do* (V-I) in another, instead of from *sol* to re (V-II). Thus, tonal unity is preserved. The balance between melodic and chordal emphasis reached a high state of refinement in the hands of such composers as Ockeghem, with rhythm as the means of organizing the use of consonance and the melodic introduction of dissonance. Thus, beauty of sound became a major preoccupation of the Renaissance composer just as visual beauty was a major preoccupation of the Renaissance painter, no matter what his subject matter.

Vocal Ranges

Vocal ranges were separated into soprano, alto, tenor, and bass. This separation was a factor in making possible the pervading imitative style by introducing the element of contrasting timbre. Imitation at the fourth and fifth made it possible to adapt the material that was being imitated to the ranges of the voices. Division into ranges also obliterated the distinction between plagal and authentic modes that had existed for the medieval theorists dealing with plainchant. Such a distinction could not be applied to a polyphonic composition as a whole.

Cadence

The older types of cadence fell into disuse and only the *ti-do* type remained (except for the mode on E). The Renaissance rationale for the leading tone was that a cadence should consist of a major sixth between the second and seventh degrees expanding to an octave (e.g. D-B expanding to C-c). In the mode beginning on E, the major sixth already exists between F and D; thus no alteration is necessary,

Rhythm

As mentioned previously, the measure as we know it today was not recognized in the Renaissance The rhythmic unit was the tactus (beat) with a length of approximately a second. Consistent grouping of beats into twos, threes, or fours should not be imposed on the music of the period. In the second half of the century French classicists (influenced by the humanistic revival of classical scansion) introduced a method of giving long syllables twice the duration of short syllables in the *chanson mesurée*.

Interpretation of Text

In association with the madrigal a device of word-painting came into existence, a method of interpreting the text undoubtedly related to the idea of imitating nature. Though it seems naive to the modern mind, it was used with the greatest artistry in the 16th century. It consists of such procedures as using a high note to represent the word *high* or *heaven* ; a low note for *low* ; an ascending scale passage to represent ascent; etc. These procedures are known as madrigalism.

Sacred Forms

Motet

In the High Renaissance secular forms achieved an equal balance with sacred forms. The most important sacred form was the motet (not to be confused with the Gothic motet). It may perhaps best be defined as a polyphonic composition with a sacred Latin text that is not part of the Ordinary of the Mass. In the 16th century biblical texts began to be used.

Word-painting as described above is often found. In addition to the imitative style most characteristic of the form, a strict chordal style-called familiar style-in which all voices move in the same rhythm was sometimes used when the composers wished to focus attention on the text. The 15th century paraphrase technique was modified early in the 16th century by adapting this technique to the style of pervading imitation. There are numerous examples of paraphrase motets in which a liturgical melody is divided into short phrases, each of which is ornamented; and each phrase is treated as a point of imitation in succeeding sections of the motet. An antiphonal style of writing was applied to the motet in Venice, inspired by the presence of two choir lofts in St. Mark's Cathedral. Polychoral motets (motets for more than one chorus) were first written by the Flemish composer, Adriaen Willaert, who was appointed *maestro di cappella* (choir master) of St. Mark's in 1527 and founded a brilliant school of Venetian composers that included Andrea and Giovanni Gabrieli.

Mass

Except for its text, the sound of a Mass movement would not be different from that of a motet. The same imitative sections and passages in familiar style would be heard. Though still to be found in the 16th century, the cantus firmus Mass declined greatly in importance. However, the 16th century Mass was still characterized by a use of preëxistent material. Paraphrase technique in the imitative manner described above plays an important role in 16th century Mass composition. In it chant melodies are borrowed from corresponding sections of the Ordinary of the Mass.

A type of Mass greatly favored in the 16th century was the parody Mass. Of the various terms now used to describe 16th century Masses, the term *Missa parodia* was the only one in use at the time. The parody Mass is based, not on a single preëxistent melody, but on all the voices of a polyphonic composition either sacred or secular. The composer might use one of his own compositions or one by somebody else. It has been noted that the parody form, so important in the 16th century, would be impossible in our time with our concept of original composition and our copyright laws. In the hands of a master, such as Palestrina it could be treated with the greatest artistry. Sometimes, treated in gradually increasing elaboration, it functioned much like a theme and variations.

Music of the Reformation

The Lutheran Chorale

There was no specifically Protestant motet style in 16th century Germany. During this period motets were written by Protestant as well as Catholic composers. Protestant composers frequently wrote motets with Latin texts, and there were settings of Lutheran texts by Catholics.

Martin Luther was himself a musically cultured person and an admirer of Josquin des Prez, a Catholic, who was the leading composer of the day. Luther had a deep appreciation of the significance of music in the service and was also devoted to the principle that the service should be in the vernacular so that the congregation could understand and participate.. He had translated the Bible into German. It was under his personal direction that the Lutheran chorale took shape. The chorale was a simple, tuneful hymn which was sung by the congregation in unison and, at this time, without accompaniment. The chief sources of the melodies were German religious songs of pre-Reformation days; Gregorian melodies with their texts translated into German; secular melodies with new texts; and songs written specifically for the

Lutheran service. The rhythm of the early chorale melodies was fluid compared with the versions that we know which stem from the 18th century. It remained for the German composers of the Baroque period (1600-1750) to make use of the chorales in polyphonic church music-a tradition which reached a glorious climax in the music of J. S. Bach.

Calvinist Psalter

Another reform movement sprang up in Switzerland in the early 16th century. First led by Zwingli, it flourished under his successor, the Frenchman Jean Calvin, who established a theocracy at Geneva. Calvin advocated an austere simplicity in the service. He also advocated use of the vernacular. He had the psalms translated into French verse and advocated singing, but he favored monophony and always opposed part singing. The French composer Louis Bourgeois (c. 1510-1561) a follower of Calvin, played the chief role in supplying melodies for the psalms. He composed new melodies and adapted preëxistent ones, mostly from chansons. Bourgeois's collection was known as the Genevan Psalter. Despite Calvin's opposition, simple chordal settings of the psalter were made, the most important of which, by Claude Goudimel, greatly influenced the Lutherans.

England

The Reformation arrived in England by two different paths: one political and one religious. On the political side Henry VIII broke with Rome in 1534 making himself head of the church in England without any significant changes in the Catholic liturgy. English was gradually introduced into the service and Henry VIII authorized the Great Bible in English (1539). Under his successor, Edward VI, the first Book of Common Prayer (1549) in English, was compiled from Catholic sources. Sacred music with Latin as well as English texts, however, continued to be written. William Byrd, the greatest English composer of the day and a composer of international standing, remained a Catholic but nevertheless held positions in Anglican churches.

On the religious side Calvinism also gained converts in England. An English psalter first appeared in 1548. The Second Prayer Book (1552) was influenced by the Reformers. During the reign of the Catholic Queen Mary, Protestant exiles developed an Anglo-Genevan psalter.

Queen Elizabeth I aimed to steer a middle course between Catholicism and Calvinism in order to prevent strife within the nation. She returned to the forms of the first Book of Common Prayer, and a service more elaborate than the Calvinist came into favor. The English anthem of the 16th century sprang from the Latin motet but had an English text. Later in the century, the verse anthem introduced by William Byrd contained parts for solo singers as well as chorus.

America

In the early 17th century a psalter prepared by Henry Ainsworth and derived from both English and Dutch Calvinist sources was brought to America by the Pilgrims in 1620.

SECULAR FORMS

Italian Madrigal

The 16th century madrigal differed from the motet in two respects: (1) The text of the motet was on a sacred subject and was in Latin, while the text of the madrigal was on a secular subject and was in the vernacular. (2) The madrigal tended to use less learned contrapuntal writing.

The early 16th century precursors of the High Renaissance madrigal were the *frottole* and *strambotti* of northern and central Italy. Half popular and half aristocratic, the *frottole* and *strambotti* were in the old tradition of Burgundian secular music with its fixed forms. The texts were trivial. The composers were native Italian and the most important center was Mantua under the Gonzagas where under the sponsorship of the cultured Marchioness Isabella d'Este, production of these secular forms flourished. *Frottole* are included among the publications of Petrucci. A form similar to the frottola was the *canto carnascalescho* (carnival song) of the late 15th and early 16th centuries. These were to be performed at the festive carnivals at Florence under the Medicis.

The first generation of madrigalists in Italy was dominated by composers of Walloon and Flemish origin, such as Adriaen Willaert (1490-1562), Jacob Arcadelt (1505-1560) and Phillippe Verdelot (d. c. 1550). Their influence played an important part in the emergence of the madrigal style from the older forms. The early generation of madrigalists included one composer of Italian birth, Costanzo Festa (1490-1545)-the first important Italian composer to fuse the northern and Italian styles.

The madrigal was noteworthy for its attention to text and the musical interpretation of text. Texts were typically of high literary quality, and the chief source of these texts was Petrarch. Poetry by Cardinal Bembo and Boccaccio was also used, as was poetry by the famous Italian poets of the Renaissance: Ariosto, Tasso, and Guarini. Bembo was influential in raising literary standards.

In the madrigal interpretation of the text took the form of portrayal of individual words rather than of the underlying content of the whole. Since the music was intended to express the text, it was non-strophic or <u>through composed</u>, i.e. it did not repeat the same musical material with different words. Declamation of the words was carefully considered in the setting. Both imitative and familiar styles were used. All voices were treated homogeneously as to musical material in the manner established by the Walloon and Flemish composers of c. 1500. Madrigals were intended chiefly for performance by solo voices, that is, one voice to each part. Some of the early pieces were serenades to a lady (the "honorable courtesans" of the large cities) and were for male voices. In this there was an echo of the troubadour-trouvère tradition.

In many ways the madrigal must be looked upon as "performer's music" since it contained many touches that were addressed to the performer. These touches included examples of eye-music (*Augenmusik*) in which a word was interpreted by means of the notation employed. For example, if the text referred to the idea of darkness or blackness, the composer might contrive his time signatures, or anything else involved, so that black notes would be used for that word. The interpretation of individual words continued to be the main preoccupation of madrigal composers throughout the 16th century. In the search for more vivid expression, chromaticism was increasingly used and reached its acme in the work of Carlo Gesualdo da Venosa of Naples who pursued chromaticism in an individual way and as a vehicle for highly emotional expression.

English Madrigal and Related Forms

A late flowering of madrigal composition took place in England in the Elizabethan period. The same cultural climate that produced Shakespeare, Marlowe, Francis Bacon, John Donne, and the architect Inigo Jones, produced a notable crop of English composers. Though the Italian influence played an important role, the English madrigal was not a mere copy of the Italian. It was less preoccupied with text than the Italian and more concerned with musical structure. Repetition of sections, so studiously avoided in the through-composed Italian madrigal, is found in the English.

A type of strophic song that flourished around the turn of the 17th century was known as the *ayre*. The ayre was meant to have all parts sung or to be performed by a solo voice with instrumental accompaniment. There was also published music of a popular character including catches, ballad airs such as *Greensleeves,* and music based on street cries. Many texts for ballads were published as broadsides (single sheets printed with the lines running along the broad side) with directions to be sung to a given ballad air. Use of street cries as well as the term *catch,* itself, seem to hark back to the 14th century Italian *caccia,* an influence which now reached the popular level. The catch was a canon at the unison (as the caccia had been). Such well-known rounds as *Three Blind Mice* come from this period.

French Polyphonic Chanson

The French polyphonic chanson of the 16th century stemmed from the medieval fixed forms, influenced now by the free imitative technique of the Walloon and Flemish composers. The rigid organization of the fixed forms was relaxed, but the principle of repetition and recapitulation that stemmed from them remained. Chanson composers showed great ingenuity in the variety of repetition schemes that were employed. Word painting as found in the madrigal played no part here, nor was there any great concern for the literary value of the texts which were usually of a light, sophisticated nature. Josquin des Prez, the first great composer of chansons, writes with great contrapuntal skill using frequent canons of various types and using concealed cadences which show motet

influence. Josquin frequently used a three-part form (*a b a*)
e.g. in *Faulte d'argent* (Lack of Money).[1]

The Paris School

In the second quarter of the century activity centering around
the French Royal Chapel produced a group of native
composers known as the Paris School   In their chansons
contrapuntal complexity was relaxed, and a mixture of chordal
and lightly contrapuntal styles was employed. Cadences
between sections became more definite and less hidden. An
opening motive with repeated notes in dactylic rhythm (a long
followed by two shorts) became almost a signature of this
school. The Renaissance desire for realism manifested itself
in the program chansons of Clément Janequin (1485-1560)
which abounded in a literal imitation of sounds of nature.
Sounds of battle with fanfares, bird calls, sounds of the hunt,
the street cries of Paris, and the chattering of women (*Le
Caquet des femmes*) are found here.

Chanson mesurée

The humanistic influence sired a group of French humanists,
the *Pleiade*, which sought to apply to French verse the
rhythmic principles of the poetry of Classical times. One
member of the group, Du Bellay, advocated nobility of subject
matter and imitation of classical forms and meters. To this
Ronsard added recommendations to the poets to make their
verse more suitable for musical setting. The result was known
as *vers mesuré a la lyre*. Baïf, following a precedent laid
down by Konrad Celtis, professor of poetry at Ingolstadt
(1492-97), advocated the application of classical scansion to

---

[1]HAM1, 91

French poetry, a procedure known as *vers mesuré a l'antique*. Baïf, together with Ronsard and Thibaut, founded the *Academie de poesie et musique* in 1570. They sought to apply the quantitative classical poetic meters to French poetry and set it to music. These settings, known as *chansons mesurées*, made use of the rigid procedure of having long syllables set to notes of twice the value of the short syllables. Associated with the group was the composer Claude le Jeune (c. 1525-1600), who produced imaginative settings of Baïf's poetry within this rigid framework. Repetition schemes are employed using refrains. The musical meters resulting from these measured settings of syllables were irregular. Simple and compound beats alternated freely and were a distinguishing characteristic of the style. (Using modern terms, a beat consisting of two eighth notes might be followed by one consisting of three eighth notes.)

Printing

Chansons were printed in great numbers by such publishers as Attaingnant in France and soon spread to Italy with Ottaviano de' Petrucci. Because the music of many of these chansons was independent of the text and autonomous in structure, chansons, especially those of the Paris school, became popular for instrumental performance in Italy where they became models for independent instrumental compositions in the following century.

Monophony-the Meistersinger

The name *Meistersinger* first appeared in the 15th century when the practice of monophony began to be cultivated by the craft guilds. The meistersingers inherited the tradition of the chivalric minnesingers from whom they claimed descent, and of whom they were the bourgeois counterpart. The type of contest which took place in their schools is accurately portrayed in Wagner's music drama *Die Meistersinger* . They had a repertory of melodies, derived more or less from the minnesong, which often had fantastic names, such as "the ape tone" or "the tone of the red bat". Sometimes texts were adapted to the old melodies, and sometimes new melodies were composed. Texts were chiefly scriptural in source. The form was the bar-form of the minnesingers (*a a b* or *a a ba*). Walther's *Preislied* (Prize Song) in *Die Meistersinger* is in bar-form. Though outside the mainstream of musical activity, the meistersingers laid a foundation for a bourgeois musical tradition independent of church or court. They thus played a part in establishing the basis upon which the musical productivity of Germany was built in later centuries.

INSTRUMENTAL MUSIC

Lute Music

Italy

Italy became the chief source of instrumental music in the 16th century, and the lute emerged as the most important instrument. The lute was a plucked stringed instrument of ancient lineage with a body rounded at the bottom and flat on top and with a flat neck on which the strings could be stopped. The mandolin is the only current survivor of the genre. Lute music was notated in tablature, a type of notation that indicated finger placement on the instrument rather than pitch. Tablature notation was important to musical research because it could show unequivocally the manner in which accidentals were used. The system of chord symbols for guitar found in popular music today is a form of tablature.

Italian lute music consisted chiefly of dances and transcriptions of vocal pieces and included some pieces of improvisational nature, possibly intended as preludes or postludes to vocal pieces. Generally, the dances were written in pairs with the first dance in slow binary meter and the second in faster ternary meter. Both dances of a given pair were based on the same musical material. The most popular of these paired dances was the pavana-gagliarda (pavane and galliard).

Later, Italian lute music came to be composed over a group of stock basses that were somewhat interrelated, such as the *passamezzo* ("step-and-a-half") *antico*; *passamezzo moderno; romanesca;* and *folia* . In such compositions the bass would be repeated (basso ostinato) with new material above it in each successive statement. Thus, these compositions belong to the family of *theme and variations*.

Spain

Beginning early in the 16th century, music for plucked stringed instruments had an important flowering in Spain. The Spanish instrument, called *vihuela,* was a guitar with six strings tuned like a lute. The earliest Spanish lute tablature was by Luis Milan (1536) and consisted for the most part of pieces called *fantasias*. These fantasias were improvisatory in character. A tablature of Luis de Narvaez (1538) contained the first examples of true theme and variation form to be found in Europe. From that time on the theme and variations played an important role in Spanish lute music. *Guardame las vacas* (Graze the Cows)- a favorite theme in the tablatures of Narvaez and later Spanish composers-was related to the *Romanesca* , one of the stock basses popular in Italy. The *Folia,* another stock bass, was also found in both Spain and Italy.

France and the Low Countries

The lute was popular also in France and in the Low Countries. In these countries music for the lute was similar to the lute music of Spain and Italy. In fact, the same types of lute compositions were found throughout Europe during the Renaissance. Lute songs found in France and the Low Countries were transcriptions of polyphonic chansons of the period.

Keyboard Music

The keyboard instruments of the 16th century included the organ, the harpsichord, and the clavichord. The organ traces its origins back to antiquity (*hydraulis*) while the stringed keyboard instruments (harpsichord and clavichord) seem to have emerged in the 14th century. In the harpsichord the strings are plucked by quills controlled by the keys and, unlike the modern piano, the performer cannot control the volume by the force with which he strikes the keys. In the clavichord the sound is produced by metal tangents which remain in contact with the strings and determine their vibrating length. The clavichord has a soft, delicate sound. Within its narrow range of volume the performer can control loudness and softness by the force with which he strikes the keys. Also, the fact that the tangent remains in contract with the string makes it possible to produce a vibrato (called *bebung*). Thus, the clavichord is a very expressive instrument.

The oldest surviving harpsichords and clavichords are of Italian construction and date from the 16th century. Italy (especially Venice) was the leading producer of harpsichords at this time.

There was little distinction between the style of organ and stringed keyboard in the 16th century. The organ was used to accompany the choir, and it was considered inappropriate to play dance music on it; but the style of writing was the same for stringed keyboard as for organ. The pedal keyboard is a distinguishing feature of the modern organ, but reference to the pedal in music of the period is almost non-existent. A known reference exists in a German tablature by Adam Ileborgh (1448).

The Germans, though backward in composition, were advanced in the art of constructing instruments. The earliest treatise on musical instruments is in German and dates from the early 16th century (1511). This treatise is by Sebastian Virdung and is entitled *Musica getutscht und ausgezogen* (A Survey of German Music). The practice of improvising undoubtedly played a part in the emergence of idiomatic writing (writing in a style that was especially suited to the instrument for which the music was written). For example, when long sustained notes were written, the performer, when playing a stringed keyboard instrument, may well have added his own ornaments such as trills, shakes, and running passages.

Sources

The earliest extensive collection of keyboard music is contained in an early 15th century manuscript found in Faenza, Italy. Its contents consist largely of organ Mass sections and ornamented transcriptions of secular vocal pieces by such 14th century composers as Machault and Landini. The organ Mass provided organ music to substitute for portions of the liturgy. In it choir and organ alternated, and the organ passages were based on the chant melodies that would ordinarily have been sung by the choir. The chant melodies were frequently treated with great freedom in these organ settings. Organ Masses are found throughout the 16th century. The Magnificat was also treated in an alternating manner, but in the case of the Magnificat, successive organ passages were variations of a single chant melody.

Preambles are found in German tablatures from the mid-15th century, and an Italian collection of 1523 contains two keyboard compositions of an improvisatory character. Keyboard dances appear in Kotter's tablature (German) of 1513. Girolamo Cavazzoni's tablature of 1524 contains the first examples of two forms of music composed directly for keyboard, forms that were to be cultivated throughout the 16th and most of the 17th centuries. These were the *ricercar*, similar in style to the motet but with more extended treatment of each theme, and the *canzona*, the instrumental counterpart of the chanson. Cavazzoni's tablature also contained organ Masses and music for the Magnificat. In these compositions he treated the chant in the imitative paraphrase manner described earlier.

In the late 16th century the improvisatory keyboard pieces evolved into an established form that was to have a long history extending well into the 18th century and beyond with a brilliant flowering in the music of J. S. Bach. The form is known as the *toccata* (fr. the Italian *toccare* to touch). The most important type was established by Claudio Merulo (1533-1604), a composer of the Venetian school. It consisted of alternations between sections in a free improvisatory style and contrapuntal sections using imitation. The sections in free improvisatory style made use of chords and scale passages.

In addition to Cavazzoni and Merulo important composers of keyboard music in the 16th century were the Venetians Andrea and Giovanni Gabrieli. Spain produced an outstanding composer of keyboard music in Antonio de Cabezon who continued the Spanish tradition of composing variations and also wrote ricercars (called *tientos*). In the late 16th century important collections of keyboard music came from England. The English composers wrote for the virginals, a type of harpsichord.   Their music shows influences of Cabezon and the Italians, with dances, variations, and pieces based on plainsong - some in cantus firmus style. The leading composers of virginal music were William Byrd, John Bull, and Orlando Gibbons.

Music for Instrumental Ensemble

Music for Voices or Instruments

Musical instruments in great variety existed in the 15th century and increased in use both in public and private gatherings during the 16th century. City bands included trombones, trumpets (without valves, which came into existence in the 19th century) and woodwind instruments of the flute and double reed families. For private gatherings the viols were favored. These were the predecessors of the modern violins but had a softer, more dulcet tone. Their shape can be seen in the modern double bass viol, the sole surviving member of a family that consisted chiefly of the three sizes corresponding to the violin, viola, and 'cello of the modern violin family. They were not held under the chin like the violins, but with the body downward like the modern 'cello. The smaller sizes would be rested on the knee.

Towards the end of the 16th century the violins began to be developed from the family known as *viole da braccia* (arm viols) which were instruments to be played while strolling through the streets and thus had to be held under the chin. The first known maker of true violins was Gasparo da Salo of Brescia (1540-1609). He was followed by G. Paolo Maggini (1580-c.1630) also of Brescia and the brothers Amati (Antonio, 1550-1638 and Girolamo, 1556-1630). It was the Amatis who created the classical violin shape. Girolamo's son Nicolo (1596-1684) was the first of the great violin makers.

In the early 16th century there was no differentiation between instrumental and vocal music; the style was predominantly vocal. There is ample evidence, however, that instrumental performance was widely cultivated though exact indications as to how the instruments were employed is lacking. Written accounts describe concerts of mixed voices and instruments as well as of instruments alone. Instrumental methods (instruction books) for flute and viol date from the first half of the 16th century. They give evidence of a highly developed viol technique and give instructions for transcribing from vocal notation to instrumental tablature. In addition, the title pages of many collections from about 1540 on state that the music may be performed by voices or instruments. It is thus evident that a given polyphonic composition of the 16th century might be performed by any combination of voices or instruments, each voice or instrument playing the part corresponding to its range. The choice of ensemble would be dictated by the conditions of performance.

The Canzona

Music intended for instrumental performance emerges in the last two decades of the 16th century. The most important form of instrumental music was the *canzona da sonar* (The name refers to pieces in chanson style to be played on instruments), also called *canzona alla francese* (French chanson). We have noted before how the French polyphonic chanson lent itself particularly well to instrumental performance because of its purely musical formal organization. Now, pieces began to be written on this model specifically for instruments. The most important composer of these ensemble canzonas in the 16th century was Giovanni Gabrieli. He favored cornetts and trombones for their performance. The cornett consisted of a straight or slightly bent tube of wood or ivory with a cup-shaped mouthpiece like a brass instrument and with finger holes like a flute or recorder to change pitches. Its sound had the timbre of a brass instrument but was very gentle. It had a long history extending from the 13th to the 19th centuries.

Dramatic and Ceremonial Music

The *Sacre rappresentazioni* were Italian religious plays performed in church with scenery of an elaborate nature. The roles were sung and instruments were used. These plays, in great favor in the 15th century, began to decline in the 16th century. The knightly tournaments of 15th century Burgundy also included music.

Secular entertainment grew in importance in 16th century Italy and led to a revival of Latin plays and the creation of Italian plays on Classical models. In the 16th century, under the influence of Italian dances, the French *ballet de cour* (court ballet) came into existence. Introduced into England, it developed into the masque, a court entertainment on allegorical or mythical subject matter, and employed both music and dancing. Music was also used in the Elizabethan drama to announce the entrance of a king upon the stage; to accompany a banquet scene; or to heighten the effect of a battle scene. The music of these stage effects was based upon actual customs of the time. For example, trumpets and drums were customarily used to announce the entrance of Queen Elizabeth and her court.

Composers

The Low Countries

The number of composers active in the 16th century increased tremendously. Recognition of the importance of the individual was a significant factor. Though the Italian city-states made prosperous by trade with the east were the chief cultural centers, the cities of the Low Countries (the Franco-Flemish School) supplied most of the composers throughout the 16th century. Much sought after by the Italian courts, they laid the foundations for the schools of native Italian composers which emerged late in the century.

Jacob Obrecht, the only prominent composer of Dutch ancestry, lived in the latter half of the 15th century (1452-1505). Most of his career was spent in the northern cities, and Erasmus was in his choir at Utrecht (1476). His style represents the transition to the style of the High Renaissance. In his secular works influences of the fixed forms are treated with new freedom. His motets are conservative, often polytextual, but sometimes material from the cantus firmus permeates the other voices. His Masses, constructed on the cantus firmus principle, show great imagination in its application. Next to Josquin des Prez he was the outstanding composer of the day.

The early 16th century produced Josquin des Prez (1450-1521), a great composer as well as a singer and one of the first in whom the High Renaissance style takes shape. He was born in Hainaut near the French border in what is now the French speaking (Walloon) part of Belgium but was until 1482 part of the Burgundian empire. Most of his career was spent in Italy. Milan, the Papal choir, and Ferrara were his chief posts. A classic purity and repose permeates his music. At his best in his motets, he also made significant contributions to the musical corpus of the Mass.

The late 16th century saw another great composer from the Low Countries, Orlandus Lassus (1532-1594). He was born at Mons, chief city of Hainaut, a city near the French border. At that time the area was part of the Spanish Hapsburg holdings known as the Spanish Netherlands. Like Josquin, a singer, he was noted for the beauty of his voice. He went to Italy at the age of 14 in the service of Ferdinando Gonzaga in Sicily, Palermo, and Milan. At the age of 24 he settled in Munich where he remained for 38 years in the service of Albert V of Bavaria. Though he composed significant Masses and chansons in addition to madrigals of great beauty, his motets are his outstanding works. Prominent among these motets are his settings of the penitential psalms. Vigor and turbulence, dramatic treatment of texts, and unexpected turns and contrasts characterize his style.

Italy

The Flemish composer Adriaen Willaert laid the foundations for a school of native Venetian composers, notable among them Andrea and Giovanni Gabrieli. He also had a follower in the Late Renaissance composer Hans Leo Hasler who inherited the polychoral style of the Gabrielis. The end of the 16th century also saw the career of the native Roman composer Giovanni Perluigi da Palestrina (c. 1525-1594) who ranks with Lassus and the Englishman William Byrd as the three greatest composers of the late 16th century. Palestrina is outstanding in his Mass composition in which he uses the old cantus firmus technique as well as paraphrase and parody techniques. His music is characterized by emphasis on the flow of contrapuntal lines and the perfection of the treatment of consonance and dissonance which became a model of its kind for succeeding centuries.

England

Though England had been a leading musical nation in the mid 15th century with John Dunstable, it stagnated soon after, and the High Renaissance style was late in reaching it. However, in the late 16th and early 17th centuries England produced some brilliant composers. Outstanding among them was William Byrd. His music is characterized by rhythmic complexity and careful treatment of text, a treatment that included word-painting. The English madrigal, lighter in tone and gayer than the Italian, was distinguished by its own melodic quality. Morley, Weelkes, and Wilbye are among the foremost English madrigal composers while Dowland was famous for his ayres.

Spain

Spain also produced an outstanding composer in the Late Renaissance in Tomas Luis da Victoria (1549-1611). He was trained in Rome, possibly by Palestrina. Unlike his contemporaries, he wrote only sacred music. This music is infused with a dark mysticism and drama that invokes comparison with his contemporary, the Spanish painter El Greco. He made use of word-painting in his motets to heighten the intensity of their expression.

HIGHLIGHTS OF THE CHAPTER

In the Renaissance polyphony became the most important medium of musical expression, as painting became the most important medium of expression in the visual arts. As music gained autonomy, the sound of the music became the chief preoccupation of musicians, rather than its liturgical function; thus were developed new techniques of dealing with consonance and dissonance. As the temporal power of the church declined, the liturgical chant ceased to exercise its *auctoritas* over music; and newly created themes, treated in pervading imitation and with canonic devices, became the chief means of musical organization. The power of music to express human emotion was recognized; and the composer became, not a mere craftsman whose only virtue lay in the accuracy with which he followed rules, but a person of talent and genius. Though instruments were widely used in the Renaissance, the style of writing was predominantly vocal. Instruments might be freely substituted in a composition for voices of corresponding range, but the only elements of purely instrumental style would be the result of improvisation. The late 16th century saw the emergence of new instrumental forms in the ricercar and canzona (both derived from vocal models) and the toccata (derived from keyboard improvisations). Dances and variations, first found in lute music, were the most important instrumental forms of the century.

Techniques

(1) Free imitation. The imitating voice does not repeat the original voice exactly. Some of the intervals may be changed and the imitating voice may begin with imitation and then go its own way.

(2) Tonal entry. To keep the tonality secure *do-sol* may be imitated by *sol-do*.

(3) Point of imitation. This is a section based on a given melodic element used in imitation. The melodic element is passed back and forth among the different voices. The basic musical form of the High Renaissance consists of a series of sections, each constituting a separate point of imitation.

(4) Imitative paraphrase. A melody is ornamented and then divided into melodic elements each of which is used as a point of imitation.

(5) Parody. A method of composition in which all the voices of a polyphonic piece are taken over as the basis of a new composition. The composer ornaments the original voices and uses them in new and different combinations.

(6) *Vers mesuré*. A method of setting texts, used mainly in France, in which a long syllable is set with a note twice as long as the note to which a short syllable is set.

(7) Madrigalism. A method of tone painting in which the word *high* may be represented by a high note; the word *low* by a low note; the idea of ascent by an ascending scale

passage; and the idea of descent by a descending scale passage, etc.

Forms

Sacred

(1) <u>Mass.</u> The Ordinary of the Mass is set using the same techniques as were used in the previous period: cantus firmus, plainsong, and paraphrase. Free imitation is imposed on these older forms. A new form is the Parody Mass, using the parody techniques described above.

(2) <u>Motet.</u> As to text, the text is sacred; in Latin; and something other than the Ordinary of the Mass. Musically, it is sectional; based on points of imitation; and the cadences are "hidden" usually by having a new point of imitation enter before the cadence is complete so that both rhythmically and melodically the music keeps moving.

(3) Full anthem. Like a motet but with English text.

(4) Verse anthem. Soloists are used as well as the full choir.

Secular

(1) <u>Madrigal:</u>

Italian. Vernacular text; through-composed; based on points of imitation.

English. Vernacular text; lighter in texture than the Italian; and makes some use of repetition and recapitulation of sections.

(2) <u>Chanson.</u> Vernacular text (French); light in nature; definite cadences between sections; various schemes of repetition and recapitulation of sections.

Instrumental

(1) <u>Canzona</u>. Instrumental counterpart of the chanson.

(2) <u>Ricercar</u>. Instrumental counterpart of the motet but with more development of each point of imitation.

(3) <u>Toccata</u>. A piece based on keyboard figurations. The most important type alternated free improvisatory passages with contrapuntal ones based on imitation.

(4) <u>Theme</u> <u>and</u> <u>variations</u>. Repetitions of a theme with changes and ornamentation introduced.

(5) <u>Varied</u> <u>couple.</u> A pair of dances, one in slow duple meter, the other in fast triple meter; both based on the same theme. The varied couple was typical of 16th century dances.

CHECK LIST FOR REVIEW

frottola	fixed form	broadside
choir book	parody	ballad
part book	chorale	catch
free imitation	psalter	program chanson
humanism	full anthem	*Pléiade*
madrigalism	verse anthem	*vers mesuré à la lyre*
familiar style	strophic	*vers mesuré `a l'antique*
paraphrase	through-composed	*chanson mesurée*
antiphonal	eye-music	Meistersinger
polychoral	ayre	

lute	*Musica getutscht*	*tiento*
pavane	*und ausgezogen*	virginals
galliard	organ Mass	viol
passamezzo antico	Magnificat	*viola da braccia*

passamezzo moderno	preamble	*canzona da sonar*
romanesca	tablature	*canzona alla francese*
basso ostinato	prelude	*sacra rappresentazione*
theme and variations	postlude	*ballet de cour*
vihuela	canzona	masque
fantasia	toccata	

Jakob Obrecht	Andrea Gabrieli	Costanzo Festa
Josquin des Prèz	Giovanni Gabrieli	Louis Bourgeois
Erasmus	Martin Luther	Cardinal Bembo
Ariosto	Tasso	Guarini
Benvenuto Cellini	Ulrich Zwingli	Boccaccio
Petrucci	Jean Calvin	Petrarch
Adriaen Willaert	Jacques Arcadelt	Carlo Gesualdo
Phillipe Verdelot	Clément Jannequin	da Venosa
Ronsard	Sebastian Virdung	Orlandus Lassus
Baïf	Hans Kotter	Palestrina
Konrad Celtis	Girolamo Cavazzoni	Hans Leo Hasler
Claude le Jeune	Claudio Merulo	Thomas Morley
Attaingnant	Antonio de Cabezon	ThomasWeelkes
Luis Milan	William Byrd	John Wilbye
Luis de Narvaez	John Bull	John Dowland
Adam Ileborgh	Orlando Gibbons	Tomas Luis da
		Victoria

LIST OF SCORES

Choral Music

Franco-Flemish

Isaac, Heinrich (1450-1517): <u>German part song (polyphonic Lied)</u>: *Zwischen Berg und tiefem Tal,* HAM1, 87; *Innsbruck ich muss dich lassen (Gross Leid muss ich jetzt tragen),* NAWM1, 52

des Prez , Josquin (1450-1521): <u>Motet</u> :*Tu pauperum refugium,* HAM1, 90; *Ave Maria,* MM, 19;*Tu solus, qui facis mirabilia,* NAWM1, 32;*Dominus regnavit,* NAWM1, 33; <u>Mass movement</u>: Agnus Dei (mensuration canon), *Missa l'Homme armé,* HAM1, 89. <u>Chanson</u>: *Faulte d'argent,* (A B A form), HAM1, 91 (see also Andrea Gabrieli);*Mille regretz,* chanson, NAWM1,49a de la Rue, Pierre (1460-1518): <u>Mass movements</u>: Kyrie I & II, *Missa l'Homme armé*, HAM1, 92

Willaert, Adrian (c. 1485-1562): <u>Motet</u>: *Victimae paschali laudes*, HAM1, 113; *O crux, splendidior*, NAWM1, 35. <u>Madrigal</u> *Aspro core e selvaggio e cruda voglia*, NAWM1,57

Gombert, Nikolaus (d. c. 1560): <u>Motet</u> *Super flumina*, HAM1, 114

Clemens non Papa (c. 1510-c. 1555): <u>Motet</u>: *Vox in Rama,* HAM1, 125

Arcadelt, Jacob (c. 1514 - after 1557): <u>Mass movements</u>: Kyrie & Gloria: *Missa Noe noe*, NAWM1, 43; <u>Madrigals</u>: *Voi ve n'andat' al cielo,* HAM1, 130; *Ahime, dov'è 'l bel viso,* NAWM1, 56

Rore, Cipriano de (1515-after 1557): <u>Madrigals</u>: *Da le belle contrade,* HAM1, 131; *Datemi pace, o duri miei pensieri,* NAWM1, 58

Lasso, Orlando di (1532-1594): <u>Motets</u>: *Penitential psalm III,* HAM1, 144; *Tristis est anima mea*, MM, 23; *Cum essem parvulus*, NAWM1, 37; <u>Mass movement</u>: Introit: *Requiem aeternam*, Mass for the Dead, HAM1, 143; <u>Chanson</u>: *Bon jour, mon coeur,* HAM1, 145a

Monte, Philipp de (1521-1603): <u>Mass movement</u>: *Missa super Cara la vita,* parody Mass, HAM1, 146b

Kerle, Jacobus de (1531-1591): <u>Motet</u>: *Exurge, Domine,* HAM1, 148

Werth, Jacob van (1536-1596): <u>Madrigal</u>: *Cara la Vita,* HAM1, 146a

German

Glogauer Liederbuch (c.1480): <u>German hymn</u>: *Nu bitten wir den heil'gen Geist*, NAWM1, 50

Hofhaimer, Paulus (1459-1537): <u>German part song (polyphonic Lied)</u>: *Mein traurens ist*, HAM1,93

Stolzer, Thomas (c. 1480-1526):<u>German</u> <u>hymn</u>: *Christ ist erstanden*, HAM1, 108

Senfl, Ludwig (c. 1490-1550):<u>Motet</u>:*Salutatio prima*, (Franco-Flemish style), HAM1, 109; <u>German</u> <u>hymn</u>:*da Jakob ne das Kleid ansah*,(Franco-Flemish style), HAM1, 110; <u>German</u> <u>part</u> <u>song</u> <u>(polyphonic</u> <u>Lied):</u> *Oho, so geb' der Mann ein'n Pfenning*, (with folksong cantus firmus),TEM, 32

Walter, Johann (1496-1570): <u>Chorale</u> <u>setting</u>: *Aus tiefer Not*, HAM1, 111a; *Komm, Gott Schöpfer, heiliger Geist* (cantus firmus), TEM, 24

von Bruck, Arnold (c. 1500-1554): <u>Chorale</u> <u>setting</u>: *Aus tiefer Not*, HAM1, 111b

Handl, Jacob (Gallus) (1550-1591): <u>Motet</u>: *Ecce quomodo*, HAM1, 156

Hassler, Hans Leo (1565-1612): <u>Motet</u>: *Quia vidisti me*, HAM1, 164; *Laudate Dominum*, polychoral motet, TEM, 28 ; <u>German</u> <u>part</u> <u>song</u> <u>(polyphonic</u> <u>Lied):</u> *Ach Schatz*, HAM1, 165

Aichinger, Gregor (1564-1628): <u>Motet</u>:*Factus est*, HAM1, 166

Praetorius, Michael (1571-1621): <u>Chorale</u> <u>setting</u>:*Vater unser im Himmelreich*, chorale bicinium, HAM1, 167a

Franck, Melchior (c. 1573-1639): <u>German</u> <u>part</u> <u>song</u> <u>(polyphonic</u> <u>Lied):</u> *So Wünsch ich dir*, Lied, HAM1, 168

Italian

Fogliano, Giacomo (1473-1548): <u>Lauda</u> :*Ave Maria*, lauda, HAM1, 94

Tromboncini, Bartolomeo (fl. c. 1500): <u>Frottola</u>: *Non val aqua* and *In Te Domine*, HAM1, 95

Cara, Marchetto, (c. 1504):<u>Frottola</u>: *O mia cieca e dura sorte*, TEM, 20; *Io non compro più speranza*, NAWM1, 55

Anon, <u>Canto carnaschialescho</u>: *Per scriptores* (c. 1500),HAM1, 96;*Orsu car'signori*, NAWM1, 51

Festa, Costanzo (d. 1545): <u>Madrigal</u>: *Quando ritrova*, HAM1, 129

Palestrina, Giovanni (1525-1594): <u>Motet</u>: *Sicut cervus*, HAM1, 141. <u>Mass movement</u>: *Missa Papae Marcelli*: Credo, NAWM1,44; Agnus Dei I, HAM1, 140. *Missa Veni sponsa Christi*: Agnus Dei,MM, 24 <u>Madrigal</u>: *Alla riva del Tebro*, HAM1, 142;

Nanini, Giovanni Maria (c. 1545-1607):<u>Motet</u>: *Hic est beatissimus*, (Roman), HAM1, 152

Marenzio, Luca (1560-1599): <u>Madrigal</u>: *Madonna mia gentil*, chromatic madrigal, HAM1, 155; *Solo e pensoso*, NAWM1, 59; *S'io parto, i' moro*, MM, 27

Gastoldi, Giovanni (c. 1556-1622): <u>Balletto (light music)</u>: *L'Accesso* , HAM1, 158

Anerio, Felice(1560-1614): <u>Song</u>:*Al suon*, song, HAM1, 160a. (See also versions for harpsichord and lute).

Gesualdo, Carlo (c. 1560-1614):<u>Madrigal</u>: *Io pur respiro*, chromatic madrigal, HAM1, 161; *Moro lasso*, chromatic madrigal, TEM, 33; *Io parto e non più dissi*, madrigal, NAWM1, 60

Spanish

Millan (late 15th c.): <u>Villancicos</u>: *O dulce* and *Durandarte*, HAM1, 97

Encina, Juan (1469- c.1530): <u>Villancicos</u>: *Congoxa mas, Pues que jamás* and *Mas vale trocar*, HAM1, 98; *Soy contento y vos servido*, TEM, 19

Morales, Cristobal (c. 1500-1563): <u>Motet</u>: *Emendemus in melius*, HAM1, 128, NAWM1, 36; <u>Magnificat</u> (Vespers, alternates choral settings with plainchant):*Magnificat octavi toni*, TEM, 23;

Guerrero, Francisco (1528-1599): <u>Antiphon BMV</u>: *Salve Regina,* antiphon BMV, (alternates choral settings with plainchant, polyphonic sections in. paraphrase) HAM1, 139

Victoria, Tomas Luis de (c. 1540-1611): <u>Motet</u>:*O vos omnes,* HAM1, 149

French

Fevin, Antoine (1437-c. 1515): <u>Mass movement</u>: Agnus Dei, *Missa Mente tota,* HAM1, 106

Mouton, Jean (c.1470-1522): <u>Motet</u>: *Noe, noe,* NAWM1, 34

Janequin, Clement (1485-c. 1560): <u>Program chanson</u>: *L'Alouette,* Paris, HAM1, 107

Sermisy, Claudin de (c.1490-1562): <u>Chanson</u>:*Tant que vivray,* NAWM1, 53

Goudimel, Claude (c. 1505-1572): <u>Psalm setting</u>: *Deba contre mes debateurs,* HAM1, 126a; *Mon Dieu me paist,* Psalm setting from French Psalter of 1564, TEM, 25; ibid. from French Psalter of 1565, TEM, 26

le Jeune, Claude (1528-1600): <u>Psalm setting</u>, *Deba contre mes debateurs,* HAM1, 126b.<u>Chanson mesurée</u>:*Revecy venir le printans,* NAWM1, 54; *D'une coline,* HAM1, 138

Bourgeois, Louis (c. 1510-after 1561): <u>Psalm setting</u>:*Qui au consil,* HAM1, 132

Costeley, Guillaume (1531-1606): <u>Chanson</u>: *Allon, gay, gay,* (Paris school) (rondo form), HAM1, 147

Crequillon, Thomas (d. c. 1557): <u>Chanson</u>: *Pour ung plaisir,* chanson (dactylic repeated note figure), MM, 20. (see also Andrea Gabrieli's *canzona francese, MM, 21*)

Fricassée, quodlibet in chanson style, taken from compositions by various composers, TEM, 31

English

Taverner, John (c.1495-1545): <u>Mass movement</u>: Benedictus, *Mass, the Western Wind,* cantus firmus Mass,

HAM1, 112; Benedictus: *Missa Gloria tibi trinitas,* NAWM1, 42

Tallis, Thomas (c. 1505-1585): <u>Responsorium:</u> (choral settings alternating with chant), *Audivi vocem,* HAM1, 127 .<u>Full</u> <u>anthem</u> : *Heare the voyce and prayer of Thy servants,* TEM, 27

Byrd, William (1543-1623): <u>Motet:</u> *Non vos Relinquam,* HAM1, 150;*Tu es Petrus,* NAWM1, 38; *Ego sum panis vivus,* MM, 25. <u>Verse</u> <u>anthem</u>: *Christ rising again,* HAM1, 151

Morley, Thomas (1557-1603): <u>Ballett:</u> *My Bonny Lass,* HAM1, 159

Dowland, John (1563-1626): <u>Ayre:</u> *What if I never speed,* HAM1, 163a; *Flow, my tears,* NAWM1, 69

Tomkins, Thomas (1573-1636):<u>Full</u> <u>anthem:</u> *When David heard,* HAM1, 169

Weelkes, Thomas (c. 1575-1623):<u>Ballett:</u> *Hark, all ye lovely saints,* HAM1, 170. <u>Madrigal:</u> *O care, thou wilt despatch me,* NAWM1, 61

Gibbons, Orlando (1583-1625):<u>Full</u> <u>anthem</u>: *O Lord increase my faith, ,* HAM1, 171. <u>Verse</u> <u>anthem</u>: *This is the record of John,* HAM1, 172

Bennet, John (fl. c. 1605): <u>Madrigal:</u> *Thyrsis, Sleepest Thou?,* MM, 28

Monophony

Meistersinger:

Sachs, Hans (1494-1576) , *Gesangweise,* TEM, 22; *Nachdem David war redlich und aufrichtig,* NAWM1, 11

Voice with Accompaniment

Spanish

Fuenllana, Miguel de (fl. c. 1554):<u>Folk-song,</u> <u>solo</u> <u>with</u> <u>lute</u>:*Paseabase el rey Moro,* HAM1, 123

English

Danyel, John (c. 1565-1630): <u>Ayre</u>, <u>solo</u> <u>with</u> <u>lute</u> <u>&</u> <u>viola</u> <u>da</u> <u>gamba,</u> *Stay, cruel, stay,* HAM1, 162

Dowland, John (1563-1626): <u>Ayre,</u> <u>solo</u> <u>with</u> <u>lute:</u> *What if I never speed,* HAM1, 163b; *My Thoughts are Wing'd with Hope,* TEM, 34

Italian

Gabrieli, Giovanni (1557-1612): <u>Motet</u> <u>with</u> <u>organ</u> <u>&</u> <u>instruments,</u> *In ecclesiis,* HAM1, 157

Music for Lute and Keyboard

Franco-Flemish

Macque, Giovanni (fl. 1584-1613), *Consonanze stravagante,* piece for organ, HAM1, 174

Sweelinck, Jan Pieterszoon (1562-1621, Dutch): <u>Echo</u> <u>fantasy</u> <u>for</u> <u>organ</u> *Fantasia in echo,* HAM1, 181

Spanish

Dalza, Joanambrosio (c. 1500):<u>Ricercar</u> <u>for</u> <u>lute</u> (non-imitative): *Tastar di corde con il ricercar,* HAM1, 99a

de la Torre, F (c. 1500): <u>Dance</u>, (*basse danse*), *Alta,* HAM1, 102a

Milan, Luis de (fl. c. 1535): <u>Fantasia</u> <u>for</u> <u>lute</u> <u>(vihuela)</u>, HAM1, 121; *Fantasia XI,* NAWM1, 64

Narvaez, Luis de (fl. c. 1538): <u>Variations</u> <u>for</u> <u>lute,</u> *Diferencias sobra O Gloriosa Domina,* HAM1, 122. <u>Transcription</u> <u>of</u> <u>vocal</u> <u>piece</u> <u>for</u> <u>lute,</u> *Mille regretz,* (chanson by Josquin), NAWM1, 49b

Valderravano, Anriquez de (fl. c. 1547): <u>Variations for</u>
<u>lute</u>, *Diferencias sobra Guardame las vacas*, HAM1, 124

Cabezon, Antonio de (1510-1566): <u>Organ</u>
<u>verse</u>,*Versos del sexto tono*, HAM1, 133. <u>Variations for</u>
<u>keyboard</u>, *Diferencias Cavallero*, HAM1, 134

German

Schlick, Arnolt (d. after 1517):<u>Hymns for organ</u>,
Salve Regina, and *Maria zart* , HAM1, 100 &101

Weck, Hans (c. 1510): <u>Dance</u> (*basse dance*),
Spanyöler Tancz, HAM1, 102b

Kleber tablature (1524): <u>Organ preludes</u>, HAM1, 84ef

Kotter tablature (1524): <u>Organ preludes</u>, HAM1, 84g

Neusidler, Hans (1508-63): Dances for lute (*Tanz und
Nachtanz*): *Hoftanz* HAM1,105a; *Der Juden Tanz*, HAM1,
105 b

Ammerbach, Nicolaus (1530-1597): <u>Dances for
keyboard</u>, *Passamezzo antico*, HAM1, 154a

anon. (c. 1550): <u>Dance for lute</u>, *Der Prinzen-Tanz:
Proportz, Tanz und Nachtanz*, MM, 22

English

anon. (c. 1525): <u>Dance for harpsichord</u>, (English
Dompe), *My Lady Carey's Dompe*, HAM1, 103

Redford, John (1485-1545): <u>Hymns for organ</u> *Veni
Redemptor* and *Lucem tuam*,HAM1, 120

Philips, Peter (c. 1560-after 1633): <u>Arrangement for
keyboard</u>, *Bon jour, mon coeur* (chanson of Lassus)

Munday, John (d. 1630): <u>Variations for harpsichord</u>,
Goe from my window, HAM1, 177

Bull, John (1563-1628): <u>Prelude for harpsichord</u>,
Praeludium, HAM1, 178. <u>Dance for virginals (harpsichord)</u>,
Pavana ,TEM, 30

Gibbons, Orlando (1583-1625): <u>Dance for harpsichord</u>, *Pavane Lord Salisbury,* HAM1,179

Farnaby, Giles (1560-1640): <u>Variations for virginals</u>, *Loth to Depart,* MM, 29

French

anon. (1530): <u>Dance for harpsichord</u>, (pavane), HAM1, 104   Titelouze, Jean (1563-1633): <u>Organ hymn</u>, *Pange lingua,* HAM1, 180

Italian

Spinaccino, Francesco (c. 1500): <u>Ricercar for lute</u>, *Tastar di corde con il ricercar dietro,* HAM1, 99b

Capirola, Vincenzo (c. 1504): <u>Transcription of vocal piece for lute</u>, *O mia cieca e dura sorte,* (frottola of Cara), TEM, 21

Cavazzoni, Girolamo (b. c. 1515): <u>Ricercar for organ (imitative)</u>, HAM1, 116. <u>Organ Mass</u>, *Missa Apostolorum (Cunctipotens)* , HAM1, 117; <u>Canzona for organ</u>, based on *Falte d'argens,* (chanson of Josquin) HAM1, 118

Ganassi, Silvestro (b. 1492): <u>Ricercars for viola da gamba (non-imitative)</u> , HAM1, 119

Gabrieli, Andrea (1510-1586) Venetian school: <u>Organ prelude,</u> *Intonazione settimo tono,* HAM1, 135. <u>Canzona francese for keyboard</u>, arrangement of *Pour ung plaisir,* (chanson of Crequillon) , MM, 21

Merulo, Claudio (1533-1604): <u>Toccata for keyboard</u>, HAM1, 153; *Toccata quinta, Secondo Tono,* for organ, TEM, 29

Anerio, Felice (1560-1614): <u>Transcription of Vocal Piece:</u> *Al suon,* arrangement for harpsichord & lute, HAM1, 160b

Picchi, Giovanni (fl. 1600-1620): <u>Variations</u> <u>for</u> <u>keyboard</u>: *Passamezzo antico*, keyboard dances, HAM1, 154b

Pasquini, Ercole (possibly) (1637-1710): <u>Canzona</u> <u>for</u> <u>keyboard</u>: (canzona d'organo), *Canzona per l'epistola*, MM, 26

Music for Instrumental Ensemble

Dances

Attaingnant, Pierre (d. 1552, publisher): <u>Dances</u> <u>for</u> <u>instrumental</u> <u>ensemble</u>: *Danseries a 4 Parties, Second Livre*, NAWM1, 62, French

Gervaise, Claude (fl. c. 1550): <u>Dances</u> <u>for</u> <u>instrumental</u> <u>ensemble</u>, (1) *Basse danse-La Volunté*, (2) *Pavane d'Angleterre-Gaillarde*, (3) *Allemande*, HAM1, 137

Praetorius, Michael (1571-1621):<u>Suite</u> <u>of</u> <u>Dances</u> <u>for</u> <u>instrumental</u> <u>ensemble</u>: *Ballet du Roy pour sonner après*, HAM1, 167b, German

Variations, Franco-Flemish

anon. (1583): <u>Variations</u> <u>for</u> <u>instrumental</u> <u>ensemble</u>: *Passamezzo d'Italie* , pub.   Phalèse, TEM, 35

Imitative Pieces

Ricercar and Canzona

Isaac, Heinrich (1450-1517): <u>Canzona</u> <u>for</u> <u>instrumental</u> <u>ensemble</u>, HAM1,88

Willaert, Adrian (c. 1485-1562) Venetian school: <u>Ricercar</u> <u>for</u> <u>instrumental</u> <u>ensemble</u>, HAM1, 115

Gabrieli, Andrea (1510-1586) Venetian school: <u>Canzona</u> <u>for</u> <u>instrumental</u> <u>ensemble</u>, *Ricercare del 12 tono*, HAM1, 136

Maschera, Florentio (1540-1584): <u>Canzona</u> <u>for</u> <u>instrumental</u> <u>ensemble</u>, HAM1, 175

In Nomine (Fantasy), English

Tye, Christopher (b. c. 1500-d. c. 1572), *In Nomine, "Crye",* Fantasia, NAWM1, 65

Tomkins, Thomas (1573-1656), *In Nomine,* HAM1, 176

Gibbons, Orlando (1583-1685), *In Nomine,* fantasia for a consort of viols, TEM, 36

"Sonata", Italian

Gabrieli, Giovanni (1510-1586), *Sonata pian' e forte,* HAM1, 173

Positive organ of the late 16th century designed to be placed on a table, as shown. (After Larousse Encyclopedia of Music, ed. Hindley.)

CHRONOLOGICAL CHART

Music	Political History	Intellectual History	Art
c. 1475-1521 Works of Josquin des Prez	1478-1492 Lorenzo de' Medici ("The Magnificent") in Florence		1478 Botticelli, *Venus*
c. 1480-1505 Works of Jakob Obrecht	1480-1500 Ludovico Sforza reigns in Milan		1481 Leonardo, *Adoration*
1484 Tinctoris, *De inventione et usu musicae*	1485-1603 Tudor dynasty in England	1484 Sir Thomas Malory, *Morte d'Arthur*	
1492 Boëthius (480-524) *Opera,* published in Venice	1492 End of Moorish Kingdom in Spain 1st voyage of Columbus Alexander VI, Borgia, elected Pope	Papal bull against witchcraft & sorcery	1493-1498 Rouen, Palace of Justice
1495 Des Prez appointed choirmaster at Cambrai	1494-1498 Ascendancy of Savonarola in Florence as reformer	c. 1494-1539 Isabella d'Este at Mantua 1495-1547 Works of Cardinal Bembo	1495 Bosch, *Temptation of St. Anthony*
1496 Gafori, *Practicae musicae,* on music theory	1497 Voyage of John Cabot Voyage of Vasco da Gama to India 1st voyage of Vespucci		
1498 License to print music granted to Petrucci the "Gutenberg" of music	1499 Milan reconquered by Sforza then lost again to the French Turks defeat Venetian fleet at Sapienza	1498 Celtes made 1st German poet laureate Comedies of Aristophanes published at Venice	1498 Leonardo, *Last Supper* Dürer, *Way to Calvary*
1500-1600 Spread of Meistersinger activity in Germany			

Music	Political History	Intellectual History	Art
1501 Petrucci's *Odhecaton*, earliest printed publication of polyphony, containing earliest polyphonic chansons	1501 Ferdinand I declares Granada a Christian kingdom French enter Rome	1501 Burning of books against the Church ordered by Papal Bull	1501 Dürer. *Life of the Virgin* Fra Filippo Lippi *St. Catherine*
1502 1st book of Masses by Josquin, pub. by Petrucci	1502 Peasants' revolt in Speyer, Germany	1502 Celtis, *Amores*, humanistic poem	1503 Henry VIII's chapel at Westminster 1504 Michelangelo, *David* 1505 Leonardo, *Mona Lisa*
1507 Petrucci's first lute tablature	1507 Diet of Constance recognizes Holy Roman Empire	1506 Reuchlin, Hebrew grammar & dictionary 1507 Martin Luther ordained	1506-1592 St. Peter's Cathedral in Rome 1507 Dürer, *Adam and Eve* 1508 Giorgione, *Sleeping Venus*
1510-1560 Janequin's works 1511 Virdung, *Musica getutscht* (German Music), treatise on instruments	1509-1547 Henry VIII, King of England	1511 Erasmus, *In Praise of Folly*	1508-1514 Michelangelo, Sistine ceiling 1509-1511 Raphael, *School of Athens*

Music	Political History	Intellectual History	Art
1513 Kotter's tablature: preludes, dances, transcriptions of vocal pieces (for keyboard) **1513-1545** Festa's works	**1513** Balboa discovers the Pacific Ocean **1513-1521** Leo X (Medici), Pope		
		1514 Machiavelli, *The Prince* **1516** Thomas More, *Utopia* Ariosto, *Orlando furioso* **1517** Luther's *95 Theses* condemning the sale of indulgences **1519-1528** Zwingli, Swiss reformer	**1514** Raphael, *Sistine Madonna* **1516-1518** Titian, *Assumption of the Virgin*
	1518 Cortes conquers Mexico **1519** Magellan circumnavigates the globe **1519-1556** Charles V, Holy Roman Emperor **1520** Diet of Worms: Luther outlawed, Reformation begun		**1523** Holbein, *Erasmus*
1524 Johann Walther, *Geistliche GesangkBuchlein* 1st Protestant songbook **1525-1550** Works of Verdelot	**1527** Sack of Rome by Charles V	**1526** Luther, German Mass **1528** Castiglione, *The Courtier*	**1525-1533** Michelangelo, Medici tomb
1528-1549 Attaingnant's publications, **1530-1585** Thomas Tallis works		**1530** Copernicus, *The Revolutions of Planets*	

Music	Political History	Intellectual History	Art
1533 First Italian madrigals 1535-1566 Works of Cabezon 1536-1561 Works of Luis Milan 1537-1566 Works of Merulo 1539 Gardano publ. chansons to be sung or played(Venice) 1539-1562 Compilation of Genevan Psalter by Louis Bourgeois 1540-1542 First publications of organ and ensemble ricercari 1542 De Rore, *1st Book of Madrigals* 1547 Glareanus, *Dodekachordon*, treatise on church modes 1550-1600 Le Jeune's works 1554-1594 Palestrina's works 1554-1603 De Monte's works	1541 De Soto discovers the Mississipi River 1542 Ireland made a kingdom	1532 Rabelais, *Gargantua* 1534-1536 Calvin,*Institutes of theChristian Religion* 1536 Library founded at Venice 1540 Loyola founds Jesuit Society 1541 Calvin's reforms at Geneva 1545-1563 Council of Trent: Catholic reform re dogma and correction of abuses c. 1553 Pléiade, Ronsard and Bäif (leaders). Promotion of the use of the French language in literature.	1539 Holbein, *Henry VIII* 1541-1548 Louvre court (Lescot) 1543 Cellini, Salt Cellar 1548 Cellini, *Perseus*

Music	Political History	Intellectual History	Art
			1554 Titan, *Danäe*
1555-1594 Lassus' works	1555 Peace of Augsburg (truce in religious wars)		
1558 Zarlino, *Istitutioni harmoniche*, theoretical treatise			
1560 Abolition of tropes at the Council of Trent			c. 1560 Breughel, Wedding Dance
1567-1600 *Musique mesurée*, le Jeune & Maudit			
1568-1623 William Byrd's works		1570 *Academie de poesie et de musique.* Bäif and Thibaut. It aimed at a closer union between poetry and music. See *Musique mésurée*	1570-1576 Titian, *Madonna*
1571 Andrea Gabrieli, *Canzoni alla francese*			1571 Warwick, Lord Leicester's hospital
1572-1611 Vicoria's works		1572-1598 Tycho Brahe's improved measurement of planets and stars	
1575 Byrd and Tallis, *Cantiones sacrae*			1576 Tintoretto, *Ascension of Christ*
1580 Vincenzo Galilei, *Dialogue between Ancient and Modern Music*		1580 Montaigne, Essays	1581 Caravaggio, Martyrdom of St. Maurice
c. 1583-1626 Thos. Morley's works			

Music	Political History	Intellectual History	Art
1586 Jakob Handl, *Opus musicum* 1587 Monteverdi, 1st Book of Madrigals 1588 Yonge, *Musica transalpina*. Italian madrigals with texts translated into English			1586 El Greco, *Burial of Count Orgaz*
	1588 Defeat of the Spanish Armada by England	1588 Christopher Marlowe, *Dr. Faustus* 1590 Edmund Spenser, *The Faerie Queen* 1590-1608 Shakespeare's works	
	1594 Henry of Navarre, crowned Henry IV of France, enters Paris	1594 Shakespeare, *Romeo and Juliet* 1596-1631 John Donne's works 1597-1625 Francis Bacon's essays	1592 Tintoretto, *The Last Supper* 1594 Caravaggio, *The Musical Party*
1597-1623 Thos. Weelkes' works 1598-1638 John Wilbye's works	1598 Boris Godunov becomes Czar of Russia		1619-1622 Banqueting Hall, London, Inigo Jones

Facsimile from Musica getutscht (On Music, in German), Virdung (1511). Left: *clavichord;* right: *virginal (harpsichord with one manual).* *(After Akademische Druck-u. Verlagsanstalt, Graz, Austria)*

Hendrick Terbrugghen (1588-1629), 'Woman Playing the Penorcon', (after Flemish & Dutch Drawings, Eisler). The penorcon was a rare form of the lute family of fretted instruments, used for accompaniment of singing and solo playing.

CHAPTER VII

THE EARLY BAROQUE

BACKGROUND OF THE BAROQUE

The period extending roughly from 1600-1750 is known as the Age of Reason in philosophic and scientific thought; as the Age of Absolutism in government; and as the Age of the Baroque in art and music. Where the Renaissance sought to discover and explore, the Age of Reason sought to explain. Man believed that he could explain the workings of the world and the universe in terms of an orderly system based on reason. Faith in the power of reason was a basic tenet of the new age. Francis Bacon (1561-1626) was the founder of the modern inductive method of reasoning - the counterpart to the deductive method which had existed in Classical Greek times.

Where centers of Renaissance culture resided in small independent city-states, the Age of Absolutism was dominated by the large nation ruled by an absolute monarch. Where Renaissance art sought to imitate nature, and Renaissance music was preoccupied with pure musical sound, Baroque art and music sought to express violent and dramatic emotion.

The Age of Reason

Spurred on by the exploration and navigation of the 16th century, the Age of Reason pursued the pure theoretical sciences of mathematics and astronomy. The seed had actually taken root early in the 16th century with the work of Copernicus who set forth the hypothesis that the sun was at the center of our planetary system. In the later 16th century Tycho Brahe was important for the accuracy of his measurements of stars and of planetary motion. The first advances in theoretical science were made early in the 17th century by Johannes Kepler with his laws of planetary motion. He was followed by Galileo, next to Newton the most important of the founders of modern science, who studied falling bodies and projectiles and formulated laws concerning acceleration, inertia, and combination of forces. The great surge of scientific thought in the 17th century included advances in mathematics, such as the invention of calculus by Newton and Leibniz; the invention of logarithms by Napier; and the invention of analytical geometry by Descartes. Medicine, physiology, chemistry, physics, biology and geology all participated in the rise of science. In science and mathematics advances of a comparable scope had not been seen since the Hellenistic period - the period of Euclid in geometry and Archimedes in physics. Francis Bacon's contribution to the reasoning process was his formulation of the method of inductive reasoning used in modern science - a method which emphasizes the gathering of facts as its beginning point. From the time of Ancient Greece the deductive method beginning with the generalization, the "self-evident" postulate, had been the dominant method of reasoning. The deductive method, very powerful as long as the beginning concept is sound, gained immeasurably by the contribution of Bacon's method of arriving at a sound postulate.

The emphasis on thought is reflected in the philosophic doubts which Descartes invoked in his proof of existence - doubts which he dispelled in his famous conclusion *"Cogito ergo sum""* ("I think; therefore I exist"). Emphasis on thought resulted in a renewed interest in philosophy and religious doctrine. The new scientific theories raised religious issues that were earnestly discussed, and many of the scientific thinkers, men such as Descartes and Leibniz, were concerned with reconciling natural science and religion. Interestingly, Kepler's work on planetary motion was motivated by his interest in astrology.

Organized religion was now impelled to enlist music and art into its service. In the 16th century the Reformation had made art and religion autonomous and independent of each other. The subject matter of a painting or a piece of music, whether sacred or secular, had little influence on the style. There had been a strong impetus toward simplicity in the service, especially in Calvinism. The Reformation had made church and state autonomous and independent of each other by bringing to an end the political power of a single religious body. Though religion was never again to occupy so powerful a political seat in the West, religious wars played a role in 17th century politics, and art and music were once more marshalled into the service of religion. The Counter-reformation (or Catholic reformation) now brought about a resurgence of creativity in sacred art. By the same token it inspired an equal effort on the part of Protestantism, and a Protestant art and music now emerged. The 16th century autonomy now gave way to a new unity in the combining of art and religion. This resulted in a differentiation of style between the sacred and the secular.

The Age of Absolutism

In the political sphere the autonomy represented by the independent city-states of Italy and the Low Countries gave way before an emerging centralization of power. Absolutism in government was the dominant method of rule in 17th century politics and was epitomized by Louis XIV (1643-

1714) of France, *"Le Roi Soleil"* ("The Sun-King"), who ruled by divine right and who was imitated by a host of greater and lesser rulers throughout Middle Europe. He organized and unified the government so that he could dominate it without the slightest challenge to his authority. In his quest for dominance the magnificent palace at Versailles (a suburb of Paris) played a most important role. By gathering the nobility around him at this court and smothering them in luxury Louis XIV was able to prevent them from having political power. Versailles, itself conceived from the ground up in accordance with a preconceived plan symbolizes this absolutism. In its design it is completely dominated by one structure - the royal palace; and nature itself, represented by the royal gardens, is completely organized and dominated by this palace.

The Age of the Baroque

Emotional Effects

Baroque art is defined as deliberate exaggeration, throwing things off balance and destroying symmetry in order to achieve dramatic and emotional effects. The Baroque artist tries to do in his own art what can more easily be done in another art - for example, the effect of motion is sought in painting and sculpture by depicting figures in strained poses or off balance. Architectural designs were planned in terms of light and shadow for emotional effect. Music represents emotional states by means of choice of instruments and other musical devices. The influence of subject matter on style is a dominant feature of Baroque art and music.

Uniting of the Arts

In the Baroque period arts are frequently combined in order to pursue their expressive aim. Architecture uses painting and sculpture as part of an architectural design in order to create spectacular effects. Opera, the most characteristic musical creation of the Baroque, welds music (vocal and instrumental) to the stage along with its dramatic action, costumes, and scenery.

Space

Another element of Baroque art was spaciousness. Perspective, light, and shadow were used to give the feeling of great physical depth to paintings. Paintings were planned so as to avoid symmetry and make the frame seem like a mere accident. Churches had sky and cherubs painted on ceilings to destroy the effect of enclosure. Space was made an actual element of musical performance in the early Venetian Baroque, notably in the polychoral motet which contrasted the sound of two or more choirs in different locations.

Baroque Music

Thoroughbass

The classic balance between voices that prevailed in Renaissance music gave way to emphasis on the top and bottom voices: a melody supported by a bass with the texture filled out by chords. This style gave greater freedom of dramatic expression and was basic to opera. In particular, emphasis on a single melodic line gave opportunity for presentation of the text in a way that could not be done within the contrapuntal web of Renaissance choral writing. The Baroque musicians developed a chordal notation called *thoroughbass* or *basso continuo*. This was a system in which numbers written under the notes of the bass line indicated the harmonic intervals which were to be added above the bass line to make a chord. During the whole period (1600-1750) a continuo instrument whose purpose was to fill out the chords was an indispensable part of any musical performance. The harpsichord was favored for this purpose though organ or plucked stringed instruments, such as the lute were also used.

In modern popular groups the guitar, organ, and/or piano frequently serve the same purpose.

Affective Representation

The emphasis on extremes of emotion in Baroque music made inevitable the emergence of new methods by which expression was attained. Baroque theorists scorned madrigalism as being pedantic and favored the expression of the underlying emotion of the text rather than the portrayal of single words. These underlying emotional states - joy, grief, exaltation, etc. - were known as the *affections*. The affections included not only what we would identify as emotional states but also such things as a pastoral affection or a military affection. Towards the Late Baroque period the means by which these affections were represented crystallized into a series of specific musical devices which marshalled all the elements of music in their service. Thus, choice of tonality or mode; use of certain rhythmic figures or time signatures; use of such devices as a basso ostinato; employment of chromaticism; choice of instruments; all aided in the representation of an affection. The association of the minor mode with sadness and the major mode with joy stems from the Late Baroque period. The trumpets of Handel's "Hallelujah" chorus or the "*Resurrexit* " of Bach's B-minor Mass represent the affection of exaltation. Modern tempo indications were originally the names of affections, e.g. *allegro* (happy), *mesto* (sad). The affections, of course, could not be applied to purely instrumental music though they might be applied to a chorale tune that the members of the congregation were expected to know, even if the text was not presented.

Instrumental Music

Instrumental music as an independent type rose to importance during the Baroque period. Though instruments in great variety existed during the Middle Ages as well as in the Renaissance, there is little indication as to how they were used; and the predominant styles were vocal. In the Baroque period there were three changes: (1) The Baroque *concertato* style was a style in which instruments had an independent role in the accompaniment of vocal music. They did not merely substitute for voice parts or double voice parts as they had done in the Renaissance. (2) Independent instrumental forms became important. These developed chiefly from the French polyphonic chanson through the *canzona da sonar* (or *sonate*) from which the modern term *sonata* is derived. (3) A specifically instrumental style emerged- a style intended primarily for instrumental performance. It developed partly from the chordal approach to Baroque polyphony, since chordal skips (skips from one member of a chord to another) were an important ingredient of the style. This aspect of the style had its origins in Renaissance lute music. Since the lute was limited in its capacity to play all the voices of a polyphonic complex, it was frequently forced to suggest them by playing in succession notes that were originally sung simultaneously by different voices. Another important ingredient of the instrumental style was contributed by the English virginalists. They used idiomatic keyboard figurations, scale passages, and repeated patterns of figuration - techniques that were called for by the fact that the stringed keyboard instruments were limited in their capacity to sustain tones. This instrumental style, once established, influenced writing for all instruments and even the human voice.

Harmonic Styles

Recognition of the chord concept made possible a freer treatment of dissonance. Since the chord was firmly established by the continuo, it was possible to play a dissonance against it, even in a rhythmically strong place, without the careful preparation demanded by the Renaissance style. Existing simultaneously with the new style, however, the Renaissance style, now considered antique (*stile antico*) was preserved in sacred choral music, especially that of the Catholic Church. Along with the old harmonic style such forms as the cantus firmus Mass and the parody Mass were also preserved. Music continued to be written in the stile antico during the 17th and 18th centuries even by such progressive composers as Monteverdi, Schütz, Alessandro Scarlatti, Antonio Lotti, and Benedetto Marcello. The Baroque fashioned its *stile antico* specifically after the music of Palestrina, which it placed on an exalted pedestal. Rules for the treatment of dissonance in his music were codified by such theorists as the Late Baroque composer J. J. Fux- though the rules were somewhat fictionalized. Fux laid out a set of exercises in the so-called Palestrina style and based on a cantus firmus in his book *Gradus ad Parnassum* (1725). Such writings became the bases for modern species counterpoint, a system of student exercises.

Performance Media

The term *a cappella* was applied by Baroque composers to the unaccompanied performance of sacred choral works in *stile antico*. The term *a cappella* (meaning "as performed in the chapel") referred specifically to the Sistine Chapel (built in 1473) where sacred choral works were performed by unaccompanied chorus in the late 16th century. Mistakenly, later ages imputed this type of performance to all Renaissance vocal music. It was, in fact, the Baroque period that gave birth to this consciousness of medium which made a distinction between vocal and instrumental performance, and in addition, assigned a different style to sacred and secular music. This differentiation of style did not exist in the Renaissance.

Traditional Harmony

In the Late Baroque a new concept of harmonic materials arose - a concept which we now consider to be traditional harmony, and which remained the basis of music composed through the 19th century. It is still the basis of most of the music that we hear today. The first theoretical treatise on traditional harmony was written in 1722 by the French composer Jean Philippe Rameau. Traditional harmony embraces (1) chord progression, (2) keys based on the major and minor modes, and (3) modulation, or change of key. It also considers that every note in a piece of music is either a member of a chord or a non-harmonic tone.

The concept of chord progression considers (1) that every chord has a root which is the lowest note of the chord when its members are arranged in a chain of thirds, (2) that the root of a chord is related to a scale or key; i.e. it is the first, second, third, etc. note of a given scale, and (3) that music can be analyzed in terms of root movement, a process known as harmonic analysis. This process of analysis leads to conclusions concerning the common practice of composers and is an example of the process of inductive reasoning that received its impetus from the theoretical scientists of the Age of Reason.

The key note of any scale is the bottom note on which the scale is built (e.g., the note C in the scale of C). A scale belongs to only one of two modes, major or minor. These modes replace the old church modes.

Modulation consists of a change of key and is brought about by means of chord progression. The tendency of chords to relate to a given key has its analogy in the law of gravity which was formulated by Newton in the same period.

Rhythm

The rhythm of Baroque music encompassed the widest extremes. Nowhere is the tendency toward exaggeration and imbalance better epitomized than in the extremes of Baroque rhythm. In the emotional, affective music, rhythm was very free. Freedom of tempo (*tempo rubato*) began to emerge with the chromatic madrigal of the late 16th and early 17th centuries. It was now applied to the new accompanied monody and to the free passage work of the Baroque toccata. At the other extreme was the rhythm of the instrumental ensemble music - a rhythm which emanated from the dance. This music was characterized by the traditional measure with its regularly recurring accents. Regularity of pulse reached a climax in the Late Baroque concerto where durational articulation all but disappeared in a driving, locomotive-like, mechanically pulsating, unceasing rhythmic flow.

Sources of Baroque Music

The beginning of the 17th century saw Italian composers dominating the scene - a dominance that began in the late 16th century with Palestrina. By the end of the 16th century the remarkable flow of talent from the area occupied by modern Belgium had dried up. The Dutch composer Jan Pieterszoon Sweelinck, the last great figure from the Low Countries, had so many German pupils that he became known as the "maker of German organists". Indeed, German music, which had lagged during the Renaissance, began to emerge; and from the Middle Baroque period on many of the greatest composers were German. Nevertheless, Italy remained the chief generating force during the Baroque period and was a constant source of fresh impulses which sustained and renewed creative activity.

Divisions of the Baroque

In the Early Baroque a reaction to the complex contrapuntal style of the Renaissance was a dominant feature. Presentation of the text in a clearly understandable way was considered the sole aim of music, and the texts chosen were such as to stress violent emotion. Free rhythm, chromaticism, and wild leaps in the melodic line all aimed at affective representation. In the Middle Baroque period interest in purely musical effect began to reassert itself. The undifferentiated monody of the Early Baroque developed into two distinct styles, one of which was essentially a vehicle for the text (recitative) and the other which put its emphasis on melodic interest (aria). The aria being solo song, however, did not obscure the text though it allowed of text repetition for melodic purposes. The wild leaps of the Early Baroque began to be organized on chordal lines, and contrapuntal texture was reintroduced in the choruses. In the Late Baroque large instrumental forms emerged and instrumental style became dominant. The internal organization of movements became unified and continuous. The *stile antico* declined except in Catholic music, and a vocal style, including virtuosity, took shape under the influence of instrumental music. Interpenetration of contrapuntal texture by tonal harmony was accomplished.

The Baroque Legacy

The Baroque period saw the arrival of modern rhythmic notation along with the measure and the barline. Strong and weak beats with regularly recurring accent were concomitant with the emergence of traditional harmony in the Late Baroque period. Opera, cantata, and oratorio came from the Baroque period. So did the concerto grosso and solo concerto; the prelude and fugue; and the chorale prelude. The Late Baroque produced two composers, Bach and Handel, whose music has for many years occupied an imposing position in our concert repertory. More recently Domenico Scarlatti and Antonio Vivaldi have received increasing attention. Radio and records have been responsible for the revival of the music of Georg Philipp Telemann. Modern interest in authentic performance of Baroque works has led to a veritable renaissance of harpsichord building. Of greater importance in the history of instrumentation is the fact that the violin family achieved its status as the most important of the stringed instruments, superseding the viols. The Baroque period was the age of the great violin makers: Nicolo Amati (1595-1684), his pupil Antonio Stradivari (1644-1737), and Guiseppe Guarneri (1666-c.1740).

EARLY BAROQUE VOCAL MUSIC

In the last quarter of the 16th century there were intellectual currents, musical and literary, that led to the emergence of opera. One group, called the Camerata (which gave its name to the whole movement) met at the house of Count Bardi in Florence, probably from c. 1576-1582. Another group was headed by Count Corsi, also in Florence; while still another group, in Rome, centered around Emilio de' Cavalieri. Count Bardi's group included the musicians Jacopo Peri and Giulio Caccini in addition to Vincenzo Galilei (father of the astronomer Galileo). A document setting forth the ideas and principles of the new movement was Vincenzo Galilei's *Dialogue between Ancient and Modern Music* (1581), which criticized contrapuntal music for the way in which it made the words impossible to understand. It also condemned madrigalism as being pedantic and set forth the idea that music should express the underlying emotions of the text and not confine itself to depicting single words. Under the influence of Humanistic thought, it addressed itself to the task of reviving the principles of Ancient Greek drama and music. The aim was to make the word supreme; to make music subservient to the text; and to portray violent emotion. Because the founders of opera invoked Greek drama, it used to be said that the invention of opera marked the beginning of the Renaissance in music many years after it had taken place in the other arts. To say this, however, is to oversimplify the cultural currents of the Ancient Greek world. The Greek drama was itself an outgrowth of the Dionysian cult with all that this implies in terms of emotional expression; and it was more in keeping with the Baroque spirit than with the Classical Apollonian spirit of moderation. The opera had more in common with the violence of the Hellenistic Laocoön group than with the calm repose of Phidias or Praxiteles. The term *baroque* is properly applied to any art when it bursts beyond the boundaries of its own limitations in its search for expressiveness. And that is what music sought to do when it made itself subservient to the delineation of text and the expression of its underlying emotions.

Accompanied Monody

The great contribution of the movement known as the Florentine Camerata was the <u>accompanied</u> <u>monody</u>. This monody was performed by a solo voice with very simple chordal accompaniment using a thoroughbass notation. The earliest surviving music of the school was a group of songs by Caccini, published in 1601, and entitled *Nuove musiche* (New Music). According to the principles of the Camerata, the monody called for a syllabic setting of the words. Caccini, however, being a skilled singer, introduced various virtuoso effects such as sliding changes of pitch; tremolo waverings of pitch; and changes of volume on a sustained tone. The texts were prose, and there was no attempt at musical form.

Prototypes

Solo singing was itself no novelty. There had been performances of contrapuntal madrigals with the top voice sung as a solo and the lower voices played on a lute. There were lute songs by Spanish composers of the 16th century and lute ayres by the English. A prototype of the use of music in a sustained dramatic context was the madrigal comedy of which the most famous was Orazio Vecchi's *L'Amfiparnasso* (The Slopes of Parnassus, 1594). The work consisted of loosely connected scenes and was not actually intended for stage production. The music was almost all part music with textures varying from chordal to contrapuntal. It was largely comic and made use of stock *commedia del arte* characters, such as Harlequin, Pulcinella, and Pagliaccio. Adriano Banchieri also wrote madrigal comedies using some of the same stock characters.

The First Opera

The first opera that called for staging and acting was composed by Peri with portions introduced into the performance by Caccini without Peri's previous knowledge. The work was entitled *Eurydice,* and it used a pastoral setting peopled by mythological characters. It was written throughout in a simple monodic manner with no use of vocal ornaments - a style known as the *stile rappresentativo.* The use of characters from Classical mythology, a legacy of the original concept of reviving Greek drama, persisted throughout the Baroque period. The story of Orpheus (the musician) and

Eurydice, upon which the first opera was based, was particularly popular and was used by composers from Monteverdi to Gluck.

Collections of Monody

In addition to its use in the opera, much monody was found as the basis of separate compositions which were published in collections. Among the composers of such collections (in addition to Caccini's *Nuove musiche*) were Peri, Grandi, Landi, and Frescobaldi. The beginnings of a purely musical organization are reintroduced in these collections, and they are the seed from which the aria grew and came to be admitted into opera in the Middle Baroque. The most important form in these collections of monody was the strophic variation. In the strophic variation a bass was repeated in more or less free fashion while a melody unfolded above it in through-composed manner. In addition to newly invented basses, there were a group of stock basses that were used in this manner. Some of them had been used in the Renaissance in lute and keyboard music - basses such as the *romanesca* and *passamezzo antico*. The composers mentioned above made use of this type, sometimes with a florid vocal line that called for virtuosity. Monteverdi, in some of his compositions entitled madrigal, used the strophic variation and the stock bass.

Monody in Sacred Music

The new monodic style was applied immediately to sacred as well as secular music. Emilio de' Cavalieri, a Roman noble and a member of the Camerata, composed a kind of sacred opera in his *La rappresentazione de anima e di corpo* (The Representation of the Soul and the Body, 1600). This work made use of choruses as well as monody. It stemmed from the tradition of the *laudi spirituali* and was written for Neri's congregation of secular priests, the Congregation of the Oratory in the New Church at Rome where *laudi* were customarily performed in services of a popular character. It was from the popular services that the oratorio got its name. The oratorio then became an aspect of the Catholic Reformation in dealing with the inroads of Protestantism. Cavalieri's monody was rather dry and lacked the affective character of Florentine monody. His work remained a somewhat isolated example but established early the principle that the *stile moderno* (modern style) was applicable to sacred music of a not strictly liturgical type.

Vocal Polyphony

Viadana's collection, *One Hundred Church Concerti* (1602), used a basso continuo which was a true bass line instead of being made up of whatever notes happened to be the lowest in the vocal parts at a particular point (*basso seguente*). His basso continuo was at times a completely independent part, and in some pieces which had only one or two vocal lines, it was an essential part of the composition. In other pieces his writing was conservative. The term *concerto* in the title of the collection refers to vocal music with instrumental accompaniment, a sense in which it was used throughout the Baroque period.

Polychoral Motet

Polychoral motets in the Venetian tradition continued to be written during the early 17th century, since their emphasis on space made them attractive to the composers of the Early Baroque. Giovanni Gabrieli was a master of the polychoral style, and those of his motets which were written after 1600 show a decidedly Baroque concept of affective writing and use of dissonance. His fellow student and friend, Hans Leo Hasler, also mastered the polychoral technique which he adapted to a German style and used for both sacred and secular works though without the depth of feeling of his Italian contemporary.

The ultimate in polychoral writing albeit, with conservative harmonic means, was achieved by the Roman school in the so-called "colossal Baroque" in which choruses were placed in balconies in various parts of the church to create the maximum of spatial effect. A Mass written by the Roman Orazio Benevoli for the consecration of the Cathedral at Salzburg in 1628 employed two eight-part choruses with soloists and six instrumental ensembles (three for each chorus). The instrumental ensembles consisted of two string groups, three brass, and one woodwind. There is a continuo part for each chorus and one for the whole composition. Despite the profusion of means, the style is the *stile antico* and affective Baroque expression is absent.

CLAUDIO MONTEVERDI

The most important composer of the Early Baroque was the Mantuan, Claudio Monteverdi. Though not associated with the original Camerata, he suffused the new style with his genius. He was a thoroughly trained musician who could compose equally well in the *stile antico* and the new style. His works included chromatic madrigals, operas, a ballet opera, a dramatic scene, and sacred music. In his sacred music he used both old and new styles.

Operas

Monteverdi's opera, *Orfeo* - performed in Mantua in 1607 - was the first operatic masterpiece. The composer used the Florentine monody but did not rely on it solely and combined it, moreover, with purely musical forms, such as strophic songs, duets, madrigals, and dances. He also succeeded in fusing these seemingly disparate musical forms and media into a unified dramatic entity. The opera was introduced by an instrumental overture in fanfare style. Monteverdi's orchestration is of interest in terms of the variety of instruments employed and the venturesome character - for his day - of the violin parts in which he set an example not soon followed.

Of his next opera, *Arianna*, only one complete number survives, the celebrated lament. The *Lamento d'Arianna* (Ariadne's lament at being left on the island of Naxos by Theseus) was greatly admired and was later arranged by Monteverdi as a madrigal. At another time its melody was set with a sacred text. Monteverdi's later operas, *The Return of Ulysses* and *The Coronation of Poppaea* (Nero's second wife), articulate the monody into recitative-like and cantabile melodic sections. Thus, they anticipate the distinction between recitative and aria within the opera.

Madrigals

The madrigal also came under the influence of the new style. It made use of the continuo, and this in turn made possible a freer treatment of dissonance and also an openwork texture in which the voices could come and go freely without bearing the burden of the harmonic structure. In this way madrigals were written in two or three voices with the voices in the upper register supported by the continuo. Madrigals of this type were known as chamber duets or trios. Instruments were used either as interludes or for accompaniment, and contrast between solo and choral sections also played a part. Strophic variation was also used in the madrigals.

Monteverdi's eighth book of madrigals, published in 1638 - the *Madrigali guerrieri et amorosi* (Madrigals of War and

Love) - contains a selection of earlier dramatic works including affective madrigals; the *Ballo delle Ingrate* (Ballet of the Damned) of 1608; and the *Combattimento de Tancredi e Clorinda* (Combat of Tancred and Clorinda) of 1624. The *Ballo delle Ingrate* is a ballet with operatic elements. The *Combattimento di Tancredi e Clorinda* is based on a portion of Tasso's *Jerusalem Delivered* and describes the combat of the Crusader, Tancred, with the pagan heroine, Clorinda. The story is set forth by a narrator (*testo*) in recitative, and the speeches of the principals are sung with appropriate actions. Note: the device of the narrator was to become characteristic of the oratorio. The work is remarkable for an innovation by the composer, known as the *stile concitato* (frantic or excited style). In vocal writing this style consisted of a portion of the text delivered rapidly in repeated notes; in string writing the *stile concitato* was represented by a tremolo which was one of the earliest examples of string tremolo. Monteverdi used a pizzicato effect during the combat scene. He made highly significant contributions to the repertory of expressive musical effects that was evolving in the 17th century.

Sacred Music

Monteverdi's *Vespro della Beata Virgine* (1610) is in "modern" style, using polychoral techniques and the new monody (*stile rappresentativo*). In it the five psalms of the First Vespers of the Feast of the Blessed Virgin Mary are set with the psalm tones as canti fermi and with voices and instruments treated in antiphony. The antiphons (not the same ones associated with these five psalms in the Liturgy) are set as emotional, dramatic affective solos in the most advanced operatic manner. Two settings of the Magnificat are included - one accompanied by instruments, the other accompanied by the organ alone. There is also included a *Sonata sopra 'Sancta*

Maria ora pro nobis' for voice and orchestra which uses the Litany (not the one from the Liturgical Vespers service) as a vocal cantus firmus. According to the composer, the *Vespers* was meant to be performed either in the chapel or in the palace and may not have been intended as a unified composition.

Monteverdi's treatment of the Ordinary of the Mass was characterized by much more conservative treatment tending towards the stile antico. He published, along with the *Vespro,* a Mass which is a parody on Gombert's motet *In illo tempore* and is in the Renaissance style. Conservative treatment also characterizes his later Masses. The posthumously published *Messa a quattro voci* (1650), though not completely independent of continuo, stresses polyphony of a predominantly vocal nature.

SUMMARY

The period of the Baroque in music and art coincided with a period of absolutism in government; with a period of notable advance in scientific theory and mathematics; and with a period of renewed vigor in philosophical thought. The term *baroque* refers to exaggeration, emotionalism, the striving after effect, and the combining of the arts to achieve effect. In music the chief legacy of the Baroque period was opera, which combined vocal music, instrumental music, stagecraft, and often ballet, to heighten the dramatic effect of a given story. Italian music predominated. Other important elements of Baroque music were: (1) interpretation of the underlying emotional content of a given text; (2) a chordal approach to harmonic style culminating in the emergence of traditional harmony in the Late Baroque; (3) the emergence of independent instrumental music and an instrumental style; (4) the existence simultaneously of two harmonic styles: an old style (*stile antico*) based chiefly on Palestrina to be used with more formal Liturgical compositions, and the new Baroque style; (5) a consciousness of medium which drew distinctions between vocal and instrumental music; (6) extremes of rhythmic flow ranging from the free tempo rubato of recitative and toccata to the mechanical pulsations of the concerto style; and (7) modern rhythmic notation.

The Early Baroque saw the rise of <u>accompanied monody</u> found in (1) opera and (2) collections of independent monodic compositions. A prominent form in the monodic collections was the <u>strophic variation</u>, important in the evolution of the <u>aria</u>. The new monody was also applied to sacred music of an informal popular kind, the point of departure for the <u>oratorio</u>.

Choral writing was influenced in the Early Baroque by the basso continuo, and polychoral writing was much admired.

The leading composer of the Early Baroque was Claudio Monteverdi. He wrote continuo madrigals, ballet opera, a dramatic scene, and the first operatic masterpieces. In his sacred music he used *stile antico* for his Masses and modern style for less formal sacred works.

CHECK LIST FOR REVIEW

Age of Reason	*Nuove musiche*
Age of Absolutism	*Eurydice*
Baroque	*Romanesca*
Counter Reformation	*Passamezzo antico*
Catholic Reformation	*La Rappresentazione di anima*
"Le Roi soleil"	*e di corpo*
Gradus ad Parnassum	Colossal Baroque
Sistine Chapel	*Lamento d'Arianna*
Dialogue between Ancient	*Ballo delle ingrate*
and Modern Music	*Vespro della beata Virgine*
Camerata	

Copernicus	Benedetto Marcello	Count Bardi
Tycho Brahe	J. J. Fux	Count Corsi
Kepler	Jan Pieterszoon	Cavalieri
Galileo	Sweelinck	Jacopo Peri
Newton	J. S. Bach	Giulio Caccini
Leibniz	Handel	Vincenzo Galilei
Des Cartes	Domenico Scarlatti	Orazio Vecchi
Louis XIV	Antonio Vivaldi	Banchieri
Monteverdi	Telemann	Orazio Benevoli
Schütz	Nicolo Amati	Grandi
Alessandro Scarlatti	Stradivari	Landi
Antonio Lotti	Guarneri	Frescobaldi

polychoral motet	madrigalism	concertato
thoroughbass	affections	canzona da sonar
basso continuo	affective representation	sonate

virginals	tempo rubato	oratorio
stile antico	toccata	laudi
a cappella	recitative	*basso seguente*
harmony	*stile rappresentativo*	concerto
chord progression	strophic variation	*stile concitato*
modulation	aria	opera
accompanied monody		

LIST OF SCORES

Choral Madrigal

Monteverdi, Claudio (1567-1643), *Cruda Amarilli*, NAWM1, 67; *Ohimè dov'è il mio ben*, NAWM1, 68; *Ohimè se tanto amate*, HAM2, 188

Madrigal Comedy

Banchieri, Adriano (1568-1634), *Il zapaione musicale*, madrigal comedy, HAM2, 186

Accompanied Monody

Collection of Monody

Caccini, Guilio (c. 1546-1618), pieces from *Le nuove musiche* (Florence, 1602): *Sfogava con le stelle,* aria, HAM2, 184; *Dovrò dunque morire*, madrigal for solo voice & lute, MM, 30; *Perfidissimo volto* , madrigal for solo voice and accompaniment, NAWM1, 66

Opera

Cavalieri, Emilio de' (1550-1602),two scenes from *La Rappresentatione i anima e di corpo,* sacred opera, "*A questi suoni* " HAM2, 183; *Via, via,,* TEM, 37. *Dalle più alte sfere*, madrigal, NAWM1, 70

Peri, Jacopo (1561-1633), Selections from *Euridice*, (opera): "*Funeste piaggi* ", recitative, HAM2, 182; *Le musiche sopra l'Euridice*, NAWM1, 71: (a) Prologo, La Tragedia: *Io, che d'altri sospir vaga e di pianti*, (b) Tirsi: *Nel pur ardor della più bella stella* (c) Dafne: *Per quel vago boschetto* Arcetro: *Che narri, ohimè,* Orfeo: *Non piango e non sospiro*

Monteverdi, Claudio (1567-1643), Selections from *Orfeo* (opera) "*Me che temi* " , recitative, HAM2, 187; "*Tu se' morta*",MM, 31; Prologo, La Musica: *Dal mio Permesso amato a voi ne vegno,* NAWM1, 72a; Act II, Orfeo: *Vi ricorda o boschi ombrosi* (excerpt), NAWM1, 72b; Act II, Messagera: *In un fiorito prato,* NAWM1, 72c; Orfeo: *Tu se' morta,* NAWM1, 72c; Choro: *Ahi caso acerbo,* chorus, NAWM1, 72c *L'Incoronazione di Poppea*: (opera) Act I,

Scene 3 , duet with ritornello, NAWM1, 73; "*Non schivar, non parar* " from *Il combattimento di Tancredi e Clorinda* , opera (1-act), solo, *stile concitato*, HAM2, 189

Cesti, Marc' Antonio (1623-1669), Orontea: Act II, Scene 17: *Intorno all' idol mio*, opera aria, NAWM1, 74

Sacred Music

Viadana, Lodovico Grossi (1564-1645), *Exaudi me Domine*, sacred concerto, HAM2, 185

Schein, Johann Hermann (1586-1630), *Erschienen ist der herrliche Tag*, Sacred Concerto (chorale concerto), cantata, TEM, 38

Carissimi, Giacomo(1605-1674), *"Afferte Gladium"*, scene from *Judicium Salomonis*, oratorio, MM, 32

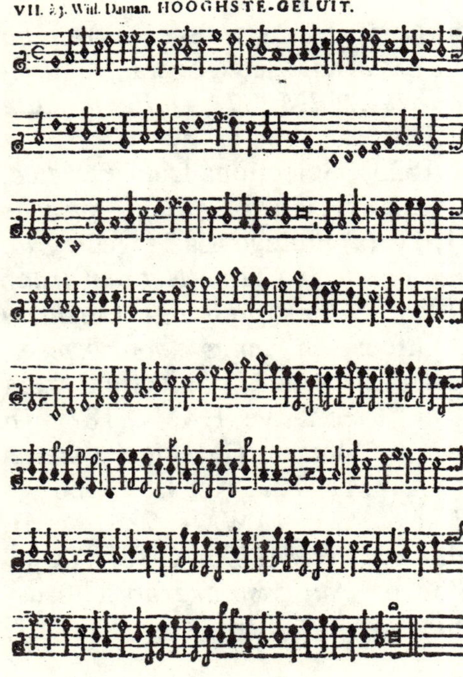

Facsimile from: *XX koninklycke fantasien . . . en noch IX fantasien . . ., Amsterdam*, P. Matthysz. Source: *S-Uppsala, Universitetsbiblioteket.*

In 1648 Matthysz published a collection of 29 fantasies for 3 violas da gamba by English composers including Lupo, Orlando Gibbons, Coprario, and Daman. (After Herman Baeten, publishers, Peer, Belgium)

CHRONOLOGICAL CHART

Music	Political History	Intellectual History	Art
1618 Schein, *Opella nova*, earliest chorale concertatos	**1618-1648** 30 years War, Protestant princes vs the Holy Roman Empire & Hapsburgs	**1618-1619** Kepler's 3rd law of planetary motion	**1618** Rubens, *Leucippus*
1619 Praetorius, *Syntagma musicum*, chief source of information on instruments	**1619-1637** Ferdinand II Holy Roman Emperor		
1620-1684 Violins of Nicolo Amati, first of the great violin makers	**1620** Pilgrims arrive at Cape Cod Mayflower Compact	**1620** Francis Bacon, *Novum organum*, application of inductive method	**1620** Velasquez, *The Water Seller of Seville*
	1621 Francis Bacon pardoned by the King	**1621** Johannes Kepler's *The Epitome of the Copernican Astronomer* banned by the Church	**1621** Van Dyke, *Rest on the Flight into Egypt*
	1621-1623 Gregory XV, Pope		
1621-1628 Schein, *Musica boscareccia*, accompanied strophic songs in 3 voices	**1621-1625** Philip IV King of Spain		
1623 Schütz, *Story of the Happy and Triumphant Resurrection*			**1623** Bernini, *David*, sculpture

Music	Political History	Intellectual History	Art
1624 Monteverdi, *Combat of Tancredi and Clorinda,* secular oratorio or semi-opera Scheidt, *Tabulatura nova,* organ collection (fugues,echoes, cantus firmus variations) 1625 Schütz, *Cantiones sacrae,* accompanied motets 1627 Schein, *Leipzig Cantional,*established the practice of organ accompaniment of the chorale 1628 Benevoli, *Salzburg Festival Mass,* "colossal Baroque", for 53 voices and instruments 1629 Schütz, *Symphoniae sacrae* sacred concertos in 3 voices 1634 Lawes, *Comus,* (masque)	1624 England declares war on Spain 1624-1642 Cardinal Richelieu in power in France 1625-1649 Charles I, King of England 1626 Manhattan Island bought by Peter Minuit 1628 La Rochelle captured, end of Huguenot power in France 1630 Puritans establish Boston 1631 Battle of Lützen, 30 Years War: Gustavus Adolphus of Sweden defeats Wallenstein, general of the Holy Roman Empire	1624 John Donne, *Devotions upon Emergent Occasions* 1625 Hugo Grotius, *De jure belli et pacis,* treatise on international law 1628 William Harvey, *Essay on the Motion of the Heart and the Blood* 1631 Galileo, *Dialogue on the Two Chief Systems of the World,* (supports Copernican planetary system with the sun as center)	1624 Frans Hals, *Laughing Cavalier* Nicolas Poussin, *Rape of the Sabine Women* 1625 Bernini, *Costanza* Inigo Jones, Covent Garden Church, 1627 Hals, *Lute Player* Rubens, *Mystic Marriage of St. Catherine* 1628 Andrea Spezza, Waldstein Palace. Prague 1631 Rembrandt, *Anatomy Lesson* 1634-1653 Taj Mahal

Music	Political History	Intellectual History	Art
1635 Frescobaldi, *Fiori musicali,* organ Mass	**1635** Colonization of Connecticut begins	**1635** French Academy founded by Cardinal Richelieu: issued dictionary and grammar; awarded literary prizes	**1635** Velasquez, *Surrender of Breda*
1636 Mersenne, *Harmonie universelle,* source for musical thought in France	**1636** Roger Williams first settlement in Rhode Island	**1636** Founding of Harvard College Corneille, *Le Cid*	**1636** Van Dyck, Children of Charles I
1637 First public opera theater in Venice	**1637-1657** Ferdinand III Holy Roman Emperor	**1637** Descartes, *Discourse on Method,* presents method of Cartesian doubt Descartes, *Essay on Analytical Geometry*	
1638 Monteverdi, *Madrigals of War and Love*			**1638** Rembrandt, *Fall*
	1639 Mazarin enters the service of Richelieu	**1639** First printing press in America, Cambridge, Mass.	**1639** Zurbaran, *St .Francis in Meditation*
1640 *Bay Psalm Book,* 1st book printed in America	**1640-1688** Frederick William, the 'Great Elector' of Hanover		

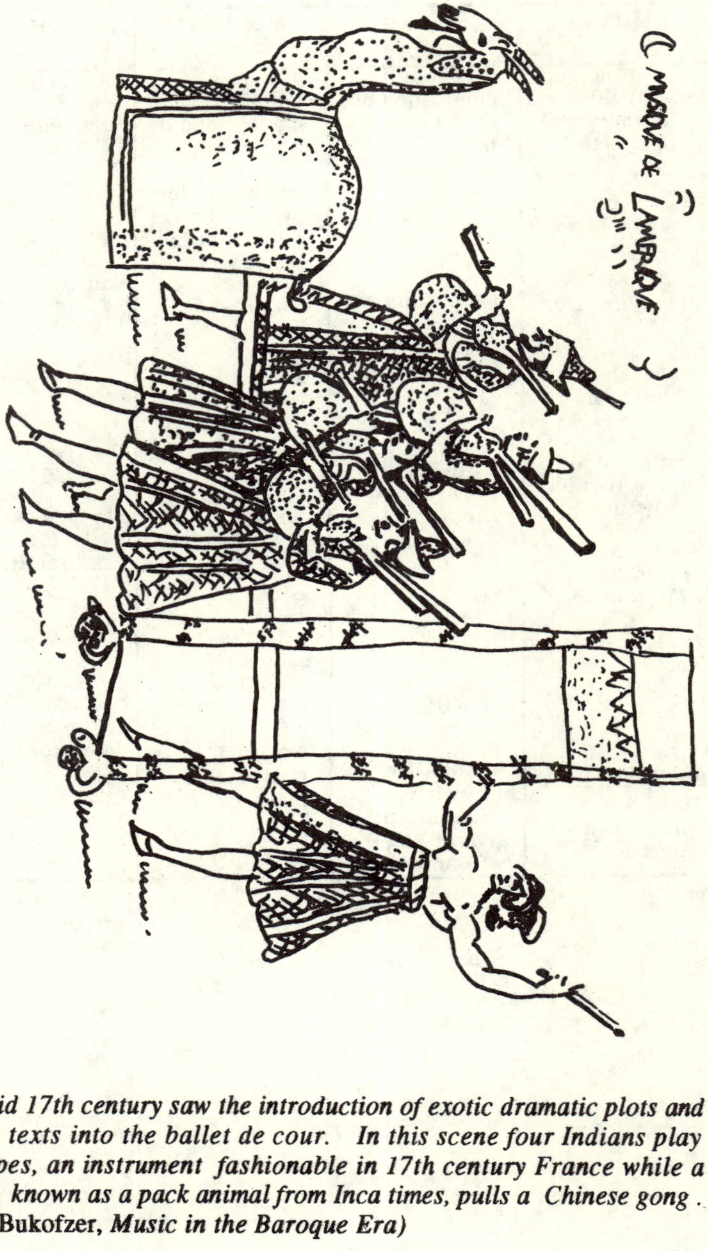

Entrance of American Music from La Dourairière de Billebahaut (a ballet de cour)

The mid 17th century saw the introduction of exotic dramatic plots and poetic texts into the ballet de cour.   In this scene four Indians play bagpipes, an instrument fashionable in 17th century France while a llama, known as a pack animal from Inca times, pulls a Chinese gong . (after Bukofzer, *Music in the Baroque Era*)

CHAPTER VIII

MIDDLE BAROQUE VOCAL MUSIC

FORMS AND STYLES

Monody had emerged as a musical device whose sole purpose was to present and interpret the text; but the Middle Baroque, taking a more balanced approach, reintroduced purely musical considerations. This did not mean, however, a return to the ideal of ensemble sound that characterized the Renaissance. Rather it meant the introduction of a new concept, namely that of beautiful singing (*bel canto*) of the solo voice. During this period the wild leaps of the Early Baroque melodic line became organized along chordal patterns; chromaticism subsided; and the musical style became harmonically simpler. Metrical organization became more symmetrical, and the emotional vocal ornaments of the Early Baroque were subdued except in the arioso.

The Aria

The desire for more purely musical effects had its impact on monody and the new dramatic forms resulting in the emergence of the aria towards the middle of the 17th century. Thus, two distinct forms grew out of the early monody - the <u>recitative</u> and the <u>aria</u>. Both were for solo voice; but the aria was characterized by: (1) its emphasis on melodic interest and beautiful singing; (2) its organized forms; (3) its repetitions of text for purely musical purposes; (4) its regular phraseology

217

which was influenced by the dance; (5) its fondness for triple meter; and (6) its use of written-out *(obbligato)* instrumental parts for its accompaniments instead of the sparse chordal accompaniments of the monody.

The prototypes of the aria had occurred in the separate collections of monodic pieces which included, in addition to the usual strophic variations, some examples of arias patterned after the French chanson forms. Frescobaldi wrote some arias in the *canzona francese* form. Another early example of repetition of melodic material in monody occurred in Monteverdi's famous *Lamento d'Arianna* on the text *lasciatemi morire*. While the strophic aria on a short basso ostinato persisted throughout the 17th century (e.g. "Dido's Lament" from Purcell's *Dido and Aeneas*, an especially distinguished example of the form), the most prominent type came to be the *da capo* aria in three-part form (A B A). Prominent in the early development of *bel canto* were Luigi Rossi (1597-1653) in Rome, and Pier Francesco Cavalli (1602-1676) in Venice.

Recitative

The <u>recitative</u>, another offshoot of the monody, existed in several styles: (1) the *recitativo secco* (dry recitative) presented narrative sections of the work in a straight-forward manner with the simplest chordal accompaniment; (2) *recitativo accompagnato* (accompanied recitative) was used in parts of the work that were more significant dramatically; and (3) the *arioso* was reserved for affective, emotional passages in which the vocal ornaments of the Early Baroque reappeared and which preserved the tradition of the original monody.

Dramatic Forms

The recitative and aria were employed in large works on both sacred and secular texts. Works on secular texts using stage settings and dramatic action were called <u>opera</u>.

Enthusiasm for staged drama "play fever" was especially characteristic of the Baroque. An extended work on a religious text performed either in church or in a concert hall but without scenery or costumes was called <u>oratorio</u>. Less extended works on either sacred or secular subjects without stage setting were called <u>cantatas</u>. In the Middle Baroque period choruses were introduced into the dramatic forms and duets also appeared.

Oratorio

The Middle Baroque saw an increase in the production of sacred music even though sacred music was not lacking in the early 17th century. The oratorio was established as a form in the works of Giacomo Carissimi (1607-1674), *maestro di cappella* in the Church of San Appollinare in Rome from 1628-1674. He wrote 16 oratorios besides Masses and motets, and his works included a large number of secular cantatas. Harmonic simplicity was characteristic of Carissimi's oratorios. *Jephtha* was his masterpiece in the oratorio form. Carissimi's recitatives were in metrical rather than free rhythm and had a melodic line which frequently outlined chords. He employed the chorus in a simple manner but with telling effect.

In the field of sacred music the oratorio and church cantata were the media which made use of the monodic forms. Cavalieri's *Anima e corpo* with its elaborate stage production had been in the nature of a sacred opera rather than an oratorio, but the sacred opera with stage settings did not establish itself as an important form. A rare example of an important sacred opera dating from the Middle Baroque period was *Il Sant' Alessio* (St. Alexis) of 1632 by Steffano Landi. Besides showing definite contrast between recitative and aria, this work also made use of an orchestral overture with a slow introduction followed by a faster canzona-like section. This structure was to be important in the history of the French overture. The sacred opera never established itself as a separate genre though a sacred opera of significance in the 20th century is Arnold Schoenberg's *Moses and Aaron.*

Cantata

The chamber or secular cantata (*cantata da camera*) had its origins in the Early Baroque strophic variation. The term *cantata* was first introduced by Grandi in his *cantade et arie a voce sola* (1620). The cantata used the same forms as the opera, but it did not have staging or action. Its subject matter was dramatic or pastoral, and as a genre it became established in Rome chiefly in the works of Luigi Rossi and Giacomo Carissimi. The strophic variation was still important, but in addition there was a form known as the rondo cantata which was given musical coherence by the recurrent use of the same aria. With Rossi, the *recitativo secco* was definitely established as a style. Carissimi, though known chiefly for his oratorios, wrote cantatas which were much more venturesome harmonically. His pupil, Cesti, made especial use of the arioso. In the generation of Legrenzi and Stradella (1642-1682) the cantata grew in size and became more contrapuntal in texture.

GERMANY

The Chorale

In the Germanic countries, infused with the spirit of the Reformation, sacred music predominated. The Thirty Years War (1618-1648) deepened both the cultural and religious rift

between the Protestant North and the Catholic South.
Lutheran chorale composition continued throughout most of
the 17th century with such collections as Michael Praetorius'
Musae Sionae (Muses of Zion), of which parts V to VIII
(published 1607-1610) contain many newly composed songs
such as "Lo How a Rose E'er Blooming" (in Theodore
Baker's translation). Other chorales were written by such
composers as Hasler, Schein, Crüger, and Scheidt. Chorales
came to be harmonized, and the practice of accompanying
chorales with the organ began in the Early Baroque. As
harmonic and tonal feeling developed, the originally irregular
meter of the Renaissance and Early Baroque was changed to
the regularly recurring accent of our traditional measure (duple
and triple meter). In addition to simple harmonizations of the
chorale, with the melody first in the tenor and later in the top
voice, chorale melodies entered into more highly developed
musical structures: one, in conservative style, was the chorale
motet; the other, using Baroque techniques, was the chorale
concertato.

Chorale Motets

Chorale motets were of two types. One using Renaissance
motet-like procedure used succeeding portions of the melody
as points of imitation. Another treated the chorale melody as a
cantus firmus. Chorale motets were written by such
composers as Praetorius, Hasler, and Scheidt, and often made
use of polychoral techniques. Scheidt made an important
contribution to the chorale cantata in cantus firmus chorale
motets in which he set succeeding verses with different
polyphony and thus constructed a set of vocal variations. In
doing so he was transferring to choral music a keyboard
variation form.

The Chorale Concertato

The foundations for the chorale cantata were laid by the chorale *concertato*. This *concertato* was written for only one or two voices, so that the presence of the continuo was essential. The chorale *concertato* emerged in the works of Johann Hermann Schein (1596-1630). In his *Opella nova* (1618-1626), chorale melodies were treated freely in order to interpret the underlying emotions of the text. The chorale melodies were ornamented; treated imitatively; divided between the voices; and broken into motives which were transposed. Counterpoint was never abandoned in the Germanic countries as completely as it had been in Italy; and the chorale, in a large class of Lutheran polyphony, occupied a place similar to that of Gregorian chant of an earlier age. The texts of the chorale *concertato* were based on chorale texts for the various days of the church year and thus, unlike Mass compositions, belonged to the proper of the service.

The Free Concertato

Another important type of concerted church music in the line of evolution which led to the church cantata was the free *concertato* (actually more widespread than the chorale *concertato*). The term *Geistliches Konzert* was used in Germany for either type. Under the influence of the Italians the free *concertato* used no preëxistent melody. It was usually written for one or two voices on German texts taken from Scriptures (Psalms or Gospels). The free (or dramatic) *concertato* achieved its greatest manifestation in the works of Heinrich Schütz.

Heinrich Schütz

The greatest German composer of the Middle Baroque was Heinrich Schütz (1585-1672). Though a Lutheran, he used no chorale melodies in his sacred compositions. He and Handel stood alone among Protestant composers of the Baroque

Period by reason of the absence of chorale melodies from their sacred music. Schütz applied the Italian styles to Protestant church music - both the grand polychoral style of the Venetians and the affective monody of the opera and oratorio. He was well versed in the style of the chromatic madrigal to which he brought a bold treatment of dissonance and an intense preoccupation with the interpretation of the text, often in madrigalistic fashion.

Biography

Though Schütz's parents had wanted him to be a lawyer, the Landgrave of Hesse, an accomplished musician himself, chose Schütz from among his choirboys to go to Vienna to study with Giovanni Gabrieli. In 1617 Schütz became choirmaster to the Elector of Saxony at Dresden and spent the rest of his life at this post, though his service was punctuated by visits to Copenhagen where he assumed the post of court conductor during some of the trying times of the Thirty Years War. He also made visits to Italy during his mature years because of his especial interest in the music of Monteverdi.

Music

Schütz's earliest work was a set of madrigals in the affective, chromatic manner of Gesualdo and Monteverdi. His dissonance treatment and interest in the interpretation of the word were in evidence even in this early work. The setting of words and the musical interpretation of text were of such importance to him that he never wrote any independent instrumental music. The vast majority of his surviving works are sacred. In 1619 he brought out a setting of the Psalms of David in the polychoral manner of the Venetians. In it he used instruments in alternation and combination with voices, and he made distinction between choral passages and passages for solo singers. He also interpreted words in madrigalistic fashion. In his *Symphoniae sacrae* (Sacred Symphonies, i.e. sacred vocal pieces with instrumental accompaniment) of 1629, 1647, and 1650, he showed influences of both Monteverdi and Giovanni Gabrieli. In these pieces Schütz included adaptations of some of Monteverdi's compositions, and he made use of the Monteverdian *stile concitato*. Several of the later *Symphoniae* are really cantatas. The *Geistliche Chormusik* (Sacred Music for Chorus) of 1648 combined an advanced harmonic vocabulary with the *stile antico* and was written in a contrapuntal style that did not depend upon a continuo.

Schütz wrote oratorios at various times throughout his career. The *Seven Words on the Cross* and the *Christmas Oratorio* (1684) use all the resources of the day: instrumental passages, choruses, recitatives, and ensembles. In his last works, the Passions, he composed in a quasi-archaic, completely individual manner, doing away with instruments altogether and using an unaccompanied recitative in a neo-Gregorian manner. This recitative, which was intended to follow the rhythm of speech, was written in plainsong notation without rhythmic indications.

Schütz's Style

Schütz followed the typical Middle Baroque practice of writing in an instrumental style that was governed by chordal skips - a style that pervaded the vocal as well as the instrumental parts. Another characteristic of his music, and one which was to become even more prominent in the Late Baroque, was his use of harmonic and melodic sequences. He combined in his music a mastery of the Italian techniques which provided the hard core of Baroque style with an individuality of approach. Thus, he produced masterpieces of Protestant music which were at once dramatic and devout. His lack of emphasis on the chorale lent an element of universality to his music

FRANCE

French composers of the 17th century held important posts at the royal court which dominated music as it dominated all other aspects of 17th century French culture. Lavish entertainments and spectacles in the palace at Versailles played an important role in the scheme of Louis XIV (r. 1643-1715) to dominate French nobility, and in this scheme music served an important function. All the arts were marshalled to his purpose and this led to a highly organized institutionalism. The Academies (Letters, Painting, and Architecture) made possible a unified control and favored an academic classicism.

Ballet

Ballet played a most important part in the music of the French court, and ballet composers held important posts there. The *Ballet de cour* (court ballet) included parts for chorus and solo singers and was based on an allegorical plot. The airs from these ballets (called *airs de cour*) were published in collections and disseminated widely. These airs were short strophic songs on the love theme and had wide appeal. They were the genesis of the solo ayre in England. The instrumental music of the ballet was supplied by the *Vingt-quatre violons du roi* (The Twenty-Four Violins of the King) which became famous under Lully and established the principle of orchestral doubling (several instruments playing the same part) that is characteristic of the modern symphony orchestra. In their form the ballet overtures foreshadowed the important French overture.

Opera

Opera was introduced to the French by Cardinal Mazarin, an Italian by birth, who was chief minister under both Louis XIII and the Regency. At the court, however, performances of Italian opera were interlarded with French ballet and were produced with the aid of Torelli's complex stage machinery, both of which attracted more attention than the opera itself. A performance of Cavalli's *Ercole amante*, (Hercules in Love) written expressly for the wedding of Louis XIV, was provided with huge ballet scenes at the end of each act. These scenes were written by Lully and overshadowed the opera to such an extent that Cavalli was infuriated.

Lully

Jean-Baptiste Lully (1632-1687), like Mazarin an Italian by birth, was nevertheless French in his musical background having been brought to the French court at the age of fourteen. His creative period coincides closely with the reign of Louis XIV, and his position in French musical life is analogous to the monarch's domination of the political sphere. At first an advocate of Italian music, Lully succeeded in making himself the leading advocate of native French music after the death of Mazarin and the ascendancy of Colbert. Under Lully the Baroque had a brief flowering in France.

Lully began his career as a composer of court ballets and brought to prominence such dance forms as the *passepied, rigaudon, bourrée,* and *gavotte,* which in his time were dances of recent origin. These dances were later to play an important part in keyboard suites, such as those of J. S. Bach. Lully also made the march an important form.

The emphasis on the dance in French Baroque music also accounts for the prominence of ballet in French opera. Lully composed operas whose plots were based on such stereotypes as the conflict between love and honor and were peopled largely with characters from Classical mythology. Extended choral and orchestral movements were favored in Lully's operas. For both chorus and orchestra the chaconne form was used (not, however, the form that was known by the same name in Bach's time). Lully's chaconne form was based on a recurrent theme alternating with contrasting themes (rondo form). The theme itself was a movement in triple meter with the accent on the second beat (sarabande rhythm). Bach, in his famous D-minor Chaconne, used a theme with this rhythm, but used it as a basis for variations. In his instrumental chaconnes Lully interpolated woodwind trio sections that were the direct ancestors of the trios of the Viennese Classical minuet of Haydn and Mozart. The French overture also achieved its definitive form with Lully. This was another form that was to recur prominently in the music of the Late Baroque. It was found in both Bach and Handel, e.g. the overture to Handel's *Messiah*. The French overture consisted of a slow section with a pronounced dotted rhythm (♩) followed by a fast section of fugal character. Sometimes, a recapitulation of the slow section, often abbreviated, rounded off the movement. In Lully's operas the arias were comparatively brief, but recitative and arioso played an important part in advancing the dramatic movement.

Lully cultivated a precise, brilliant style of orchestral performance without improvised ornamentation. His harmony was conservative, and his vocal lines frequently outlined triads. Nevertheless, in his work he achieved a pomp, grandeur, and scope that matched well the grandiose concepts of *le roi soleil* (the "sun-king", Louis XIV).

Church Music: Charpentier

Church music took second place in France. Marc-Antoine Charpentier (1634-1704), a pupil of Carissimi and next to Lully the leading French composer, was the most important composer of sacred music. His chief contribution was his establishment in France of the oratorio, a form in which he was greatly influenced by his teacher. In his harmonic vocabulary, however, he was more advanced than Carissimi was in his oratorios. In melodic invention he was superior to Lully but lacked his grandeur of conception. Mass composition was little cultivated in France, but motets were composed by both Lully and Charpentier. These motets were cantatas on a large scale using chorus, soloists, and orchestra.

ENGLAND

The French ballet had its parallel in the English masque which achieved high artistic levels in the writings of John Milton and Ben Johnson. The movable set, imported from Italy, became as popular in England as it had become in France. Opera, lacking the impetus of court patronage, was limited to a few isolated successful works. Early Baroque monody in England lacked the affective expression of the Italian. By the time the Baroque took hold in England, the Middle Baroque tonality had become established, and the English combined this incipient tonality with the chromaticism of the Early Baroque. Affective monody emerged in the work of such late 17th century composers as Matthew Locke(1630-1677), John Blow (c. 1648-1708), and Henry Purcell (c. 1659-1695), one of the greatest musical geniuses ever produced by England.

Anglican Church Music

The liturgical music of the Anglican Church, which used English texts, consisted of chorale-like metrical psalms (the only music accepted by the Puritans) and Anglican chant. The latter had short, simply harmonized melodies repeated for each verse (or two) of a prose psalm or canticle. The metrical psalms might be accompanied or not, or they might be sung with simple harmonizations. Important 17th century psalters were those by Ainsworth (1612), Ravenscroft (1621), and Playford (1677).

The freely-composed music consisted of anthems and services, of which the anthems were the more numerous. The full anthem in the Renaissance was basically a motet with English text. It was the verse anthem (in which soloists and choir alternated) that predominated in the Baroque period. With the advent of monody the verse anthem became essentially the same as the church cantata. It differed from the cantata only in that its text was restricted to the psalms, but both anthem and cantata belonged to the Proper of the service and were intended for specific times in the church calendar. Among the most important of the Baroque anthem composers were Pelham Humfrey (1647-1674), Locke, Blow, and Purcell.

The services were musical settings of rites for the morning service, the evening service, and the Communion service. These were rites taken over from the Catholic Church, and the parts were referred to by their Latin names (*Te Deum, Jubilate)* even though the texts were in English.

Henry Purcell

Henry Purcell, the genius of Restoration music, accomplished much in a short life of 36 years. A pupil of Humfrey and Blow, he achieved recognition in his own time in a number of important posts some of which he held simultaneously. He was organist at Westminster Abbey and the Royal Chapel and court composer under Charles II, James II, and William III. Music at the Restoration court had as its main purpose pure entertainment without the pomp of the French, the religious fervor of the German, or the affective emotionalism of the Italian. Within this framework Purcell was immensely effective. His vocal music includes anthems written in the early part of his career; odes and welcome songs written throughout his career; and stage works written mainly in the last six years of his life.

Anthems

Purcell's anthems were mostly verse anthems, that is, anthems for soloists and chorus, though he also wrote full anthems (for chorus alone). His full anthems retained the motet form and showed his ability to master contrapuntal technique. Harmonically, they used dissonance and chromaticism as elements of musical style as well as for affective purposes. Though his early verse anthems were for voices with only organ accompaniment, the later ones used other instruments as well - frequently strings. Instrumental interludes often came between the verses and were linked thematically to the choral sections. The accompaniments were at times quite independent of the vocal lines though doubling of voice parts did occur. Recitative and arioso were found in the solo verses, and pictorial and affective devices were exploited to the full. Thus, Purcell's late verse anthems were essentially cantatas. The use of dotted rhythms to represent the affections of joy, praise, or triumph was a frequent occurrence.

Odes and Welcome Songs

The odes and welcome songs were written for court occasions and St. Cecilia's days. Their texts were frequently weak, though Purcell set Dryden's *Ode on St. Cecilia's Day* . In form the odes are similar to the verse anthems and are thus

cantatas. They use string orchestras for accompaniment -
sometimes with trumpets, recorders (end-blown flutes), and
oboes. Choruses are in both chordal and contrapuntal styles,
and ground basses are frequent in the arias. Major and minor
modes are associated with the affections of grief and joy
respectively.

Dramatic Works

Purcell's first dramatic work, *Dido and Aeneas*, produced in
1698, was his only opera and the only significant English
opera of the period. In writing it he was influenced by Blow's
Venus and Adonis (c. 1682) - entitled a masque, but actually a
short opera written for the court. Purcell's opera was
composed, not for the court, but for an amateur performance
at a boarding school for girls though it is certainly worthy of
professional performance. It contains an especially fine
example of the ground bass (strophic) aria, "Dido's Lament",
from the last act. Based on a descending chromatic ground
bass to represent the affection of grief, it contains a fascinating
interplay between the phraseology of the short bass figure and
the long line of the solo part. The libretto, written by Nahum
Tate, (frequently a librettist of Purcell's) was of inferior literary
quality, especially in some of its motivations; but it made for
effective theater and served well as a vehicle for Purcell's
music. The chorus, which was used extensively, was in the
manner of a Greek tragedy, commenting upon and
participating in the action. Other dramatic works by Purcell
include masques, operatic scenes, and songs for plays.

Later Works

Purcell's later works are greatly extended in scope and show
mastery of organization on a large scale. *Da capo* arias (A B

A form) appear in his later works along with influences of the Italian instrumental concerto style (as distinguished from the accompanied vocal music with which the term *concerto* was associated earlier). In the last few years of his life the developed tonality of the Late Baroque - the traditional harmonic idiom of our own day - began to emerge in his music. It is discernible in such works as the music written for the play *The Fairy Queen* (1692), an adaptation of Shakespeare's *A Midsummer Night's Dream* and another Shakespearian play, *The Tempest,* which was arranged for Purcell by Dryden and Davenant.

Purcell's Style

Italian influences came to Purcell's music by way of his teachers, Humfrey and Blow. Purcell mastered the affective monody of the Early Baroque with its wide skips and chromaticism; and towards the end of his life he adopted the Late Baroque style which also emanated from Italy. He also used such practices of affective representation as the descending chromatic ground bass to represent grief; the dotted rhythms to represent joy and triumph; the major mode for joy; and the minor mode for sadness. He was influenced by the French, and by Lully in particular, in such areas as orchestral technique and idiomatic writing for violins. He also made use of the French overture form and the chaconne which he treated in the extended rondo manner of Lully. His use of dissonance and chromaticism purely for their sonorous affect and as elements of musical style was characteristic of the English. Purcell was a master of his craft when it came to setting English words to music. He could match the accents of the text with the notes in a way that followed the natural flow of the English language; and his music heightened the dramatic impact of his text.

SUMMARY

After the innovations of the Early Baroque, the Middle Baroque became more conservative. It became aware, anew, of essentially musical considerations and introduced the melodic *bel canto* style. This style formed the basis of the aria, so that the early monody now branched into two distinct styles: the recitative and the aria. Music began to show organization in terms of chord progression; the major and minor scales replaced the ecclesiastical modes; music became less dissonant; and the wild leaps of the melody were organized along chordal lines. Harmonic organization and the reintroduction of counterpoint made it possible to have large forms. Instrumental music (to be discussed in the next chapter) became as important as vocal music.

The following styles emerged in the Middle Baroque:

(1) Recitative: (a) *recitativo secco*, (b) *recitativo accompagnato*, (c) *arioso*.

(2) Aria: (a) strophic bass aria, (b) *da capo* aria.

The following dramatic vocal forms established themselves in the Middle Baroque using recitative, aria, duet, and chorus.

(1) <u>Opera</u>: secular text, stage action, scenery, and costumes.

(2) <u>Oratorio</u>: non-liturgical religious text; concert type of performance (either in church or concert hall); frequent use of narrator (*testo*).

(3) <u>Cantata</u>: Sacred or secular text; church or chamber performance without stage setting; less extended than opera or oratorio and using smaller groups of performers.

The following national schools were significant in the Middle Baroque:

(1) Germany: leading composer Heinrich Schütz (1585-1672). The forms were:

   (a) Chorale settings (not found in Schütz): chorale motet (imitative style and cantus firmus style) and chorale concertato (free setting of chorale for 1 or 2 voices and continuo).

   (b) Free concertato: no chorale melody; for 1 or 2 voices and continuo. Scriptural text.

(2) France: leading composer, Jean-Baptiste Lully (1632-1687)

   (a) Emphasis on ballet in court ballet and opera.

   (b) Established French overture and perfected orchestral performance.

   (c). Oratorio. introduced by Marc-Antoine Charpentier.(1634-1704).

(3). England: leading composer, Henry Purcell (1659-1695)

   (a) Masque: similar to court ballet in France.

   (b) Solo Songs (Blow and Purcell) and catches (rounds for group singing, often on ribald subjects).

   (c) Odes: large works for chorus, soloists, and orchestra for special festivities.

   (d) Opera: Blow (*Venus and Adonis*) and Purcell (*Dido and Aeneas*).

   (e) Music for plays: in some of Purcell's later works these come close to being operas, though spoken dialogue is included.

   (f) Anglican church music.

Liturgical: <u>Anglican</u> <u>chant</u> (a harmonized chant), <u>service</u>(rites for morning service, evening service, and Communion); and <u>metrical</u> <u>psalms</u> (similar to Lutheran).

Non-liturgical: <u>full</u> <u>anthem</u> (a motet with English text): <u>verse</u> <u>anthem</u> (similar to a cantata); and private <u>devotional</u> <u>songs.</u>

CHECK LIST FOR REVIEW

obbligato	French overture
recitativo secco	recitativo accompagnato
arioso	cantata
rondo cantata	chorale
chorale motet	chorale concertato
oratorio	testo
ballet de cour	

march	chaconne	Anglican chant
passepied	rondo	devotional song
rigaudon	trio	service
bourrée	masque	ode
gavotte	metrical psalm	welcome song

Heinrich Schütz	Steffano Landi
Henry Purcell	Johann Crüger
Luigi Rossi	Samuel Scheidt
Pier Francesco Cavalli	Jean-Baptiste Lully
Giacomo Carissimi	Marc-Antoine Charpentier
Marc' Antonio Cesti	Giovanni Legrenzi
Matthew Locke	Alessandro Stradella
John Blow	Michael Praetorius
Henry Ainsworth	Hans Leo Hasler
Thomas Ravenscroft	Johann Hermann Schein

John Playford   Pelham Humfrey
vingt-quatre violons du roi

Lamento d'Arianna   *Symphoniae sacrae*
Dido and Aeneas   *Kleine geistliche Konzerte*
"Dido's Lament"   *Geistliche Chormusik*
Jephtha   SevenWords on the Cross
Il combattimento di   Christmas Oratorio
    Tancredi e Clorinda   Te Deum
Il Sant' Alessio   Jubilate
Cantade et arie a voce sola Ode on St. Cecilia's Day
Musae sionae   Venus and Adonis
Opella nova   The Fairy Queen
                             The Tempest

LIST OF SCORES

Italy

Cavalli, Francesco (1602-1676), "*Ecco la lettra* ", from *Xerxes*, recitative & aria from opera, HAM2, 206

Carissimi, Giacomo (1605-1674), "*Miserunt ergo sortem*" from *Jonas* recitative & chorus, HAM2, 207

Landi, Steffano (1590-1655), sinfonia from *Il San Alessio*, opera overture (canzona), HAM2, 208; duet from *Il San Alessio*, HAM2, 209

Rossi, Luigi (1597-1653), *Io lo vedo*, chamber cantata, HAM2, 203

Cesti, Marc'Antonio (1623-1669), , "*Di belleza e di valore*" from *Il pomo d'oro*, opera, Venetian, HAM2, 221

Provencale *Il schiavo di sua moglie*, opera aria (ostinato), HAM2, 222

Stradella, Alessandro (1645?-1682), *Tra cruci funeste* from *Il Carispero*, opera aria, HAM2, 241

Steffani, Agostino (1653-1728)., *Un balen* from *Henrico Leone*, opera aria (da capo), HAM2, 244

Germany

Schütz, Heinrich (1585-1672), "*Da Jesus an dem Kreuze stund* " from *Die sieben Worte*, chorus from sacred concerto, HAM2, 201; aria from ibid., HAM2, 202a; *Saul, was verfolgst du mich*, double chorus from sacred concerto, HAM2, 202b; *O Herr, hilf,.* sacred concerto, MM, 33

Albert, Heinrich (1604-151), *Auf mein Geist*, aria, HAM2, 205

Hammerschmidt, Andreas (1612-1675), *Wende Dich, Herr*, dialogue, HAM2, 213

Tunder, Franz (1614-1667), *Wachet auf, ruft uns die Stimme*, aria from chorale cantata, HAM2, 214

Rosenmüller, Johann (c. 1620-1684), "*Aleph. Ego vir*" from *Lamentationes Jeremiae*, sacred cantata, HAM2, 218

Krieger, Adam (1634-1666), *Adonis Tod*, aria with ritornellos,HAM2, 228

Buxtehude, Dietrich(1637-1707), *Liebster Herr Jesu*, sacred cantata, HAM2, 235

France

Cambert, Robert (1628?-1677), overture from *Pomone*, opera overture, HAM2, 223

Lully, Jean-Baptiste (1633?-1687), overture from *Alceste*, opera overture, HAM2, 224; *Le Ciel protège les héros* , from *Alceste*, recitative & aria, HAM2, 225. Selections from *Armide*, opera: *Ouverture*, opera overture, NAWM1, 75a, MM, 36; Act II, Scene 5: "*Enfin il est en ma puissance*", NAWM1, 75b

Charpentier, Marc Antoine (1633-1704), *Dialogue entre Madeleine et Jésus* from *Le Reniement de St-Pierre*, oratorio, HAM2, 226; scene from ibid., TEM, 42

England

Lawes, Henry (1596-1662), "Sweet echo" from *Masque of Comus*, air, HAM2, 204

Humphrey, Pelham (1647-1674), *O Lord, my God*, verse anthem, HAM2, 242

Blow, John (1648-1708), "*Mourn for thy servant* " from *Venus and Adonis*, opera chorus, HAM2, 243; *Jubilate Deo*, hymn-Anglican, canticle from the Anglican Service, TEM, 43

Purcell, Henry (c. 1659-1695), selections from *The Fairy Queen*, masque: "Thus the ever grateful Spring", air, NAWM1, 76a; "Hark the ech'ing air", air, NAWM1, 76b. Selections from *Dido and Aeneas*, opera: Act III, recitative, "Thy hand, Belinda"; aria, "When I am laid in earth", NAWM1, 77a, HAM2, 255; "With drooping wings", chorus, NAWM1, 77b

Spain

Cererols, Joan (d. 1676), *Señor mio Jesu Cristo*, villancico, HAM2, 227

CHRONOLOGICAL CHART

Music	Political History	Intellectual History	Art
1642 Monteverdi *L'Incoronzione di Poppea*	1642-46 English Civil War "Roundheads" under Cromwell defeat Cavaliers (royalists) 1643-1715 Louis XIV, King of France at age 5	1643 Molière founds *Illustre Théatre*, in Paris (*Théatre de la Comédie Française* from 1689) 1645 John Milton, *L'Allegro, Il Penseroso*	1642 Rembrandt, *The Night Watch*
1645 Schütz, *The Seven Words of Christ on the Cross*, oratorio			1644 Bernini, *Cornaro Chapel*, S. Maria della Vittoria, Rome incl. *Ecstasy of St. Teresa*, sculpture
	1648 Treaty of Westphalia, end of 30 Years War		
1649 Cavalli, *Giasone*, opera Cesti, *Orontea*, opera	1649 England declared a Commonwealth		
1650 Athanasius Kircher, *Musurgia unversalis*, theory Carissimi, *Jephtha* Schütz, *Symphoniae sacrae, Part III* Scheidt, *Chorales for organ* Emergence of da capo aria as preferred form of aria		1650 Corneille, *Andromède*, tragedy DesCartes, *Musicae compendium*	1649 Terborch, *Philip IV of Spain*, portrait Velasquez, *Pope Innocent X*, portrait
	1651 Louis XIV attains majority	1651 Thomas Hobbes, *Leviathan*	

Music	Political History	Intellectual History	Art
1653 Jean-Baptiste Lully, court composer at Paris Locke, *Cupid and Death*, masque 1658 1st French overture (Lully) 1660 Cavalli, *Serse*, opera 1661 Cesti, *Dori*, opera 1662 Cavalli, *Ercole amante*, opera	1653 Cromwell dissolves Parliament 1654 Coronation of Louis XIV at Rheims 1660 Restoration of Charles II 1661-1715 Absolute reign of Louis XIV	1654 Pascal & de Fermat, theory of probability 1660 Pepys, *Diary*	1653 Borromini, *S. Agnese in Agone*, Rome 1656 Velaszuez, *The Maids of Honor* Vermeer, *The Procuress* 1660 Zurbaran, *The Young Virgin* 1661 Rembrandt, *Syndics of the Cloth Hall*
1664 Schütz, *Christmas Oratorio* 1665 Schütz, *St. John Passion* 1667 Rosenmüller, 12 sonate da camera a 5 1669 Paris Acdemy of Music founded 1670 Chambonnières, clavecin pieces	1663-4 Turks war on Holy Roman Empire 1664 New Amsterdam becomes New York 1666 Great fire of London 1668 British East India Co obtains control of Bombay 1671 Turks declare war on Poland	1662 Molière, *École des femmes* Revised English Prayer Book 1665 Spinoza, *Ethics* 1667 Milton, *Paradise Lost* 1668 La Fontaine, *Fables* 1670 Molière, *Le Bourgeois gentilhomme* Pascal, *Pensées*	1663 Bernini, *Scala Regia*, Vatican, Rome 1664 Christopher Wren, Sheldonian Theatre, Oxford Vermeer, *The Lacemaker* 1667 Bernini, colonnade of St. Peter's

Music	Political History	Intellectual History	Art
1675 Lully, *Thésée* Locke, incident- al music to *Psyche* 1676 Thomas Mace, *Musick's Monument* 1678 Lully, *Isis*, opera 1679 First German opera house opens in Hamburg Alessandro Scarlatti's first opera ,*Gli Equivoci nell' amore, Rome*	1679 Peace of Nijmegen between France and the Dutch, and France & Spain	1677 Racine, *Phèdre* 1678 Bunyan, *Pilgrm's Progress* Corneille, *Le Comte d'Essex* Huygens dis- covers polari- zation of light 1680 Comédie Française formed	1675 Sir Christopher Wren begins St. Paul's Cathedral 1676 Sir Christopher Wren, Trinity College Library Cambridge 1678 Murillo, *Mystery of the Immaculate Conception*

COSTUME FOR A BALLET IN TURIN, ITALY, 1647

(From Dr. Attilio Bigo, Turin, after the
Larousse Encyclopedia of Music, ed.
Hindley)

English viol music of the middle baroque was of high quality. Divisions were improvised variations. This illustration, from Christopher Simpson's The Division Violist *(1659) shows two forms of the viol. The one on the left, which according to Simpson was "better for sound" has the shape of a violin though its six strings and frets are characteristic of the viol. (After Bukofzer,* Music in the Baroque era.*)*

CHAPTER IX

EARLY AND MIDDLE BAROQUE

INSTRUMENTAL MUSIC

The instrumental music of the Baroque arose from Renaissance music by a process of evolution that was essentially continuous. The Baroque saw the transfer of vocal forms to instrumental media. Instrumental techniques were developed, and the influence of affective expression was felt; but there was nothing to correspond to the revolutionary impact of vocal monody. Independent instrumental music grew greatly in importance; and in ensemble music, the strings eclipsed the wind instruments. Among stringed instruments, the newly emergent violin family with its more brilliant tone gradually displaced the delicate sounding viols of the 16th and 17th centuries. As domestic solo instruments, the stringed keyboard instruments - the harpsichord and clavichord - began to supersede the lute.

The types of instrumental music were: (1) forms derived from vocal models, for which the chanson was by far the most important model; (2) toccatas - keyboard compositions that had their origin in improvisation; (3) variations (important both as the basis for a form and as a technique which had wide application): and (4) dances.

Forms Derived from Vocal Models

As we have seen, the French polyphonic chanson because of its purely musical organization independent of text, was favored for instrumental performance in the 16th century. Such performances were particularly popular in Italy where chansons were made widely available in numerous publications. The chief characteristics of this form were: (1) a lightly contrapuntal texture: (2) definite cadences between sections; (3) various schemes of repetition and recapitulation of sections; and (4) a first subject that began with repeated notes in dactylic rhythm (♩ ♩ ♪ ♪) a device that amounted to a signature. Independent compositions with the chanson as a model were given the Italian name for chanson (canzona) since the development took place mainly in Italy. In being applied to instrumental music the canzona evolved in two different directions: (1) All sections came to be based on the same theme, and in the Late Baroque the fugue emerged, a mono-sectional as well as monothematic form. This development took place in the field of keyboard music by a gradual process which was anticipated in various individual compositions. (2) The individual sections became expanded to the point where they became separate movements. Thus, the sonata emerged as a form for chamber ensembles, and in the field of opera, the expanded canzona became the basis for a two-movement orchestral overture.

Keyboard Canzona

While ornamented transcriptions of chansons for keyboard had been numerous in the late 16th century in Germany (the "colorists"), France (Attaingnant), and Italy (Andrea Gabrieli), it remained for the 17th century to develop the possibilities of independent composition with the chanson as model. The earliest steps in this direction had been taken by Girolamo Cavazzoni in his collection of keyboard compositions published in 1542. Though he took preëxistent compositions as his point of departure, he did not merely ornament these compositions but rather reworked the themes in new contrapuntal combinations.

Variation Canzona

An important development in the evolution of the form was taken in the variation-canzona. This was a monothematic canzona in which the theme was altered in accordance with the changes in meter and tempo associated with the various sections of the canzona. In the Early Baroque period the most important composer in this form was Girolamo Frescobaldi (1583-1643), the distinguished organist of St. Peter's in Rome. In the Middle Baroque period his pupil, J. J. Froberger (1616-1667), a composer of cosmopolitan background, also wrote variation canzonas in the more settled, harmonically organized idiom of the Middle Baroque. J. S. Bach's Canzona in d-minor is also an example of the form, and its theme is based on a theme of Frescobaldi.

Ricercar

The contrapuntal ricercar, a form also established by Cavazzoni in his publication of 1542, was the keyboard counterpart of the motet with more extended development of sections. As compared with the canzona it tended toward more learned contrapuntal treatment. Frescobaldi applied the monothematic treatment to the ricercar as well as the canzona and wrote variation ricercars. He brought to these forms the bold harmonies of the Early Baroque and sometimes used themes of unusual chromatic structure.

Sweelinck

In the north, Calvinist restrictions on sacred vocal music which was limited to congregational singing caused musical expression to be channeled into the instrumental field. The leading composer of the Early Baroque was the Dutchman Jan Pieterszoon Sweelinck (1562-1621) who, though conservative in his vocal writing, was influenced in his keyboard composition by the Italian forms of the Baroque and by the keyboard style of the English virginalist (harpsichord) composers. The English virginalists made an important contribution to Baroque instrumental style in their variations, in which they introduced idiomatic keyboard figures used in repeated rhythmic patterns. These figures were used in a purely abstract way unrelated to affective expression. Sweelinck's most important music was for keyboard and for sacred use. His fantasies were similar to the ricercars of the Italians. They were monothematic compositions of sectional structure and were thus related to the variation ricercar; but instead of the rhythmic transformation of the themes which was characteristic of the variation ricercar, it was the figuration patterns of the other voices that changed. When the theme was introduced in long notes against rapidly moving patterns in the other voices, the result was very much that of the cantus firmus variation.

Keyboard Forms in Sacred Music

The canzona, ricercar, and toccata were used in the Catholic Church service. Organ Masses continued to be written during the Baroque period, and they made use of these forms. The practice of using the organ to alternate with the choir and substitute for parts of the sung service dates back to the 14th century. Organ music was also used to accompany liturgical actions. One of Frescobaldi's best-known works, the *Fiori musicali* (Flowers of Music) published in 1635, provided music for alternating and accompanying use in three specific Masses. This work so impressed J. S. Bach that he made his own handwritten copy of it. Organ music was also used to substitute for alternate verses of psalms and of the *Magnificat.* Such compositions were called versets and made use of chant melodies, sometimes as canti fermi, sometimes in imitative paraphrase.

Canzona for Chamber Ensembles

Canzonas for groups of solo instruments were cultivated in the Early Baroque period, especially in Venice. Some of them used the polychoral principle found in Venetian motets. These early ensemble canzonas were characterized by a relatively large number of short sections, and for this reason were called quilt or patchwork canzonas. The sections were organized into ingenious schemes of repetition and recapitulation and were written for keyboard as well as for instrumental ensemble.

Baroque Sonata

Canzonas for few voices (one, two, or three) evolved into the various types of chamber sonata, which were categorized in accordance with the number of voices for which they were written. The trio sonata, the chief type, was thus written not for three instruments, but for three obbligato (obligatory) parts with continuo. The three parts might be played by one, two, or four instruments. There are trio sonatas for organ alone by J. S. Bach; and a characteristic trio sonata ensemble might consist of two violins, a cello, and a harpsichord. The harpsichord plays the bass line with the cello and fills in the chords. The sonata *a due* had two obbligato parts, a melody and a figured bass (i.e.,with continuo). The sonata *a due* frequently became the vehicle for virtuoso violin writing with the accompaniment of a keyboard instrument and often a bass instrument. In this version it was called <u>violin</u> <u>sonata</u> or <u>solo</u> <u>sonata</u> for violin. There are also true sonatas for unaccompanied violin or cello of which the most famous are those by J. S. Bach.

The chamber sonatas developed from the canzona in a process whereby the individual sections of the canzona were lengthened and decreased in number and evolved into separate movements. This evolution took place in Italy in the second quarter of the 17th century, chiefly within a group of composers centering around the Church of San Petronio in Bologna. The term *sonata da chiesa* (church sonata) was applied to this form since it was intended for performance in the church. The violins achieved a prominent position in the chamber sonatas, and a violinistic style of counterpoint was cultivated there. Four or five movements was the rule, and they alternated slow and fast. The slow movements were influenced by the *bel canto* style.

Trio Sonata

The trio sonata, which was to become the most important chamber music form of the Baroque period, first made its appearance in the *Sinfonie e gagliarde* (Mantua, 1607) of Salamone Rossi who appended *Ebreo* (Hebrew) after his name. The first example of the violin sonata (*a due*) was found in the *Affetti musicali* (1617) of Biagio Marini who, like Rossi, was associated with Monteverdi in Mantua. Frescobaldi also wrote chamber sonatas. In the Middle Baroque period outstanding contributions to the music for chamber ensembles were made by Giovanni Legrenzi (1626-1690) in Venice and Giovanni Battisti Vitali 1644-1692) at the Church of San Petronio da Bologna. In Legrenzi's hands the canzona sections increased in length and attained the status of separate movements, though repetitions of musical material in more than one movement recall the canzona form. Tone repetitions in his subjects go far beyond the simple dactylic rhythm of the standard canzona theme though they recall it. Legrenzi's counterpoint shows firm harmonic roots. Counterpoint is also characteristic of the instrumental writing of Vitali and the Bolognese school.

English Viol Music

The English continued to write for viols far into the 17th century at a time when Nicolo Amati 1596-1684), the first of the great violin makers, was already building his instruments. The 17th century from about 1625-1675 was, in fact, the "golden age" of viol construction and viol music in England. A chamber music ensemble of viols was known as a consort of viols, and sets of viols of different ranges were frequently stored in chests constructed for the purpose.

The most important form for viol music was the <u>fancy</u>. The term was derived from the Italian *fantasia* which at this time was essentially synonymous with the ricercar. The fancy was written in an austere Renaissance style without continuo - a style well suited to the soft delicate, remote sound of the viols. Middle Baroque English music was of high quality, and the most important composer of fancies was John Jenkins (1592-1678). The violin began gradually to supplant the viols after the Restoration, and the Restoration composer Henry Purcell contributed the last examples of the fancy for viols.

The French Overture

The overture to Monteverdi's *Orfeo* (1607) consisted merely of a written-out fanfare entitled "Toccata"; and the overture to his *L'incoronazione di Poppea* (1642) was a varied couple in the Renaissance manner. The earliest independent instrumental music in opera was trivial and all related to the dance. The first overture of a more highly developed character was the overture to Landi's sacred opera *Il Sant' Alessio* (1632). The overture to this opera consisted of a slow, stately *Praeambulum* followed by a canzona of three sections in lively tempo. The name overture was first applied in the French ballet which was also the source of the characteristic heavy, ponderous, dotted rhythm that was to be found in the opening slow section of the overture. In its fully developed form the French overture consisted of a slow opening section with the dotted rhythm followed by an imitative section in lively tempo in which the canzona influence was predominant. It was in this form that it was found in the works of Lully. Lully's familiarity with the Venetian canzona as well as the overture to the *ballet de cour* is evident in the overture to his opera *Armide* (1685) where the repeated note theme is evident even in the opening slow section. An imitative beginning is soon obscured by heavy chords and the appearance of the dotted rhythm.

The Toccata for Keyboard

The toccata form as established by Merulo in the 16th century consisted of free improvisational sections alternating with contrapuntal sections. Frescobaldi infused the form with the dramatic, emotional spirit of the Early Baroque. In the toccata he made use of affective chromaticism and of freely changing tempo. In the introduction to his *Toccate e partite* (1614) he compares his freedom of tempo to that of the madrigalists. In addition to toccatas of the Merulo type, Frescobaldi also wrote toccatas in which he eschewed all virtuosity and expressed moods of quiet, devout contemplation. Toccatas could be used as preludes to other pieces or as independent compositions. The *Fiori musicali* includes toccatas to be played during the performance of such ritual acts as the Elevation of the Host. A worthy successor to Frescobaldi in the writing of toccatas was the Middle Baroque German composer J. J. Froberger, primarily a composer of keyboard music. He was a pupil of Frescobaldi but surpassed him in the scope of his toccatas. He, too, wrote short liturgical toccatas for the Elevation.

The Dance

The Renaissance had established the principle of the varied couple in such dances as the pavane and galliard - a stepped dance and a leaped dance - the first in a slow duple meter, the second in a fast triple meter. In the varied couple both dances used the same melody. The Early Baroque added some new types, such as the <u>allemande</u> which was in moderate duple meter and the <u>courante</u> which existed in two versions: the Italian *corrente* , in fast triple meter; and the French *courante*, in a slower six-unit measure which alternated between a division into two threes and three twos. From the English virginalists came the variations on a single dance, each of whose sections was repeated and ornamented on the repetition. The chief media for dances were the plucked stringed instruments: the guitar and the lute. The guitar, which was imported from Spain, came to supersede the more subdued lute in popularity. In France, music for lute and clavecin (harpsichord) was cultivated. The lute flourished mainly in the Early and Middle Baroque; the clavecin in the Middle and Late Baroque. French lute and clavecin music had far-reaching influences on Baroque style. The most important of the lutenists was Denis Gaultier (c. 1603-1672). His most famous work was a collection entitled *Rhétorique des dieux*, published posthumously. His collections consisted mostly of dances - but idealized rather than true dances. He grouped them in suites of three or more. Of great significance was the technique by which he suggested a polyphonic texture within the limited possibilities of the instrument. He used a free-voiced texture in which voices were added or dropped as required; he used an arpeggio (or broken-chord) technique, to suggest the polyphonic web; and he used numerous ornaments to compensate for the lute's inability to sustain tones. All these devices, arising from the nature of the instrument, became elements of style in a style-conscious period such as the Baroque was. Although lute music declined in importance after Gaultier, the clavecinists made use of the devices which he had perfected and to which the English virginalists had also contributed. The first of the clavecinists to follow Gaultier's lead was Jacques Champion de Chambonnières (1602-1672) who expanded the resources of ornamentation and the possibilities of suggested part-writing.

Keyboard Dance Suite

The style of the dances (as idealized rather than true dance compositions) was established in France. The concept of organizing these dances into a unified composition which was meant to be performed as a group took place in Germany. Froberger, a South German, had visited France and was influenced by Gaultier and Chambonnières. He mastered the free-voiced style of the French and used their idealized dance style; but Froberger organized the dances into a suite that was sometimes, though not always, unified by a transfer of musical material from one dance to another. His suites consisted of an allemande, a sarabande (in slow triple meter, often with the accent on the second beat), a courante, and a gigue (in fast compound meter). It was actually not until after his death that his suites were published with the gigue last - the position in which the gigue came to be placed customarily. In the suites of Gaultier and Chambonnières, as well as Froberger, all dances were in the same key, but to the French the suite was more a collection of dances than a sequence of dances. A so-called "suite" of Chambonnières, for example, contained 5 allemandes, 11 courantes, 4 sarabandes, 2 gigues, 5 courantes, and 1 chaconne - obviously not a grouping that was meant to be performed as a unit.

Dances for Chamber Ensemble

In the Early Baroque in Italy dances were written for various combinations of instruments (wind and string), and violins were very popular. Dances were not grouped into suites though varied couples were found. Often dances of a single kind were grouped together. In the Middle Baroque the sonata da camera emerged as a free combination of dances to be performed as a unified composition.

Under English influence quartets or quintets of viols became popular in Germany for the performance of dances. Here, the concept of a group of dances as a unified composition developed early with the variation suite, in which all dances used the same thematic material. Schein, in his celebrated *Banchetto musicale* (Musical Banquet) of 1617, not only uses the variation technique but makes a distinction between stylized dances and true dances, a distinction that was to persist in the Late Baroque suite.

Variation Techniques

There were four types of variation technique to be found in the Baroque era: (1) the cantus firmus variation (2) the ornamentation of a melody (3) the repeated harmonic scheme with or without a bass melody, and (4) the application of changes in rhythm and tempo to a given melody. In the cantus firmus variation the melody appears in its original form while new figural patterns are woven around it in the other parts. In the ornamentation of a melody the original notes of the melody are kept more or less intact while new ornaments and passage work are interspersed between them. A repeated bass melody is known as a <u>basso</u> <u>ostinato</u> or <u>ground</u> <u>bass</u>. These variation techniques played a very important role in the 17th century. They were applied in the variation ricercar; in the variation- canzona; in the strophic aria; in the chorale motet; in sets of dances; and in self-styled sets of themes and variations.

Italy

In the varied couple, changes in tempo and meter were applied to the same melody used for two different dances; whereas in the keyboard dances of the English school, ornamentation of the melody was applied to the repetition of sections of the dance. Both types were to be found in the Italian music of the Early Baroque. In addition, variations based on stock bass melodies were common. These stock basses, which included the *ruggiero*, the *passamezzo antico*, and the *passamezzo moderno* , etc. had been found in 16th century Spanish music. In Italy these stock basses were used in compositions for keyboard or for keyboard and violin.

England

In England variations were applied to both secular and sacred melodies in the music of the virginalists. In the case of secular songs and dances the melodies were ornamented while plainsong melodies were treated as *cantus fermi*. The English use of scale passages, arpeggios, and repeated rhythmic patterns - though without any affective connotations - were of great importance in establishing the Baroque instrumental style. The prominent English virginalists, John Bull (c. 1562-1628) and Peter Philips (1561-1628), spent time on the continent (Antwerp and Brussels) and their influence spread throughout Europe through the work of Sweelinck, a Dutchman. He taught so many prominent German organ composers that he became known as the "Maker of German Organists".

Low Countries and Germany

Like the English, Sweelinck wrote variations on both sacred and secular melodies, and he followed the English practice of treating the sacred melodies as *cantus fermi*. He used psalm tunes and chorales as bases for his sacred variations. In his ornamentation of secular melodies he never allowed the contours of the original melody to become obscured. Sweelinck's influence spread to Central Germany through the work of his pupil Samuel Scheidt (1587-1654). Like his teacher, Scheidt wrote variations on hymns and chorales which he treated as *cantus fermi*. He was the first German composer to make extensive use of chorale melodies, as he did in his organ collection *Tabulatura nova* (New Tablature, 1624). This collection occupied an important position in the establishment of a German school of organ composition - a school which reached a brilliant climax in the organ works of J. S. Bach. The *Tabulatura nova* included variations on both sacred and secular melodies, the secular melodies being songs and dances of English and Flemish origin.

Middle Baroque: Biber

The violin sonatas (*a due*) of the Middle Baroque German composer Heinrich Biber (1644-1704) of Salzburg made frequent use of variation techniques. His sonatas included dance movements with embellished *doubles*   in the French manner (dance movements repeated and ornamented in the repetition). Arias with variations in the Italian manner and stock basses were also to be found in the Biber sonatas. Biber made use of repeated figures and rhythmic patterns in the manner of Sweelinck and Scheidt, but related these figures to the affections. In the virtuosity of his violin writing he surpassed even Biagio Marini and was so celebrated in his own day that he was elevated to the nobility.

SUMMARY

Independent instrumental music increased greatly in importance in the Early and Middle Baroque periods. It was the time when the violins and stringed keyboard instruments came into prominence. The sources of Baroque instrumental forms were:

I. Vocal models:

A. The French polyphonic chanson. Independent instrumental compositions modeled after the chanson were called <u>canzonas</u> (the Italian name for chanson). The canzona evolved in two directions:

1. In keyboard music the trend was toward unification: the variation canzona was based on one theme; and in the Late Baroque the fugue emerged as a thematically unified and rhythmically continuous form.

2. Individual sections were expanded into separate movements. In chamber music this line of evolution led to the Baroque sonata. In orchestral music it led to the operatic overtures - the Italian and (more important in the Baroque period) the French.

a. Sonatas were classified in accordance with the number of obbligato parts as being <u>sonatas *a due*</u> or (more important) <u>trio</u> <u>sonatas</u>. There were also sonatas for unaccompanied violin or cello. The term <u>sonata</u> <u>da</u> <u>chiesa</u> (church sonata) was also applied to the Baroque sonata. Movements alternated fast and slow and the number was not standardized before the Late Baroque period.

      b. The French overture consisted of a slow introductory movement emphasizing a dotted rhythm followed by an imitative allegro. The allegro was frequently given a slow ending.

B. The Motet

    1. The <u>ricercar</u> was the keyboard counterpart of the vocal motet. It was characterized by a more extended and learned contrapuntal treatment than the canzona. The <u>variation</u> <u>ricercar,</u> like the variation canzona, treated one theme, modified by changes in rhythm and tempo in the various sections of the composition. In the Late Baroque period the ricercar and canzona merged in the fugue.

    2. The fantasies of Sweelinck for organ were related to the variation ricercar.

    3. Fancies for viols in England were written in an austere Renaissance style in the ricercar tradition.

II. Toccatas for keyboard influenced by the affective Baroque idiom. There were two different forms:

A. The form established by the Renaissance composer Claudio Merulo consisted of improvisational sections alternating with imitative sections.

B. A contemplative type without virtuoso display, found especially in Frescobaldi, though he used both types.

III. Dance forms

A. The French established the Baroque dance style.

    1. Free-voiced texture.

    2. Idealized dance style - an art form rather than a true dance.

3. Found first in lute music, later transferred to stringed keyboard.

B. Froberger grouped the dances into a suite to be performed as a unit.

1. His dances were written for stringed keyboard.

2. His suites consisted of, <u>allemande, sarabande, courante,</u> and <u>gigue</u>.

<u>3.</u> He used the free-voiced texture and idealized dance style of the French.

4. The dances of his suites were sometimes, but not always related melodically.

C. Ensemble dances

1. In Italy dances were written for winds and strings but were not grouped into suites until the Middle Baroque. The term <u>sonata da camera</u> (instrumental piece to be played in the chamber) first appeared in connection with these dances in their later grouping.

2. In Germany dances were written for viols and grouped into variation suites.

IV. Variation - important as a basis for form and as a technique to be used in various forms.

A. Types of variation technique:

1. Cantus firmus

2. Ornamentation of a melody

3. Changes in rhythm and tempo applied to a given melody

4. Repeated harmonic scheme with or without a bass melody

B. Forms to which they were applied:

1. Variations on sacred melodies for keyboard in England, the Low Countries, and Germany used cantus firmus technique.

2. Secular variations in England, the Low Countries, and Germany, written for keyboard, used ornamentation of a

melody, as did *doubles* found in French dances and the repeated sections of English dances.

   3. The varied dance couple, the German variation suite, the variation ricercar, and the variation canzona used changes in rhythm and tempo applied to a given melody.

   4. The stock basses such as the *passamezzo antico, passamezzo moderno, ruggiero,* and *la folia* used a repeated harmonic scheme, as did the strophic bass aria.

   C. Types of themes to be varied:

   1. The fully developed theme with a definite melody, such as a dance or a folk song, with definite pauses between presentations.

   2. The brief theme, usually a scheme of harmonies or a *basso ostinato,* repeated without pauses.

CHECK LIST FOR REVIEW

chanson	"Colorists"	Magnificat
toccata	variation canzona	verset
variation	virginals	quilt canzona
dance	harpsichord	chamber sonata
canzona	fantasia	trio sonata
overture	ricercar	sonata a due
sonata	organ Mass	violin sonata
sonata da chiesa	French overture	allemande
bel canto	ballet de cour	courante
viol	madrigal	corrente
consort of viols	pavane	guitar
chest of viols	galliard	lute
fancy	varied couple	clavecin

sarabande

gigue

variation suite

cantus firmus variation

basso ostinato

ground bass

variation ricercar

strophic aria

chorale motet

ruggiero

passamezzo antico

passamezzo moderno

psalm

chorale

Attaingnant

Andrea Gabrieli

Girolamo Cavazzoni

Girolamo Frescobaldi

J. J. Froberger

Jan Pieterszoon Sweelinck

Salamone Rossi

Biagio Marini

Giovanni Legrenzi

Giovanni Battisti Vitali

Nicolo Amati

John Jennings

Henry Purcell

Claudio Monteverdi

Steffano Landi

Jean-Baptiste Lully

Claudio Merulo

Denis Gaultier

Jacques Champion de Chambonnières

Johann Hermann Schein

John Bull

Peter Philips

Samuel Scheidt

Heinrich Biber

Fiori musicali

Sinfonie e gagliarde

Affetti musicali

Orfeo

L'Incoronazione di Poppea

Il Sant' Alessio

Armide

Rhétorique

Banchetto musicale

Tabulatura nova

LIST OF SCORES

Canzona for keyboard

Trabaci, Giovanni Maria (1580-1647), canzona francese (variation canzona), keyboard, HAM2, 191

Frescobaldi, Girolamo (1583-1643), canzona, keyboard, HAM2, 194

Ricercar

Frescobaldi, Girolamo (1583-1643), *Ricercar dopo il Credo,* from *Fiori musicali*, ricercar for organ, MM, 34

Canzona for Chamber Ensembles

Merula, Tarquinio (b. c. 1600), *Canzon detta la Vesconta*, canzona (sonata) for instrumental ensmble, HAM2, 210

Sonata

Cazzati, Maurizio (c. 1620-1677), *Sonata prima La Pellicana*, sonata for vln & continuo, HAM2, 219
Vitali, Giovanni Battista (c. 1644-1692), *Sonata La Graziani,* sonata, 2 vlns & cont, HAM2, 245
Legrenzi, Giovanni (1626?-1690), *La Buscha*, sonata for instrumental ensemble, HAM2, 220; *La Rasponsa*, trio sonata, NAWM1, 92

English Viol Music

Locke, Matthew (c. 1632-1677), *Fantazia*, fancy for strings, HAM2, 230
Purcell, Henry (1659-1695), *Fantasia*, for viols, HAM2, 256

Opera Overture

Landi, Steffano (1590-1655), sinfonia from *Il San Alessio*, opera overture (canzona), HAM2, 208

Cambert, Robert (1628?-1677), overture to *Pomone*, opera overture, HAM2, 223

Lully, Jean-Baptiste (1633?-1687), overture to *Alceste*, HAM2, 224; *Ouverture*, overture to *Armide*, NAWM1, 75a, MM, 36

Toccata

Frescobaldi, Girolamo (1583-1643), *Toccata IX*, toccata, organ, HAM2, 193

Froberger, Johann Jakob (1616-1667), *Toccata II*, toccata, organ, HAM2, 217

Buxtehude, Dietrich (1637-1707), *Praeludium cum fuga*, toccata for organ, HAM2, 234

Pachelbel, Johann (1653-1706), Toccata in E-minor for organ, MM, 37

Dances for Lute and Keyboard

Gaultier, Denis (1600-1672), *Tombeau de Mademoiselle Gaultier*, dance, stylized, for lute, TEM, 39; *Mode sous-ionien*, dance,stylized, lute, HAM2, 211

Reusner, Esajas (1636-1679), prelude for lute, HAM2, 233

Chambonnières, Jacques Champion de (b. c. 1602-1672), *Chaconne*, dance,stylized, keyboard, HAM2, 212

Froberger, Johann Jakob (1616-1667), *Lamento*, movement fr suite, harpsichord, HAM2, 216; Suite in E-minor for clavichord, dance suite, MM, 35

Couperin, Louis (1630-1665), *Menuet de Poitou*, minuet for harpsichord, HAM2, 229

d'Anglebert, Jean Henri (c. 1628-1691), *Prélude, Allemande, Sarabande* from dance suite, harpsichord, HAM2, 232

Variations for Keyboard

Frescobaldi, Girolamo (1583-1643), *Partite sopra l'aria della Romanesca*, variations, keyboard, HAM2, 192

Le Bègue, Nicolas Antoine (1630-1702), Noël,"*Une Vierge pucelle* ", variations on Christmas tune for organ, HAM2, 231

Poglietti, Alessandro (d. c. 1683), *Aria allemagna con alcuni variazioni* , variations fr harpsichord, HAM2, 236

Cabanilles, Juan (1644-1712), *Paseos*, chaconne, organ, HAM2, 239

Muffat, Georg (c. 1645-1704), "*Passacaglia*" (without ground bass), organ, HAM2, 240

Purcell, Henry (c. 1669-1695), *A new Ground*, variations for harpsichord, MM, 38

Variations for Solo with Continuo

Biber, Heinrich Franz (1644-1704), *Surrexit Christus hodie*, variations for violin & continuo, HAM2, 238

Chorale Prelude

Scheidt, Samuel (1587-1654), *Vater unser im Himmelreich*, chorale prelude, HAM2, 190a

Preludes and Fugues

Tunder, Franz (1614-1667), *Praeludium*, prelude & fugue, organ, HAM2, 215

Poglietti, Alessandro (d. c. 1683), *Capriccio über dass Hennengeschrei*, fugue, TEM, 40

Bach, Johann Christoph (1642-1703), *Praeludium und fuge ex dis*, prelude & fugue, organ, HAM2, 237

CHRONOLOGICAL CHART

Music	Political History	Intellectual History	Art
1618 Schein, *Opella nova*, earliest chorale concertatos	1618-1648 30 years War, Protestant princes against the Holy Roman Empire & the Hapsburgs	1618-1619 Kepler's 3rd law of planetary motion	1618 Rubens, *Leucippus*
1619 Praetorius, *Syntagma musicum*, most important source of information on instruments	1619-1637 Ferdinand II Holy Roman Emperor		
1620-1684 Violins of Nicolo Amati, first of the great violin makers	1620 Pilgrims arrive at Cape Cod Mayflower Compact		
1621-1628 Schein, *Musica boscareccia*, accompanied strophic songs in 3 voices	1621-1623 Gregory XV, Pope 1621-1625 Philip IV King of Spain		
1623 Schütz, *Story of the Happy and Triumphant Resurrection*			
1624 Monteverdi, *Combat of Tancredi and Clorinda*, secular oratorio or semi-opera Scheidt, *Tabulatura nova*, organ collection:fugues, echoes, cantus firmus variations	1624-1642 Cardinal Richelieu in power in France		1624 Frans Hals, *Laughing Cavalier*

Music	Political History	Intellectual History	Art
1625 Schütz, *Cantiones sacrae*, accompanied motets 1627 Schein, *Leipzig Cantional*, established the practice of organ accompaniment of the chorale	1625-1649 Charles I, King of England 1626 Manhattan Island bought by Peter Minuit		1625 Bernini, *Costanza* 1627 Hals, *Lute Player*
1628 Benevoli, *Salzburg Festival Mass*, "colossal Baroque", for 53 voices and instruments 1629 Schütz, *Symphoniae sacrae* sacred concertos in 3 voices	1628 La Rochelle captured, end of Huguenot power in France 1630 Puritans establish Boston 1631 Battle of Lützen, 30 Years War: Gustavus Adolphus (Sweden) defeats Wallenstein, general of theHoly RomanEmpire	1628 William Harvey, *Essay on the Motion of the Heart and the Blood* 1631 Galileo, *Dialogue on the Two Chief Systems of the World*, (supports Copernican planetary system with the sun as center)	1631 Rembrandt, *Anatomy Lesson*
1634 Lawes, *Comus*, (masque)			1634-1653 Taj Mahal
1635 Frescobaldi, *Fiori musicali*, organ Mass		1635 French Academy founded by Cardinal Richelieu: issued dictionary and grammar; awarded literary prizes	1635 Velasquez, *Surrender of Breda*

Music	Political History	Intellectual History	Art
1636 Mersenne, *Harmonie universelle*, source for musical thought in France	1636 Roger Williams first settlement in Rhode Island	1636 Founding of Harvard College Corneille, *Le Cid*	
1637 First public opera theater in Venice	1637-1657 Ferdinand III Holy Roman Emperor	1637 Descartes, *Discourse on Method*, presents method of Cartesian doubt	
1638 Monteverdi, *Madrigals of War and Love*			1638 Rembrandt, *Fall*
1640 *Bay Psalm Book*, 1st book printed in America	1640-1688 Frederick William, the "Great Elector" of Hanover	Descartes, *Essay on Analytical Geometry*	
1642 Monteverdi, *L'Incoronazione di Poppea*	1642-46 English Civil War "Roundheads" under Cromwell defeat Cavaliers (royalists)	1643 Molière founds *Illustre Théatre*, in Paris (*Théatre de la Comédie Française* from 1689)	1642 Rembrandt, *The Night Watch*
1645 Schütz, *The Seven Words of Christ on the Cross*, oratorio	1643-1715 Louis XIV, King of France at age 5	1645 John Milton, *L'Allegro, Il Penseroso*	1644 Bernini, *Cornaro Chapel*, S. Maria della Vittoria, Rome incl. *Ecstasy of St. Teresa*, sculpture
	1648 Treaty of Westphalia, end of 30 Years War		
	1649 England declared a Commonwealth		1649 Terborch, *Philip IV of Spain*, portrait Velasquez, *Pope Innocent X*, portrait

Music	Political History	Intellectual History	Art
1650 Athanasius Kircher, *Musurgia universalis,* theory Carissimi, *Jephtha* Emergence of da capo aria as preferred form of aria Schütz, *Symphoniae sacrae, Part III*		**1650** Corneille, *Andromède,* tragedy DesCartes, *Musicae compendium* **1651** Thomas Hobbes, *Leviathan*	
1653 Jean-Baptiste Lully, court composer at Paris Locke, *Cupid and Death,* masque	**1653** Cromwell dissolves Parliament **1654** Coronation of Louis XIV at Rheims	**1654** Pascal & de Fermat, theory of probability **1660** Pepys, *Diary*	**1653** Borromini, *S. Agnese in Agone,* Rome **1656** Velaszuez, *The Maids of Honor* Vermeer, *The Procuress*
1660 Cavalli, *Serse,* opera **1661** Marc' Antonio Cesti, *Dori,* opera **1662** Cavalli, *Ercole amante,* opera	**1660** Restoration of Charles II **1661-1715** Absolute reign of Louis XIV **1663** Turks declare war on Holy Roman Empire	**1662** Molière, *École des femmes* Revised English Prayer Book	**1660** Zurbaran, *The Young Virgin* **1661** Rembrandt, *Syndics of the Cloth Hall* **1663** Bernini, *Scala Regia,* Vatican, Rome
1664 Schütz, *Christmas Oratorio* **1665** Schütz, *St. John Passion*	**1664** New Amsterdam becomes New York **1666** Great fire of London	**1665** Spinoza, *Ethics*	**1664** Wren, SheldonianTheatre, Oxford Vermeer, *The Lacemaker*
1667 Rosenmüller, *12 sonate da camera a 5 stromenti*		**1667** Milton, *Paradise Lost*	**1667** Bernini, colonnade of St. Peter's

Music	Political History	Intellectual History	Art
	1668 British East India Co obtains control of Bombay	1668 La Fontaine, *Fables*	
1669 Paris Acdemy of Music founded			
1670 Chambonnières, clavecin pieces	1671 Turks declare war on Poland	1670 Pascal, *Pensées* Molière, *Le Bourgeois gentilhomme*	
1675 Lully, *Thésée* Locke, incidental music to *Psyche*			1675 Sir Christopher Wren begins St. Paul's Cathedral
1676 Thomas Mace, *Musick's Monument*		1677 Racine, *Phèdre*	1676 Wren, Trinity College Library, Cambridge
1678 Lully, *Isis*, opera		1678 Bunyan, *Pilgrm's Progress* Corneille, *Le Comte d'Essex* Huygens discovers polarization of light	1678 Murillo, *Mystery of the Immaculate Conception*
1679 First German opera house opens in Hamburg Alessandro Scarlatti's first opera ,*Gli Equivoci nell' amore, Rome*	1679 Peace of Nijmegen between France and the Dutch, and France & Spain	1680 Comédie Française formed	

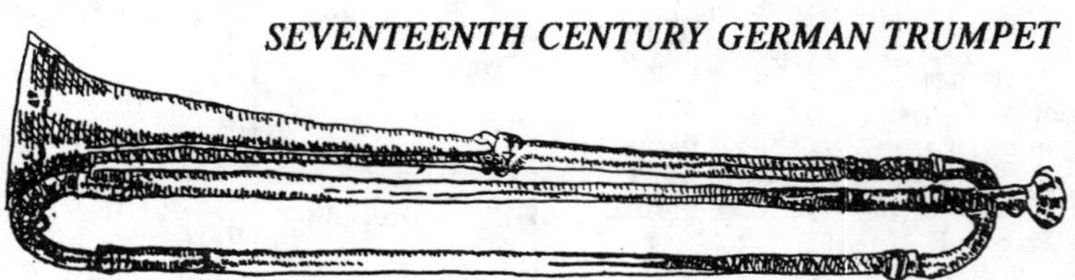

The trumpet did not acquire valves until the 19th century. (After the Larousse Encylopedia of Music, ed. Hindley)

CHAPTER X

THE LATE BAROQUE

SOCIAL BACKGROUND

Two trends existed in the period which saw the Late Baroque in music (1685-1750): the closing phases of the Age of Reason and the emergence of the Enlightenment. Likewise, new trends in music (to be discussed in Chapter 13) and art were emerging while some of the greatest masterpieces of the Baroque were being created. Perhaps the most brilliant creation of the Age of Reason was Newton's *Principia* (1687). In it Newton "harmonized the universe" by showing how gravitation on earth was the same force which controlled the movements of the planets and thus brought awe-inspiring order to the cosmos. The philosophical orientation of the period, as we have seen before, took thought as its point of departure. Thus, Descartes took thought as the starting point from which existence is deduced: "I think, therefore I exist" (*cogito ergo sum*).

The foundations of the Enlightenment, which reached fruition in the late 18th century, were laid with the triumph of parliamentary rule in England (1688). It was here that the emphasis began to shift from thought to experience, and the theoretical advances began to be applied to human affairs. The philosopher Locke (1632-1704) taught that all knowledge is derived from experience. Voltaire (1694-1788) brought the English influence to France where it took firm root. These

269

currents were beginning to make their presence felt in art and culture while some of the greatest monuments of the Baroque were still being created, as will be discussed in the last chapter.

The revolution in thought was for a long time, however, a "quiet revolution". In government autocracy reached a peak from the mid-17th century on. The power of kings who ruled by divine right soared unrestrained, and the social position of the aristocracy reached new heights. Autocracy held sway at the courts of the cultured Hapsburg emperor Charles VI (r. 1711-1740) and the soldier-king Frederick William I of Prussia (r. 1713-1740). As we have seen, the arch-autocrat of all and the model for the other sovereigns was Louis XIV of France (r. 1643-1714). He organized and unified the government so that he could dominate it without the slightest challenge to his authority. The unified structure of Versailles itself symbolizes this absolutism.

The subjective and inward-turning aspects of the Baroque mystique saw a resurgence of emphasis on religion. The Catholic Reformation was active during the Early Baroque period, and in Germany the Thirty Years War (1618-1648) had a strong religious component. Baroque art and music were deeply involved with both aristocracy and religion. Protestant music, in particular, flowered in the Late Baroque period and reached its greatest heights with J. S. Bach.

A spirit of unity and organization hovers over the art and culture of the Late Baroque. This spirit constitutes the link between the absolutism of Louis XIV; Newton's theory of gravitation; and the large-scale, thematically unified musical forms of the Late Baroque. Just as Louis XIV organized and unified the French government, so Newton organized and unified the cosmos; Rameau unified and organized polyphony with his treatise on harmony; and the Late Baroque composers unified and organized the movements of musical forms on a large scale. In this sense opera is perhaps the most representative form of the Late Baroque. It unites music both instrumental and vocal; dramatic art; the visual arts in scenery; and ballet - all in the service of presenting a drama on the stage. With Alessandro Scarlatti it became the most widespread form of the period though little of it survives today.

With the decline of French Absolutism which began in France with the death of Louis XIV in 1714, the French Baroque began to give way to the lighter Rococo. Grandeur in expression gave way to taste - everything was done in good taste, but the underlying dramatic spirit was gone. Rococo art associated itself with a dying aristocracy which maintained its social position but not its relevancy. Nevertheless, from this, new directions took shape while the last and greatest monuments of the Baroque were still to be created in Germany by Bach and in England by the cosmopolitan, transplanted Saxon, G. F. Handel.

LATE BAROQUE MUSIC

Both Italy and France contributed to the style of Late Baroque music. The Italian contributions consisted of: (1) the concerto allegro style; (2) the instrumental forms of the concerto, and sonata; and (3) the vocal *bel canto* style of Italian opera, combining lyrical melody with the influence of the generalized instrumental idiom. The French contributions were: (1) the cultivation of orchestral performance; (2) the French overture; (3) the stylized dances ; (4) the use of melodic ornaments; (5) the keyboard technique (to which the English also contributed); and (6) the introduction of programmatic and coloristic devices into music. German music partook of both French and Italian influences and was characterized by the firm foundation of its harmonic and contrapuntal structures. German music tended toward the contemplative, the subjective, and the religious.

The Late Baroque period extended from about 1685-1750, and it is from this period that many works survive in the modern repertory. The traditional harmonic style that remained the basis of art-music throughout the 19th century - and still pervades much folk and popular music to the present day - stems from this period. Because of the importance of this traditional harmonic style, it will be useful to bear with the following description of its salient features. In addition, much of the music of the Late Baroque was contrapuntal in texture, that is, it emphasized the melodic independence of the different voice parts of a composition.

Harmony

The counterpoint of the Late Baroque period was supported by a harmonic framework organized in terms of chord progression. The awareness of chord progression centered around the concept that a chord had a root above which it was constructed by proceeding upward in thirds. The changes in chord roots were the source of chord progression. Harmony made possible a freer use of dissonance in two ways: (1) Building upwards in thirds gave rise to the <u>seventh chord</u>, a chord with three thirds in which the interval between the root and the upper note of the top third is a seventh. Seventh chords could be absorbed into the harmonic scheme as being chords of tension requiring progression to a chord of rest. (2) The harmonic framework made possible a freer treatment of ornamental, or non-harmonic tones, through the establishment of a vocabulary of harmonic progressions which, through their familiarity, made themselves more easily perceptible to the hearer. In addition, the use of a supporting instrument - a keyboard or plucked stringed instrument- supplied a harmonic, chordal support for the melody instruments. This kind of instrumental support, first established in the Early Baroque as accompaniment for the vocal monody, remained in use throughout the Baroque period. It was similar in function to the kind of support provided in popular groups of today.

Harmony also made possible the absorption of chromatically altered notes into the system. The most characteristic progression was that in which the root moved up a fourth or down a fifth (e.g. sol-do) . By progressing in a chain of fifths while preserving the interval structure of the chords, chromatics could be introduced.

Sequence

The repetition of harmonic progressions at various pitches gave rise to harmonic sequences. Along with the harmonic sequences melodies could also be repeated at different pitch levels (transposition). Harmonic and melodic sequences played a very important part in the expansion of musical forms in the Late Baroque period. These sequences played an important role in the episodic (subsidiary) passages that came between presentations of the main themes. It should be pointed out that the term sequence is here being used in a different sense than it had been used in naming a Medieval chant form.

Modulation

With the advent of harmony, change of key became an element of form. A given scale (or key) could be established as the basis of a musical passage by means of chord progressions which created a feeling of ending or relaxation (cadence) on the chord whose root was the same as that of the scale. Therefore, key changes, *modulations,* could be established by harmonic means; and these modulations became an element of musical form in the Late Baroque period. The shrinking of the modal system to two modes (major and minor) also aided in the use of modulation, since the basing of the scales on different pitches brought new sets of sharps or flats into the musical web. In the modal system all the modes could be played using only the white notes of the piano, simply by beginning the different modes on different white keys so that the order of whole and half steps would change. The element of contrast brought about by these new sharps or flats became an element of musical form in the Late Baroque period. The ability to modulate into all keys also depended upon the acoustical problem of devising a tuning that would make all scales sound satisfactory on a keyboard instrument. If, for example, the key of C-major were tuned to the natural diatonic scale, other keys would be out of tune. A satisfactory compromise consisted of dividing the octave into 12 equal semitones so that all scales were equally tempered. The principal of equal temperament was advocated by the German organist and theorist Andreas Werckmeister in 1691. In his *Well-Tempered Clavier,* J. S.. Bach was the first composer to present compositions in all available keys in a systematic collection.

Instrumental Forms

The forms of the movements were not only extended by means of harmonic and melodic episodes and the use of modulation, but they were also unified in their use of melodic material. Also, the combinations of movements in the composite (multi-movement) forms became standardized. The *sonata da chiesa* came to consist of four movements (slow-fast-slow-fast); and the *sonata da camera* came to consist of a prelude and two or three dances. At the same time the character of the movements in the *sonata da chiesa* and *sonata da camera* were influencing each other. The *sonata da camera* was given an abstract prelude, and the *sonata da chiesa* adopted features of the stylized dance, especially in its last two movements. In the area of keyboard music the dance suite for keyboard attained a standardized grouping of movements. In France, Italy, and Germany a large production of individual harpsichord pieces emerged. These were characterized by a new emphasis on keyboard technique. In Germany the Italian *sonata da chiesa* was also transferred to keyboard. In addition, the Germans led in organ music with passacaglias, organ chorales, toccatas, and fugues. Like the fugue, the Baroque concerto for orchestra was a product of the Late Baroque period. Among the stringed instruments the lower instruments of the violin family, namely the viola and cello, came into their own. At the same time the number of wind instruments was reduced, and their construction was standardized as to size and range.

Vocal Forms

In vocal music the style of writing was for the first time dominated by instrumental style. A definite distinction was now made between comic opera and serious opera; recitative was clearly distinguished from aria; and the aria itself was limited to a single affection. The *da capo* aria became the leading aria form, and the internal organization of the sections was influenced by the ritornello form of the allegro movement of the concerto. The concerto also sparked the emergence of an Italian form of operatic overture in the Late Baroque. Among secular vocal forms the chamber cantata received important emphasis, while in Catholic church music, a conservative type of contrapuntal choral writing reflected the influence of the *stile antico*. Aria and recitative, however, were the basis of the Late Baroque Protestant church cantata.

Ritornello

The basic form which took shape in the Late Baroque period was the *ritornello* form. The term ritornello (It., the diminutive of the word *ritorno* , meaning return) was used to refer to the periodic returns of the main idea. These returns, however, were not literal, but were typically transposed to different keys and abbreviated - hence the use of the diminutive. Modulations to a series of related keys was an important aspect of the architecture of this form. The ritornello form achieved its most characteristic manifestation in the concerto. (Note, however, that in the Late Baroque period the term concerto referred to a purely orchestral composition, and not to a vocal composition with instrumental accompaniment.) In the concerto grosso (grand concerto) the statements of the main theme, whole or abbreviated, were played by the whole orchestra, while the modulating episodes were played by a small group of solo instruments called the <u>concertino.</u> In the solo concerto a solo instrument with continuo played the episodes. It is interesting to note that in extended concerto movements the main theme itself could be constructed on the ritornello pattern after which the concertino would enter with episodes based on new melodic material.

Fugue

The main theme of a ritornello form might be either homophonic or imitative. The fugue was the most characteristic example of the application of the ritornello principle to imitative form. In the fugue a melodic idea, or subject, was imitated throughout all the voices - usually four - of a composition at such transpositions and with such minor changes in intervals as would serve to establish the main key of the composition. This opening group of imitative presentations of the subject would constitute the main theme of a ritornello form. It was followed by a modulating episode leading to another group of entries of the subject (in imitation) but this time usually not a complete set. This incomplete set of entries constituted the first ritornello, and it was followed by other episodes and entries in similar fashion. In the fugue contrasts in instrumentation were not characteristic, but it was customary to have one of the voices drop out during the episodes to provide contrasts in texture. Fugal episodes were usually based on subsidiary melodic ideas taken from the main subject.

Other Applications

The ritornello form had widespread applications. It might be used to extend the structure of the individual sections of a two-part dance form. It could be used to extend the separate sections of the *da capo* (A B A) aria where the instrumental ensemble might play the main theme while the voice sang the episodes; or the whole form might be executed by the voice part. It can thus be seen that the ritornello form, using new tonal concepts, provided the Late Baroque period with a vital and fruitful basis for the construction of musical forms of large scope, independent of extra-musical aids or preëxistent material.

Variations

In its variation forms the Late Baroque favored a continuous type of variation using a brief theme repeated without pauses between presentations. Two types were distinguished which nowadays are termed <u>chaconne</u> and <u>passacaglia</u> though the application of these terms in their present meaning is not justified by 18th century practice. The passacaglia is defined as being a variation form based upon repetitions of a bass melody above which the musical material keeps changing. The chaconne is defined as a series of harmonies which are used as the fixed element of the variations. This use of a harmonic scheme as the "theme" for a set of variations was made possible by the firm establishment of tonality. The terms *chaconne* and *passacaglia* as they are now used seem to be based on two justly famous compositions by J. S. Bach: The Chaconne from the Fifth Sonata in D-minor for unaccompanied violin and the Passacaglia for Organ in C-minor. There were also variations on fully developed themes, such as the Aria with Thirty Variations for harpsichord, by J. S. Bach, known as the "Goldberg" Variations.

Chorale Settings

Organ

In Lutheran church music, notably in the works of J. S. Bach, chorale melodies played an important part. They were used not only in church cantatas but also in works for organ where they were set in various ways. Among the forms of the organ chorale were: (1) The <u>chorale</u> <u>partita</u> (o r chorale variation) modeled after the secular variation in which the chorale was the theme for a set of variations; (2) The <u>chorale</u> <u>fantasy</u> of the North German school - a toccata-like composition in which the chorale melody often appeared and disappeared in fragmentary fashion; (3) The <u>chorale</u> <u>fugue</u> in which the opening phrase of the chorale served as a fugue subject, after which the whole chorale was introduced as a cantus firmus. In another type of chorale fugue each phrase of the chorale became the subject of a fughetta (short fugue) - a procedure closely related to that of the motet; (4) The chorale prelude. The true chorale prelude had a liturgical function since it was used to introduce the singing of the chorale by the congregation. In it the chorale was presented phrase by phrase, usually in the top voice. The voices below moved in faster rhythms with complex interweavings of harmonic figurations or counterpoint. There were pauses between presentations of the lines of the chorale while the figuration continued; and often the lower voices introduced the chorale phrase that was to follow. This introduction consisted of a brief imitative passage based on the chorale melody which was presented in short note values. The generation of Buxtehude and Pachelbel, which represents the transition to the Late Baroque, was the first to cultivate the chorale prelude.

Thus, the chorale melody might be treated in various ways in organ music: as a cantus firmus in long notes with faster moving figures in the other voices in ornamented form in the soprano; or divided into phrases with each phrase used as a fugal subject. The figures which accompanied presentation of the chorale in long notes might be purely abstract, but frequently they were meant to represent the affection of the chorale. In the chorale variation, the variations might correspond to verses of the chorale with figures to represent the affection of each verse.

Chorale Cantata

The chorale cantata was a type evolved by J. S. Bach himself in collaboration with the poet Picander. It usually begins with a choral setting of the chorale melody in the style of a chorale fantasy or a chorale prelude and ends with a simple four-part setting of the chorale. In between, the text of the chorale is paraphrased in recitative and aria. In the most severe application of the principle, the cantata *Christ lag in Todesbanden* (Christ Lay in the Bonds of Death), the chorale melody itself pervades each chorus, aria, and recitative - a technique which recalls the chorale concertato.

Toccata

The toccata survived as an important keyboard form inherited from the Renaissance and transformed by both the affective spirit of the Baroque and by Late Baroque tonality. The form as developed by Merulo and consisting of alternations between virtuoso passages and contrapuntal passages was still to be found. There also emerged a new type of free rhapsodic toccata of a particularly boundless and unrestrained nature that emanated from North Germany. The term *fantasy* was now used as being virtually synonymous with toccata, whereas it had previously been used for compositions of a contrapuntal nature similar to the ricercar. The change recalls Shakepeare's lines from *The Merchant of Venice* (III, ii):"Tell me where is fancy bred, or in the heart or in the head."

Interchange of Forms Between Media

The tendency of Baroque art to burst boundaries between different kinds of expression extended also to the treatment of forms and styles. Forms were freely transferred from one medium to another - vocal to instrumental and vice versa. Thus, we find the *da capo* aria form used for instrumental pieces, such as the slow movements of concerti and the concerto form used in an aria, such as the *"Cara Sposa "* from

Handel's *Rinaldo*. In this aria the orchestra plays the ritornello while the solo voice sings the episodes. The fugue, though it evolved from the keyboard canzona and ricercar, was used for choral and instrumental ensemble compositions as well as for keyboard works. The passacaglia, the chorale fantasy, and the chorale prelude were all adapted from instrumental to vocal media.

Predominance of Instrumental Style

In the Late Baroque period instrumental style became predominant. This predominance was aided by the chordal concept which made possible the use of the broken chord as a melodic device. The resultant employment of wide intervals, unified and organized by harmony, were more idiomatic for instrumental than vocal performance. However, instrumental style influenced vocal writing and, in fact, aided in the development of a virtuoso vocal technique particularly suited to solo performance. This generalized instrumental style - freely interchanged between various media - had its inception in early Spanish and later French lute music and received great impetus in the keyboard music of the English virginalists. Influences of lute, keyboard, and violin music all played their part in the formation of the style; and it was style itself that was the chief preoccupation of the Baroque composer. In J. S. Bach's *Well-Tempered Clavier*, a collection of keyboard preludes and fugues, examples can be found of clavichord, harpsichord, and organ styles; but the composer used them for their stylistic and expressive qualities and did not attempt to specify which keyboard instrument was to be used.

Stile antico

Vocal music was now customarily accompanied by fully developed and independent instrumental parts which constituted an indispensable part of the music. The *stile antico* and the *a cappella* ideal of unaccompanied vocal music still survived in Catholic church music along with the Renaissance Mass forms; but it was practiced much less frequently than before. Examples are found in such composers as Antonio Lotti (1667-1740), Benedetto Marcello (1686-1739), and the Austrian J. J. Fux (1660-1741). It was Fux who codified the quasi-Renaissance cantus firmus technique into the system known to music students as the five species. His textbook on species counterpoint, the *Gradus ad Parnassum* (1725), presented his system.

Rhythm

The rhythm of Late Baroque music was organized in the regularly recurring accents of our traditional music with its duple and triple meters. A characteristic feature which created an effect of unity and continuity within a movement was the mechanically pulsating rhythm of the fast movements of the concerto. The influence of this concerto rhythm was widespread, and Late Baroque counterpoint is characterized by the fact that there is consistent movement carried on at all times in one or another of the parts, which produces a continuous flow in the ensemble.

At the other extreme was the very free rhythm of the recitative and toccata. This rhythmic concept stemmed from the Early Baroque and was associated with affective dramatic expression.

Affective Representation in Vocal Music

In the Late Baroque period the doctrine of affections crystallized in an elaborate systematization of the figures which represent these affections in music. Unity was achieved by means of the consistent use of such a figure throughout a movement. The affection could also influence such considerations as the choice of mode (minor for sadness, major for joy); choice of keys; the use of such technical devices as the chromatically descending ground bass to represent grief; rhythmic figures; and choice of instruments. An instrument thus chosen as obbligato for an aria would continue its function throughout the aria. Examples of the chromatically descending ground bass are to be found in "Dido's Lament" from Purcell's opera *Dido and Aeneas* and in the *Crucifixus* of Bach's Mass in B-minor. In its final bars the Bach *Crucifixus* turns suddenly to cadence in the relative major key to represent the idea of salvation. Trumpets in the *Resurrexit* from the same Mass and in the *Hallelujah* chorus from Handel's *Messiah* represent the affection of exaltation. The recorder obbligato to the aria, known (in English translation) as "Sheep May Safely Graze" from Bach's secular cantata *Was mir behagt ist nur die muntre Jagd,* represents a pastoral affection. Often, a slow compound meter is found in pastoral movements, such as the *Pastorale* from Corelli's *Christmas Concerto*, in G-minor, op.6 no.8 and the aria "He shall Feed His Flock" from Handel's *Messiah.* In his settings of organ chorales the affections of the text are often observed by Bach in his choice of motives for the accompaniment. When Bach took a movement from one cantata and transferred it to another, he was careful not to violate the affection. The complex structure of affective representation reflects the rationalist atmosphere of Baroque culture - the fondness for structures based on thought.

Composite Forms

Composite forms (multi-movement forms) became stabilized in the Late Baroque period. These were the church sonata; the chamber sonata; the dance suite; the concerto; the

French and Italian opera overtures; and two-movement forms, such as the prelude (toccata) and fugue, or recitative and aria. Unity and continuity characterized the internal organization of the individual movements in such aspects as : thematic unity in the forms; unity of affection in music of dramatic import; unity in the handling of instrumental combinations which remained unchanged within a movement; continuity in the rhythmic flow of the concerto-allegro; continuity in the structure of such variation forms as the passacaglia and chaconne. This unity of concept within movements made for greater contrast between the movements of the composite forms.

Influence of Late Baroque Forms

The opera was, of course, the great contribution of the Baroque period; but the Late Baroque gave birth to the fugue which has had a wide influence on instrumental forms. From the time of Beethoven and throughout the 19th and first half of the 20th centuries the fugue has occupied an important place in the music of many composers. Another Late Baroque form, the Baroque concerto, reappeared in the neo-Baroque revival that took place during the first half of the 20th century. Noteworthy examples are found in the works of Igor Stravinsky (Concerto for Piano and Wind Instruments and Dumbarton Oaks Concerto) and Ernst Bloch (Concerto Grosso).

Instrumental Music

The four-part string orchestra established itself during the last quarter of the 17th century superseding the five parts that had been customary in Lully's scores. In the lower strings the members of the violin family - the violas and violoncellos (cellos) - replaced the viols, though the latter were still to be found in solo parts. The double basses, still found in the modern symphony orchestra, are the only survivors of the viol family. Violin technique made significant strides in the last two decades of the century. French horns (without valves, which only appeared in the 19th century) made their first appearance in the orchestra at the beginning of the 18th century with Alessandro Scarlatti among the first to use them. Flutes, oboes, bassoons and trumpets, previously made in many different sizes, now came to be built in the sizes we know today and with their present ranges. These wind instruments, along with the drums, were being established as regular members of the orchestra by the end of the 17th century. During the first half of the 18th century the transverse, or modern flute, replaced the recorders, or end-blown flutes.

In instrumental as well as vocal music the importance of the individual artist received increased emphasis and as a result, the solo sonata and solo concerto became established. As counterpoint reappeared in music, composers were no longer satisfied with pure continuo keyboard parts and began to write obbligato parts for keyboard accompaniments. Greater differentiation began to be made between chamber and orchestral music.

Keyboard Dance suite

Among the composite forms using movements derived from the dance the keyboard suite was the most definitely established in its make-up. Thematic connections between dances, such as were found in the variation suite of the middle Baroque, e.g. Schein's *Banchetto musicale* were no longer used. Each movement of the suite now had its own independent musical material though all movements were in the same key. The dances were of various origins. For the most part they received their stylistic features from France though Italian versions of some of the dances were used. The main impetus for the Late Baroque style came from Italy, but France was the chief source of the stylized dance as found in Late Baroque dance suites. Following, is the structure of the keyboard suite:

1. Allemande - moderate duple meter
2. Courante (Fr.) - moderate triple or compound duple meter, with frequent shifts from one to the other, or
    Corrente (It.) - fast triple meter
3. Sarabande - slow triple meter with frequent accents on the second beat and endings on weak beats (feminine endings)
4. Optional group - such contemporary dances as the gavotte, minuet, bourreé, passepied, rigaudon, anglaise, hornpipe, and polonaise. These were more in the nature of true dances, not stylized.
5. Gigue (Fr.) - fast compound duple meter, or
    Giga (It.) - much faster than the French version

The allemande (*allemande* is the French word for German) first appeared in the mid-16th century and together with the courante was found in such keyboard tablatures as B. Schmid's Tablature of 1577 and the *Fitzwilliam Virginal Book* (1629). But by the 17th century the allemande had lost its dance character and had become stylized. The 16th century courante was a dance of great vitality with jumping movements. It became stylized in two versions, Italian and French. The Italian type was established first and is closer to the original dance in character. In the French type the alternation between duple and triple meter is accomplished by means of a rhythmic device called *hemiola*. In this device a group of six beats is divided in two different ways: (1) three beats of two units each and (2) two beats of three units each:

$$(1)\ \underline{1\ \ 2}\ \ \underline{3\ \ 4}\ \ \underline{5\ \ 6}$$

$$(2)\ \underline{1\ \ 2\ \ 3}\ \ \underline{4\ \ 5\ \ 6}$$

Both the courante and corrente are common in Bach's keyboard suites. The 2nd movement of Bach's *French Suite* no. 5 is a corrente, while the 2nd movement of *French Suite* No. 3 is a good example of a courante using hemiola. Note: In modern editions of the Bach *French Suites* the title courante is often used even though the movement may actually be a corrente.

The sarabande was originally a wild and uninhibited love dance introduced into Spain (probably from Mexico) at the beginning of the 16th century. In the early 17th century it began to appear in English and French keyboard collections in stylized form and thereafter was taken into the suite in its stylized version.

The gigue originated in the British Isles as the Irish or English jig - a form in which it still survives in Irish folk music. Like the courante the gigue was stylized in both an Italian and a French version. The French version - the more common of the two - tends to be fugal with the second part often treating the subject in inversion (cf. Bach's *French Suite* no. 5). The non-fugal *giga* which appears as the last movement of Bach's *Partita* no. 1 is an Italian type, as is the final movement of Bach's *English Suite* no. 2.

The allemande, courante, sarabande, and gigue were the unchanging components of the keyboard suite. These were the stylized dances, and they constituted the complete suite as found in the works of Froberger. Before the gigue (the last movement of the suite) one or more of a group of true dance movements was introduced in the Late Baroque period. These dances first appeared in the *ballet de cour (court ballet)* at Versailles under the patronage of Louis XIII (r. 1610-1643) and his successor Louis XIV. During the reign of Louis XIV, Lully perfected these dances and brought them to prominence in performances by the *Vingt-quatre violons du roi* (Twenty-Four Violins of the King).

The dances of this optional group were mostly of French provincial origin and came from such regions as Auvergne (bourreé), Dauphine (gavotte), Provence (rigaudon), etc. The most important for the future history of music was the minuet (from Poitou). There were also dances of foreign origin, such as the anglaise and hornpipe from England and the polonaise from Poland. Occasionally, the first regular movement of the suite, the allemande, would be preceded by a prelude, as in the Bach *Partitas* which begin with movements entitled *Ouverture, Preambule, Fantaisie*, etc. Preludes are also found in Bach's *English Suites*.

Orchestral Dance Suite

The orchestral suite had its origins in the French *ballet de cour.* In France the custom arose of performing the overture and dances from a court ballet or opera in orchestral concerts. In the Late Baroque period composers began to write independent suites consisting of a French overture followed by dances of the type that were found in ballet and opera; and frequently such suites were entitled "overture". Orchestral suites of this French type were written by such German composers as Georg Muffat (1690-1779) and J. F. K. Fischer(1665-1746). Bach's orchestral suites, such as the Suite in B-minor for flute and strings, are of the French type, as is the *Water Music* of Handel.

Dances for Chamber Ensemble

In the field of chamber music the dance suite was known as the *sonata da camera* (chamber sonata). It consisted of four or five dances both stylized and true dances, and grouped in no standardized order. It frequently began with a prelude.

Internal Form of Dance Movements

Individual dance movements were in two-part form. The first part began in the tonic and cadenced in the dominant; the second part began in the dominant and modulated back to the tonic. As was typical of the Late Baroque period, the form was based on a single theme, and within each section episodic structure might be used for expansion.

Forms Derived from the Canzona

Of greater importance than the dance forms were the forms which evolved from the canzona. In many cases the individual sections of the canzona evolved into separate movements. In the Early and Middle Baroque the movements were short and frequently had melodic interconnections, but by the Late Baroque period these thematic connections had disappeared and the movements had been expanded through the use of episodic techniques. The forms involved here are (1) for orchestra: the French overture; the Italian overture; and the concerto; and (2) for chamber music: the church sonata.

The Baroque Concerto

In the Early and Middle Baroque periods the term *concerto* referred to a composition for voices and instruments. However, in the Late Baroque the concerto came to be a composition in which a few instrumentalists or a solo performer were contrasted with the orchestra. The former is termed concerto grosso, and the latter, solo concerto. Both types existed in the Late Baroque period. An element of possible confusion exists in the fact that the term *concerto* is used both as the name of the composite form - a form that consists of three movements (fast-slow-fast) - and as the name of the internal form of the allegro movements (also known as the ritornello form). The allegro movements are, to be sure, the most important movements of the concerto and the basis for the genre - a fact which is proven by the omission of slow movements or their reduction to merely a few chords in some concerti by Bach, Handel, and others. In the terminology of the Baroque concerto grosso the *concertino* is the small body of sound. The large body of sound is known as the *ripieno,* the *tutti,* or the *concerto.*

The elements that went to make up the concerto came from various sources. Some of the basic elements and their sources were :(1) <u>Style.</u> The style of writing was predominantly homophonic, but this homophony differed from the later Viennese Classical homophony of Mozart and Haydn which consisted of a single melodic line with its accompaniment. The Baroque chords were based on the use of a continuo, or thoroughbass - a bass line with figures indicating the harmonies. Thus, the Baroque chords were governed by two poles, namely melody and bass. The harmonies changed more rapidly than in the later homophonic style. Arcangelo Corelli (1653-1713) was one of the earliest composers whose works reflect the style of continuo-homophony. (2) <u>Contrast between bodies of sound.</u> The contrast between two bodies of sound had its ancestry in the polychoral motet of the Venetian school from which it was transferred to the canzonas of such Venetian composers as Giovanni Gabrieli. (3) <u>Form</u>. In the ritornello form, or - more strictly - formal procedure, the contrast between the concertino and the ripieno was not merely a contrast between bodies of sound but an alternation of passages with different musical significance. In the concerti of Guiseppe Torelli (1658-1709) the ripieno became the bearer of the main theme while the concertino played the episodic material. In this form the main theme appeared complete and in the tonic key only in its first and last presentations; in the others it was abbreviated and transposed. In Torelli's concertos the solo part had virtuoso figuration. Antonio Vivaldi (c. 1669-1741) brought the form to the point at which Bach adopted it. Vivaldi expanded the allegro movements; increased the number of ripieno passages; and sometimes gave material from the main theme to the concertino. His concertinos consisted sometimes of pure virtuoso figuration; sometimes figuration derived from the main theme; and sometimes figuration based on a new melodic idea. (4) <u>The orchestra.</u> The orchestra owed its state of development to Lully. He established the principle of orchestral doubling on a firm basis, and his orchestra was the model on which the larger body of sound could be based. Furthermore, a frequent type of concertino consisted of the trio as employed by Lully in his chaconnes. (5) <u>Rhythm</u>. The upbeat patterns and driving mechanical rhythm was a product of the concerto-allegro style itself and emerged in the concerti of Torelli.

Sonata da Chiesa

The *sonata da chiesa* (church sonata) of the Late Baroque became established as a four movement form (slow-fast-slow-fast). Corelli and the Bologna school played a leading role in the establishment of the Late Baroque form of the church sonata. In Corelli's sonatas the opening slow movement treated the two upper voices imitatively against a running bass. The second movement was a fugal allegro with the bass participating in the imitation The third movement was homophonic, in slow triple meter with a cantabile melody, and in sarabande rhythm (with a strongly emphasized second beat). The final movement was a gigue. Idiomatic string writing is to be found in these sonatas though no great virtuosity is required.

French Overture

The French overture of the Late Baroque was also expanded by means of the episodic techniques which emerged in the late 17th century. This expansion was applied principally to the allegro movements. The overture began with a stately slow movement in dotted rhythm. This was followed by a fugal allegro, often with a slow section at the end. This closing section (or coda) made use of the characteristic dotted rhythm of the French overture and frequently contained actual references to the musical material of the first section. The allegro, in triple meter, was more fully developed in its contrapuntal texture than it had been in Lully's overtures. The French overture had a dual ancestry: (1) The stately dotted rhythm of the adagio movements from the overture of the ballet de cour and (2) the imitative character of the allegro and the over-all concept of the genre emerged from the canzona. The French overture was used frequently as an overture even for Italian operas; it served as the first movement of the orchestral suite; it was used occasionally as the opening movement of the keyboard suite; and it constituted the overture in such major works as Handel's oratorio, *The Messiah.*

Italian Overture

The Italian overture was specifically a product of the Late Baroque period, and its earliest examples were to be found in operas of the Neapolitan school by Alessandro Scarlatti (1660-1725). The order of movements was fast-slow-fast, and the texture was the Baroque homophony governed by the continuo. In form and style the Italian overture was influenced by the concerto. Both the French and Italian overtures existed side by side in the first half of the 18th century, but the French overture was of greater musical significance in this period. The Italian overture, usually called *sinfonia,* was of great historical significance since it was one of the ancestors of the classical symphony which emerged in the second half of the 18th century.

Vocal Forms

The vocal forms of the Late Baroque continued the Baroque tradition of opera, cantata, and oratorio. However, the structures that made up these composite forms were expanded by means of the ritornello technique and were imbued with the harmonic language of the time. The individual sections of the *da capo* aria were expanded to the point where the form tended to become unwieldy. Contrast between recitative and aria was the basis of the structure of the opera and cantata. In the case of the cantata, which was of smaller scope and written for fewer performers than the opera, the overall key scheme was given consideration by the composer. Modulations away from and back to the tonic key was the basis of this structure.

Opera

Opera was the most widespread form of the Late Baroque period ever since the time of Alessandro Scarlatti whose main sphere of activity was in Naples. The Neapolitan style of opera founded by him spread throughout Europe. This opera relied for its effectiveness on the virtuosity of the singer who was expected to add improvised coloraturas (runs, trills, etc.) to the arias. This eventually resulted in a situation whereby the opera became dominated by the singer to the detriment of dramatic considerations. The singers of the period were rigorously trained and among the most famous were the *castrati*, or male sopranos, who were so sought after and idolized that they were able to exert a tyrannical control over opera in a way comparable to the "star" system in Hollywood movies of a recent era. Chorus and orchestra, on the other hand, received little emphasis in these opera scores.

The centers of musical instruction in Naples were the conservatories which were originally orphanages whose inmates were trained to sing sacred choral works. In addition to the tradition of vocal training which these conservatories established, they also preserved the tradition of composition in the *stile antico* in sacred choral music. The vast operatic culture which emerged from this background produced works which are virtually unperformed today because of their dependence on *castrati* parts and because of the abuses to which many of these operas became increasingly subjected in performance.

The chamber cantata (or secular cantata) was by contrast free of the excesses to which much of the operatic literature was subjected, and here vocal skills were used for high artistic purposes. Baroque opera has perhaps been too readily condemned without being thoroughly evaluated. The operas of Handel, a composer of the highest rank, have long been disregarded or cursorily dismissed. All his operas were written to Italian libretti, and their financial failure in his own time was due not so much to artistic considerations as to lack of a public. In England the scandalous collapse of the South Seas Company (1720) brought about the financial ruin of many of the noble class, the class which was the source of the operatic public. The rising mercantile class was not interested in opera in a foreign language.

Libretti

The most important librettists of the Late Baroque were Zeno and Metastasio. Some of Metastasio's libretti received upwards of 50 different settings. Both librettists used the Classical subject matter which dominated opera throughout the Baroque period, but they shifted their emphasis to Ancient history and legend rather than mythology. Some of their subject matter was adapted from the great poets of the Italian renaissance, such as Ariosto, Tasso, and Guarini. Zeno's heroes were noble and rigid; Metastasio's heroes were tragic. In their operas the action was carried by recitative while the arias portrayed feeling. Each scene fell into two parts: the first characterized by action; the second, by the expression of the feelings generated by the action. Arias fell into definite types. Some of these types were: (1) the *aria da bravura* which was a virtuoso showpiece meant to express such violent emotions as passion, revenge, joy or triumph; (2) the *aria di mezzo carattere*, a calm type of aria meant to express the calmer feelings; (3) the *aria cantabile,* a slow aria expressing sad emotions. Conflict of emotions was the chief motivating force of these libretti. A quite frequent figure in Late Baroque opera was the magnanimous ruler who acted to ensure the triumph of justice and virtue. It should be noted that this opera was a court institution so that the performance of an opera depended upon the decision of a ruler, and the audience consisted of those invited by him. Performance based on the sale of tickets to the public still lay in the future. It was intended that the ruler be able to perceive himself as the noble figure portrayed on the stage.

Opera Companies

While the larger courts could afford to stage their own operas, such ostentation was beyond the reach of the petty rulers who, nevertheless, still wished to compete in lavishness. Thus, travelling opera companies arose, companies which could produce operas in the smaller courts without straining the resources of these rulers.

Opera in Vienna

Italian opera spread to Germany where it flourished, especially in the Catholic South. The most important center in Germanic lands was at Vienna under the patronage of the music-loving Hapsburgs; others were at Munich and Dresden. At Vienna the musical level was particularly high - a circumstance due in no small measure to J. J. Fux, whose dramatic power, prodigious contrapuntal mastery, and skilful orchestration kept Viennese opera from the pitfalls of superficiality to which some of the Neapolitan works were prey. Italian artists formed the hard core of the personnel who produced and performed the works. The imperial opera came to an end in 1740 - a date which marks the passing of Baroque opera in Vienna. In Munich Johann Kaspar Kerll (1627-1693) wrote Italian operas as did Johann Adolf Hasse (1699-1783) in Dresden which was the Catholic capital of the Protestant province of Saxony. Hasse was unsurpassed in the esteem of his contemporaries, towering above Bach and Handel in repute. The leading composer of Italian opera in Berlin, the capital of Prussia, was Carl Heinrich Graun (c. 1703-1759).

Italian opera also flourished in England with Bononcini and Handel until the collapse of the South Sea Company sparked the financial difficulties of the nobility. With the end of

patronage by the nobility, English opera companies also came
to ruin.

Opera in North Germany

A public opera house was established in Hamburg in 1678,
and the leading opera composer of that city was Reinhard
Keiser (1647-1739). He was the first composer to write opera
using the German language. A particular characteristic of
German opera to be found in his music was his use of
strophic songs of popular character. He was the most
significant operatic composer in Germany before Hasse. For
many years he managed the Hamburg opera; and the opera
house closed in the year of his death. He had no immediate
successors writing opera to German texts, and the Neapolitan
opera made its influence felt here as in the rest of Europe.

Catholic Church Music

Late Baroque forms and styles made their way into church
music. Catholic church music took on all the paraphernalia of
the period and introduced the affections, the vocal style, the
orchestra, the soloists, and the operatic forms into the church.
The Mass was composed in Baroque style, and the Neapolitan
school occupied a leading role in the production of sacred, as
well as secular music. Side by side with the new style, works
continued to be composed in the *stile antico* - a style that
purported to preserve the conception of Palestrina's style. In
reality the *stile antico* became infused with the harmonic
concepts of the Late Baroque as well as with the affections
though it continued to make use of the forms and contrapuntal
techniques of the Renaissance. Fux was the greatest composer
of Catholic church music in the Late Baroque. He was a
master of Renaissance Mass forms, and his *Missa canonica*
is a tour de force of contrapuntal complexity. At the height of

the ascendancy of Neapolitan opera, counterpoint began to return to music and became a resource of the Late Baroque style.

Lutheran Church Music

In the late 17th century a movement called Pietism became active in the Lutheran Church. It opposed art in the church and ceremony in worship. In music it favored only the simplest kind of devotional songs, preferring the "religion of the heart" to dogma and intellectuality. It tended to undermine the orthodox view which maintained traditional forms and public worship and encouraged the use of choral and instrumental music in the church. Despite the conflict between Orthodoxy and Pietism, influences of Pietist sentiment are found in some of the Orthodox cantata texts. Like the Catholic Church the Orthodox Lutherans made use of all the operatic forms of the Baroque. From the Catholic liturgy the Lutheran church retained the *Missa brevis* (Short Mass), a Mass in which only the Kyrie and Gloria were set to music. (The *Missa brevis* was the starting point for what finally emerged as Bach's Mass in B-minor). Now, however, as the sermon began to be the focal point of the service, the *Missa brevis* declined in use and the church cantata became the most important musical part of the service. The cantata, unlike the musically composed items of the Mass, belonged to the Proper of the service, and thus a different cantata had to be supplied for each date of the church calendar and for each special ceremony, such as a wedding or a funeral.

The Lutheran Church Cantata

The free concertato, that is, the concertato without chorale melodies was common in the music of the late 17th century Lutheran composers. Other forms used were the strophic variation and chorale variation. In the latter of these, successive verses of the chorale were set as vocal variations.

After 1700 the mature Baroque church cantata dominated the field. This form was created by an Orthodox Lutheran pastor from Hamburg, Erdman Neumeister (1671-1756), who described it as consisting of recitatives and arias like "a part of an opera". While the concertato texts had consisted of scriptural words or chorale texts, Neumeister made extensive use of free paraphrase and commentary. To describe the irregular character of this poetry the term *madrigalian* was used, though the form stemmed from the secular cantata rather than from the madrigal. Each of Neumeister's recitatives and arias was designed to express a single affection in characteristic Late Baroque manner.

The Passion in Lutheran Music

Like the church cantata, the Passion took over operatic elements and textual additions. By taking on these textual additions, the Passion began to transcend liturgical limits and began to resemble the oratorio in both form and scope.

Important Composers

The Late Baroque period is climaxed by the work of Johann Sebastian Bach and George Frideric Handel. Though these two names have dominated our view of the period, their contributions were built upon foundations laid by many excellent musicians whose work has only begun to be rediscovered in recent years.

Lutheran Composers

Among the leading Lutheran composers of the late 17th century was Dietrich Buxtehude (c. 1637-1707), organist at St. Mary's Church in the city of Lübeck in northern Germany. He was a performer of such reputation that J. S. Bach traveled many miles on foot to hear him play. His cantatas were of the older, concertato type. Most of them were free concertatos and had an arioso melodic line. Sometimes, he would use the chorale text without its corresponding melody. The free concertato also played a prominent role among the church compositions of Johann Pachelbel (1653-1706), a leading composer in Nuremburg, in Southern Germany. Among the earliest composers of the new reform cantata were Philip Krieger (1649-1725) and J. S. Bach's predecessor at Leipzig, Johann Kuhnau (1660-1722).

Arcangelo Corelli

The earliest composer to cultivate the Late Baroque harmonic counterpoint in his instrumental works was Arcangelo Corelli (1653-1713). The traditional harmony, which emerged in the Late Baroque, emerged at about the same time in Neapolitan opera and in the instrumental music of the Bolognese school; and Corelli stood at the very beginning of this development. He established the Late Baroque style in music and created many works of more than merely historical interest. Trained in Bologna, he represented the Bolognese tradition though the location of his main activity was Rome. He also played an important role in developing violin technique. Though he was a violin virtuoso himself, Corelli eschewed virtuosity for its own sake and exploited the singing qualities of the instrument. The period of his activity coincided with the creation of the greatest instruments of the violin maker Antonio Stradivarius.

Corelli, along with Giuseppe Torelli (1658-1709), established the Baroque concerto form. He created the earliest known examples of the concerto grosso (1682). In his concerti he contrasted the sound of a string trio or a solo violinist with the sound of the entire body of strings. He applied this principle of contrast to the then existing forms of the sonata da chiesa and sonata da camera. Conservative in form, these concerti were progressive in harmony and tonality and in a violinistic style of writing. Among his more famous works are the *Christmas Concerto* (concerto no. 8 of his op. 6) with a pastorale finale. The church concerti were actually performed in church with the High Mass. Another well-known composition of his is the *la Folia* variations for solo violin and continuo. The *Folia* was a stock melody used as the basis for continuous variations by many composers of the late 17th century. Though the variations are treated in the continuous manner of the Late Baroque, they are in a line of tradition (in the use of stock themes for variations) that stems from the Spanish lutenist composers of the early 16th century.

Alessandro Scarlatti

The Neapolitan opera was raised to a position of importance by Alessandro Scarlatti (1660-1725). His output included some 115 operas (of which about 50 have survived) and an enormous number of chamber cantatas (ca. 600). These secular cantatas were to the composer of that day what the string quartet was to a later period. Here, freed of the demands made by the public, the composer could express his own fancy; confide his innermost thoughts; and indulge in harmonic or formal experiments. Of his sacred music 14 oratorios are known, and he is supposed to have written more than 200 Masses. He possessed contrapuntal skill, but his chief preoccupation was beauty of melody expressed through the medium of the singing voice. He brought the Late Baroque to opera and made a clear distinction between recitative - which he endowed with harmonic richness - and aria. The *da capo* aria became of prime importance in his later works. The affections also found expression in his music. His orchestration was colorful, and he was the composer who introduced the Italian overture. Notable was his use of coloraturas in which can be seen the influence of instrumental writing on the voice. His outstanding operas were *Tigrane* (1715) and *Griselda* (1721), the latter on a libretto by Zeno.

Antonio Vivaldi

With Vivaldi (ca. 1676-1741), the center of concerto production shifted to Venice. Ordained a priest (called "the red priest" because of his hair), he devoted himself principally to the composition of concerti grossi. He established the three-movement form (fast, slow, fast) and developed and perfected the internal organization of the allegro movements. He increased the number of returns of the tutti with its main theme and even gave fragments of the main theme to the concertino. Besides concerti grossi he wrote solo concerti. In fact, in his work there is a growing emphasis to be found on the soloist, and he tends to treat even the concertino as a group of soloists. His treatment of the concerto form influenced Bach to such an extent that Bach wrote a group of 16 concerti after Vivaldi, of which six are actual transcriptions of Vivaldi's works. The mechanical beat of the concerto allegro style is firmly established in Vivaldi's works. Vivaldi was fond of whimsical titles for his concerti; *Il Cimento dell'Armonia e dell'Inventione (The Contest between Harmony and Invention)* includes a group of four concerti entitled *Le Stagioni* (The Seasons). For each of the seasons he composed a sonnet and wrote the words underneath the score. With naïve whimsy he depicts storms, bird-calls, brooks, and inebriated weaving about. In the second movement of the concerto entitled "Spring" the violas depict (according to the annotation) the barking of dogs, while a beautiful arioso soars above. These dogs, in true Late Baroque fashion, bark gently but inexorably twice per bar throughout the entire duration of the movement. In his concerti Vivaldi greatly expanded the resources of virtuoso writing for the violin. In addition to his concertos for violin are concertos for flute, oboe, bassoon, horn, and even lute and mandolin. Wide skips, broken chords, scale passages, and outlining of harmonic progressions were all exploited to the utmost. Widely influential in his own time, his music after long neglect has recently seen a revival of public interest.

In addition to his overwhelming production of concerti he wrote operas (about 40) and also church music. Some of the latter has been revived, including a Gloria in F and one in D. Only a very small portion of Vivaldi's music has been published.

Jean-Philippe Rameau (1683-1764)

Jean-Philippe Rameau's contributions were both as a theorist and as an operatic composer. His operas represent a notable climax in the history of French opera. His treatise on harmony (*Traité de l'Harmonie,* 1722) was the first writing on traditional harmony. In it he presented the concept of the fundamental bass (*basse fondamentale)* of a musical composition which consisted of the succession of the roots of the chords - the roots being determined by transposing the chord members so that they were arranged in ascending thirds.

As an operatic composer he stood at the threshold between the serious drama of the Late Baroque and the lightness of the Rococo. His earliest operas were products of his mature period - he wrote his first opera at the age of 50- and represent his greatest achievements in the operatic field. These were the lyric tragedies (*tragédies lyriques*): *Hippolyte et Aricie* (1733), *Castor et Pollux* (1737) and *Dardanus* (1739). Also among his Late Baroque works was the heroic ballet (*ballet héroique*), *Les Indes galantes* (The Gallant Indies, 1735), an opera-ballet

In these operas of the 1730's Rameau put his preoccupation with harmony to significant dramatic use and coupled it with wide-ranging modulations. He continued and built upon the tradition established by Lully. He included significant instrumental programmatic pieces and overtures in his operas and made important contributions to the art of orchestration.

In his keyboard works he summed up and expanded upon the resources of keyboard technique in three books of *Pièces de clavecin* (Harpsichord pieces, 1683-1764). In the French tradition he concerned himself with programmatic (extra-musical) representation.

. . . .

The Late Baroque period produced Georg Frideric Handel and Johann Sebastian Bach, two towering figures whose music has retained an unchallenged position in the present. Their music will be the subject of the next two chapters.

SUMMARY

General Characteristics of the Music

1. National Styles

a. The Italian contribution was: (1) traditional harmony; (2) the concerto-allegro style; (3) concerto and Baroque sonata forms; (4) the Neapolitan opera; and (5) the *bel canto* singing style.

b. The French contribution was: (1) orchestral performance; (2) the French overture; (3) the idealized dance styles; (4) keyboard and lute ornaments; (5) keyboard technique; and (6) programmatic devices.

c. The German style was influenced by both the Italian and the French. It was characterized by harmonic and contrapuntal skill as well as religious fervor.

2. Harmony (traditional harmony)

a. Harmonic materials were organized in terms of chord progression (root changes).

b. The root of a chord was obtained by transposing the chord members to within an octave so that they formed a chain of thirds (the root being the lowest member of the chain).

3. Scales

a. The number of modes was reduced to two (major and minor). These modes, or scales, could be transposed to begin on different pitches.

b. Modulation. Within a given composition the change from a scale based on one pitch to a scale based on another is called modulation. Modulation became an element of musical organization in the Late Baroque period.

4. Interchange of forms and styles between vocal and instrumental media.

a. Vocal forms, such as the aria, were written for instruments.

b. Instrumental forms, such as the passacaglia, were adapted to vocal music, which was also influenced by the concerto.

c. A generalized instrumental style pervaded both instrumental and vocal music. In vocal music it became the basis of the vocal virtuosity of the opera. The *stile antico* (antique style) of vocal writing - a deliberate archaism applied to sacred music - was an exception.

5. Rhythm

a. Strict rhythm. The traditional measure and bar-line used today, characterized by consistent duple or triple meter, was established. The concerto-allegro and dance both contributed to it.

b. The free rhythm of the recitative and the toccata survived from the Early Baroque.

Instrumental Music

1. Instruments

a. The lower instruments of the violin family (the cellos and violas) came into use.

b. the number of wind instruments was reduced, and their construction was standardized as to size and range.

2. Distinction was made between chamber music (one player to a part) and orchestral music (several players to a part).

3. Composite forms (forms of several movements): various composite forms were given a definitive structure in the Late Baroque period.

a. Chamber music forms: (1) sonata da chiesa (church sonata: slow-fast-slow-fast); (2) sonata da camera (chamber sonata: prelude and two or three dance movements); (3) stringed keyboard dance suite (allemande, courante, sarabande, optional group, and gigue).

b. Orchestral music: (1) concerto grosso and solo concerto; (2) Italian overture (The concerto and Italian overture were both products of the Late Baroque period); (3) French overture; (4) orchestral dance suite (a French overture and several modern dances).

4. Forms of single movements or pieces were unified as to melodic material.

a. Ritornello form. This form emerged with the concerto-allegro movement, but it had wide influence. It consisted of periodic returns of a main theme separated by episodes. The returns of the main theme were modified by being abbreviated and transposed. In the concerto the main theme was played by the tutti and the episodes were played by the concertino or soloist as the case might be.

b. Fugue. The fugue applied the ritornello form to the imitative form of the canzona and ricercar. The main theme of the ritornello form was represented by imitative presentations of the fugue subject. The modified and transposed returns of the main theme were represented in the fugue by new imitative combinations of the fugue subject in new keys. Sets of presentations of the fugue subject were separated by episodes.

c. Variation. Late Baroque variations were largely of the continuous type (presentations of a brief theme following each other without pause). In the chaconne the theme was a series of harmonies; in the passacaglia the theme was a bass melody.

d. Toccata (also called fantasia in the Late Baroque period). Merulo's form was infused with Late Baroque tonality and with the affective, dramatic spirit of the Baroque.

e. Two-part dance form. As its name suggests, this form was found in the individual movements of the dance suites. It was based on one melodic idea . It modulated to the dominant at the end of the first part and back to the tonic at the end of the second. The two parts were symmetrically constructed.

Vocal Music

1. Affective Representation

a. In the Late Baroque period affective representation crystallized in a system of melodic and rhythmic figures, choice of keys, choice of instruments, and use of technical devices, such as the ground bass.

b. Each separate movement, such as a chorus or aria, had a single affection.

2. Opera. Neapolitan opera spread throughout Europe.

a. There was strict division between recitative and aria.

b. Aria. The *da capo* aria (three-part form, A-B-A) became the predominant form. The A section was frequently expanded by using the ritornello procedure under the influence of the concerto.

c. Neapolitan opera was dominated by the virtuoso singer.

3. The secular cantata tended to be conceived on a high artistic plane.

a. It was based on recitative and aria (like the opera).

b. It was frequently organized in an over-all key scheme.

4. Catholic church music

a. Catholic church music used recitative and aria in Passions, oratorios and even Masses. The Passion began to transcend liturgical limitations and to resemble the oratorio.

b. The *stile antico* was still used. This style preserved the Renaissance Mass forms and ostensibly the Renaissance vocal style, though inevitably, influences of Late Baroque tonality and dissonance treatment crept in.

5. Lutheran church music

a. Most important was the church cantata which used operatic forms and was related to the Proper of the service, thus requiring a separate cantata for each date of the church calendar.

b. Settings of chorales. The chorale played an important role in all forms of Lutheran church music. Types of chorale settings were (1) the chorale partita, a set of variations on a chorale; (2) the chorale fantasy, a fragmentary treatment of the chorale in a toccata-like setting; (3) the chorale fugue, of which there were two kinds: in one the chorale melody is divided into separate fugue subjects in the manner of a motet, and in the other there is only one subject derived from the chorale melody, but the whole melody is introduced as a cantus firmus in the course of the fugue; and (4) the chorale prelude in which the chorale is presented phrase by phrase while the other voices move in faster rhythms with harmonic or contrapuntal figurations.

CHECK LIST FOR REVIEW

Deists	Age of Enlightenment
Counter-Reformation	Sir Isaac Newton
Versailles	René Descartes
Thirty Years War	John Locke
Pietism	Voltaire
Orthodoxy	Picander
Metastasio	Benedetto Marcello
Erdman Neumeister	J. J. Fux
J. S. Bach	Alessandro Scarlatti
G. F. Handel	Georg Muffat
Guiseppe Torelli	J. F. K. Fischer
Antonio Lotti	Arcangelo Corelli
Johann Kaspar Kerll	Philip Krieger
Johann Adolf Hasse	Antonio Vivaldi
Reinhard Keiser	Johann Kuhnau
Dietrich Buxtehude	Georg Philipp Telemann

Christ lag in Todesbanden
"Cara Sposa"
Rinaldo
Well-Tempered Clavier
Gradus ad Parnassum
Water Music

"Sheep May Safely Graze"
Was mir behagt ist nur die muntre Jagd
La Folia
Tigrane
Griselda

B-minor Mass
Messiah
Missa canonica

Il Cimento dell'Armonia e dell'Inventione
Le quattro stagione

viola
cello
French horn

concerto-allegro
concerto
sonata

seventh chord
harmonic sequence
melodic sequence

recorder
transverse flute

traditional harmony
chord root

episode
scale

modulation
major and minor
equal temperament

toccata
fantasia
fugue

continuous variation
chaconne
chorale fantasia

sonata da chiesa
prelude
passacaglia

Italian overture
concerto grosso
concertino

chorale fugue
chorale prelude
fughetta

obbligato
allemande
courante
corrente
sarabande

gavotte
minuet
bourrée
passapied
rigaudon

anglaise
hornpipe
gigue
giga
hemiola

two-part form
key scheme
bel canto
da capo aria
chamber cantata

stile antico　　　　　　　　*aria di mezzo caraterre*
chorale cantata　　　　　　*aria cantabile*
a cappella　　　　　　　　strophic song
affective representation　　*style galant*
castrato　　　　　　　　　*Missa brevis*
conservatory　　　　　　　church cantata
aria di bravura

LIST OF SCORES

Instrumental Forms

Chorale Prelude

Buxtehude, Dietrich (1637-1707), Chorale preludes: *Nun komm, der Heiden Heiland*, TEM, 41; *Danket dem Herrn denn er ist sehr Freundlich*, NAWM1, 98; *Vater unser im Himmelreich*, HAM2, 190b

Pachelbel, Johann (1653-1706), *Vater unser im Himmelreich*, chorale prelude, HAM2, 190c

Bach, Johann Sebastian (1685-1750), *Vater unser im Himmelreich*, chorale prelude, HAM2, 190d

Toccata

Buxtehude, Dietrich (1637-1707), *Praeludium cum fuga*, organ toccata, HAM2, 234; NAWM, 97

Concerto

Torelli, Guiseppe (1650?-1708), Opus 8, No 8, concerto for violin, HAM2, 246; Op. 8, No. 8 (last movement); Concerto for violin, NAWM1, 94

Vivaldi, Antonio (1680?-1743), Opus 3, No 6 (1st mvt),concerto grosso, strings, HAM2, 270; Concerto grosso in G-minor, Op. 3, No., 2, NAWM1, 95; Op. 9, No. 2 Concerto for violin, NAWM1, 96; *La Primavera,* (Spring) (1st movement), solo concerto *Le Stagioni* (The Seasons), TEM, 47

Scarlatti, Alessandro (1659-1725), Concerto No 3, concerto grosso for strings, HAM2, 260

Keyboard Dance Suite

Fischer, Johann Kaspar Ferdinand (c. 1660-c. 1738), Suite for harpsichord, HAM2, 248

Pachelbel, Johann (1653-1706), *Suite ex gis*, HAM2, 250

Keyboard Preludes, Fugues

Fischer, Johann Kaspar Ferdinand (c. 1660-c. 1738), Prelude & fugue, keyboard, HAM2, 247

Krieger, Johann (1649-1725), ricercar-organ, HAM2, 249a: *Fuga*, fugue- organ, HAM2, 249b

Pachelbel, Johann (1653-1706), *Magnificat fuga*, fugue-organ, HAM2, 251

Buxtehude, Dietrich (1637-1707), *Praeludium*, BUxwv 141, organ prelude, NAWM1, 97

Program Sonata for Harpsichord

Kuhnau, Johann (1660-1722), *Der todtkranke und wieder gesunde Hiskias*, program sonata, harpsichord, HAM2, 261

Sonata da Camera

Corelli, Arcangelo (1653-1713), Opus V, No 8, violin and continuo HAM2, 253

Sonata da Chiesa

Corelli, Arcangelo (1653-1713), Opus V, No 3, sonata da chiesa-vln & orch, HAM2, 252; Opus V, No 8, sonata da camera- vln, HAM2, 253; Sonata da chiesa in E-minor, Op. 3, No. 7, MM, 39; Op. 3, No. 2, Trio sonata, NAWM1, 93
Vitali, Tommaso Antonio (c. 1665-c. 1747), Sonata No 4, trio sonata, vlns & continuo, HAM2, 263
dall' Abaco, Evaristo (1675-1742), Opus 3, No 2, trio sonata for vlns, 2nd movement, HAM2, 269
Leclair, Jean Marie (1697-1764), Opus V, No 12, sonata for violin & continuo, HAM2, 278

French Overture

Cambert, Robert (1628?-1677), Overture to *Pomone*, HAM2, 223
Lully, Jean-Baptiste (1632-1687), Overture to *Alceste*, HAM2, 224; overture to *Armide*, MM, 36; NAM1, 75

Italian Overture

Scarlatti, Alessandro (1659-1725), *Sinfonia avanti l'opera* from *La Griselda* , HAM2, 259; *Sinfonia* to *La Caduta de Decem Viri*, TEM, 44

Vocal Forms

Opera

Bononcini, Giovanni Battista (c. 1672-c.1752), "*Deh lascia, o core*" from *Astianatte*, opera aria, HAM2, 262

Keiser, Reinhard (1674-1739), *"Fahret wohl"* from *Adonis*, opera, duet, HAM2, 267; Aria, *"Hoffe noch"*, from *Croesus*, opera seria, TEM, 46

Rameau, Jean-Philippe (1683-1764), *"Séjour de l'eternelle paix"*-scene from *Castor et Pollux*, opera, MM, 41; *"Ramage des oiseaux "* from *Le Temple de la gloire*, opera scene, HAM2, 276; *"Sommeil"*, *Rondeau tendre* from *Dardanua*, opera-instrumental interlude, HAM2, 277

Graun, Karl Heinrich (1701-1759), *"Godi l'amabile"* from *Montezuma,* opera cavatina (aria), HAM2, 282

Chamber Cantata

Scarlatti, Alessandro (1659-1725), *Mitilde, mio tresore,* HAM2, 258

Marcello, Benedetto (1686-1739), *"Amor tu sei"*, from *Stravaganze d'Amore*, chamber cantata, recitative and aria, TEM, 49

Durante, Francesco (1684-1755), *Fiero acerbo*, chamber duet, HAM2, 273

Sacred

Campra, André (1660-1744), *Cantate Domino*, motet fr 2 solo voices, HAM2, 257

Erlebach, Philipp Heinrich (1657-1714), *Himmel, du weisst meine Plagen*, aria with ritornello, HAM2, 254

Hasse, Johann Adolph (1699-1783), *"Ma giunge appunto"* from *La conversione di Sant' Agostino*, oratorio, recitative, HAM2, 281

Croft, William (1678-1727), *Put me not to rebuke,* verse anthem, HAM2, 268

Greene, Maurice (1696-1755), *Acquaint thyself with God,* verse anthem, HAM2, 279

Music	Political History	Intellectual History	Art
1681 Corelli, Arcangelo, first trio sonatas Beginning of traditional harmony	1682 La Salle sails the Missisippi Philadelphia est. Wm Penn 1682-1725 Peter the Great, r. Russia	1681-82 Dryden, *Absalom and Achitophel*, satiric poem 1682 Forced conversion of 58000 Huguenots	1680 Christopher Wren, St. Mary-le-Bow completed, London
1685 Legrenzi at San Marco Playford, *The Division Violist* 1686 Lully, *Armide*	1685 Revocation of Edict of Nantes 1685-1688 Reign of James II, England	Pierre Bayle, *Thoughts on the Comet of 1680*, against superstition 1687 Newton, *Principia mathematica*	1685 Kneller, *Philip Earl of Leicester*, painting
1689 Steffani, *Richard the Lion-Hearted*, opera Henry Purcell, *Dido and Aeneas*, opera Johann Kuhnau, *Clavier sonatas* 1690 Georg Muffat, *Apparatus musico-organistica*	1689-1725 William and Mary, rulers of England 1692 Salem witchcraft trials	1689 Racine, *Esther*, tragedy 1690 John Locke, An Essay concerning Human Understanding	1689 Hobbema, *Avenue at Middleharnis*
1695 Muffat, *Flori-legium I* Keiser, director of Hamburg opera 1696 Kuhnau, *Frische Klavierfrüchte*	1696 New coinage in England under Locke and Newton	1695 Congreve, *Love for Love*, comedy	1694 Christopher Wren designs Greenwich hospital

Music	Political History	Intellectual History	Art
1697 Campra *l'Europe galante* 1698 Torelli,Violin Concertos, Op. 5 1700 Johann Sebastian Bach at Lüneberg 1701 Muffat, *12 Concerti grossi*		1697 John Dryden, *Alexander's Feast*	1698 Hardouin-Mansart, *Place Vendôme* , Paris
	1700-1746 Philip V , King of Spain 1701-13 Frederick I , King of Prussia	1700 Congreve, *The Way of the World,* comedy 1701 Yale College founded	
1703 Handel at Hamburg 1704 Handel, *St. John Passion* first Bach cantatas Telemann begins Collegium musicum at Leipzig	1703 St. Petersburg founded 1702-14 Queen Anne, r. England War of the Spanish succession aims to extend French power	1704 Daniel Defoe, in prison, begins *The Review,* weekly newspaper	1702 Watteau arrives in Paris 1703 Work begun on Buckingham Palace, London
1706 Rameau, 1st book of clavecin pieces Handel in Italy 1707 Alessandro Scarlatti, *Mitridate eupatore,* opera 1708 Bach at Weimar 1709 1st pianoforte built *opera buffa* in Italy	1706 Charles XII of Sweden defeats Russians and Saxons at Franstadt	1709 *The Tatler* & *The Spectator* founded	1707 Fischer von Erlach, Kollegen-Kirche in Salzburg complete

Music	Political History	Intellectual History	Art
1710 Campra, *Fêtes venitiennes* Handel in England **1711** Keiser, *Croesus*, opera Handel, *Rinaldo*, opera **1713** Fr. Couperin, *Pièces de Clavecin I* **1714** Bach, cantata, *Ich hatte viel Bekümmernis*, **1715** Founding of *opéra comique* A. Scarlatti, *Tigrane*, opera **1716** Handel, *Water Music* Couperin, *L'Art de toucher clavecin* **1717** Bach at Cöthen, *Orgelbüchlein* **1720** Marcello, *Il teatro alla modo*	**1711-1740** Charles VI, Holy Roman Emperor **1713** Peace of Utrecht **1714-27** George I, Handel's patron in Hanover, r. England **1715** Louis XIV dies **1718** Quadruple Alliance, England, France, the Empire, & Holland **1720** Collapse of the South Seas Company	**1710** George Berkeley, *The Principles of Human Understanding* **1711** Alexander Pope, *Essay on Criticism* **1712** Pope, *Rape of the Lock* **1714** Leibniz, *Monadologie* **1715** Alain Lesage, *Gil Blas*	**1710** Sir Christopher Wren, completes St. Paul's Cathedral, London, **1711** Kneller founds London Academy of Arts **1713** Watteau, *L'Indifférent* **1715** Beginning of Rococo **1717** Watteau, *Embarkation for Cytherea*, major Rococo art work

Music	Political History	Intellectual History	Art
1721 Bach, Branden- burg Concer- tos; French & English Suites 1722 Bach, *Well- Tempered Clavier I* Rameau, *Traité de l'harmonie* 1723 Bach, *St. John Passion* 1724 Handel, *Giulio Cesare* 1725 *Concerts spirituel,* Paris, 1st important in- stitution of concerts Johann Fux, *Gradus ad Parnassum* 1726 Vivaldi, *The Seasons* Rameau, *Nouveau système de musique théorique* 1727 Handel, Corona- tion Anthem 1728 Gay and Pepusch, *Beg- gar's Opera* 1729 Bach, *St. Mat- thew Passion*	1724 Paris Bourse opens 1727-60 Handel's patron, the Elector of Hanover, reigns as George II of England	1723 Voltaire, *La Henriade*, epic poem on Henry IV 1726 Jonathan Swift, *Gulliver's Travels*	1724 Figueroa, West entrance, St. Telmo Palace, Seville, Spain 1726-28 Tiepolo, frescoes in the Palace, Udine 1728 Chardin, *Rain*

Music	Political History	Intellectual History	Art
1730 Bach, cantata, *Ein feste Burg* Hasse, *Artaserse*, opera **1731** Bach, *Clavier-übung* Part I			
		1731 Abbé Prévost, *Manon Lescaut* **1732** Voltaire, *Zaïre*	**1731** Hogarth, *Harlot's Progress*
1733 Giovanni Pergolesi, *La Serva padrona* **1734** Bach, *Christmas Oratorio* Tartini, Sonatas Op. 1 for violin	**1733** Founding of Georgia War of the Polish Succession		**1734** Boucher, *Rinaldo and Armida*
1735 Rameau, *Les Indes galantes*	**1735** William Pitt elected member of Parliament	**1735** Linnaeus, *Systema naturae*, origin of the modern system of classifying plants and animals	**1735** Hogarth, *A Rake's Progress*
1736 Handel, *Alexander's Feast* **1737** Rameau, *Castor et Pollux*, opera Domenico Scarlatti, first published sonatas San Carlo Opera established in Naples	**1736-39** Russo-Turkish war	**1737** First lodge of Masons in Germany	**1737** Boucher, designs for Beauvais tapestries
1738 D. Scarlatti, *Essercizi*, (sonatas) Bach, B-minor Mass Handel., oratorios: *Saul; Israel in Egypt; Serse*		**1738** Methodist Church founded by Wesley and Whitefield	**1738** Chardin, *La Gouvernante*

Music	Political History	Intellectual History	Art
1739 Handel, *Concerti grossi* Mattheson, *Der vollkommene Kapellmeister*	1739 Turks threaten Belgrade, Emperor Charles VI signs treaty 1740-48 War of the Austrian Succession 1740-86 Reign of Frederick the Great, of Prussia	1739 David Hume, *A Treatise of Human Nature* 1740 Samuel Richardson, *Pamela*, first novel	1740 Giovanni Tiepolo, *Triumph of Amphitrite*
1741 Gluck, *Artaserse*, opera 1742 Bach, *Goldberg Variations* for 2-manual harpsichord Handel, *Messiah*, oratorio, performed at Dublin C.P.E. Bach, *Prussian Sonatas* for piano	1740-96 Age of Enlightened Despots 1742-45 Charles VII, Holy Roman Emperor	1741 Voltaire, *Mahomet*, tragedy	1741 Boucher, *Autumn*
1743 Handel. *Samson*, oratorio 1744 C.P.E. Bach, *Württemberg Sonatas*, piano 1745 Gluck in England Johann Stamitz at Mannheim 1746 Handel, *Judas Maccabeus*	1746-1759 Ferdinand I of Spain	1743 Voltaire, *Mérope*	1746 Boucher, *Toilet of Venus*

Music	Political History	Intellectual History	Art
1747 Handel, *Joshua* 1749 Rameau, *Zoroastre* Bach, *Art of Fugue* 1750 Quantz, Flute Concertos		1748 Montesquieu, *The Spirit of Law* Voltaire, *Zadoc* Klopstock, *Der Messias* 1750 Fielding, *Tom Jones* George Buffon, *Histoire naturelle*	1747 Fredrick the Great's castle at Potsdam, *Sans souci*

George Frideric Handel (1685-1759). From a painting in the Metropolitan Museuam of Art. (After Bukofzer, Music in the Baroque Era.)

Johann Sebastian Bach (1685-1750) From a painting by Elias Gottlieb Hauptmann. (After Bukofzer, Music in the Baroque Era).

CHAPTER XI

JOHANN SEBASTIAN BACH

BIOGRAPHY

The culmination of the German Baroque in all its religious fervor is to be found in the works of Johann Sebastian Bach (1685-1750). As organist and director of church music, the greater part of his output consisted of keyboard works and cantatas. In both of these categories the Lutheran chorale played a vital role.

Coming from a family of musicians and living in the Thuringian environment where music flourished, Bach was able to draw on all the masters of Europe for his musical precepts. Copies of works by Italian, French, and German masters are found in his handwriting and encompass the Baroque period from Frescobaldi (1583-1643) to Bach's own contemporaries. Bach's professional lineage can be traced to Hans Bach, called "the minstrel" (d. 1626), son of the miller Veit Bach (d. 1619). J. S. Bach was of the third generation of composers of the Bach name, and among his own offspring there were also eminent composers. Bach was born in Eisenach, home of the Wartburg castle where the famed "battle of song" of the Minnesingers had taken place in the 13th century and where, in the 16th century, Martin Luther had flung an ink pot at a vision of the devil. Music and religion were to dominate the life of Johann Sebastian Bach, a giant among giants in the field of musical composition.

At 15 Bach was singing in the choir of St. Michael's school in Lüneburg where the repertoire included works by Lassus, Heinrich Schütz, and Monteverdi. Prominent among his early influences was the organist of St. John's in Lüneburg, Georg Böhm, noted for the originality and expressiveness of his music. Böhm influenced Bach to visit Hamburg to hear Johann Adam Reinken and also to visit the city of Celle where he became familiar with the music of the French composer Couperin. At Lüneburg he became acquainted with the music of such Italian masters as Monteverdi, Carissimi, and Frescobaldi. Lüneburg proved to be a fruitful experience for a young and eager musician. It was a place where he could become familiar with much music from varied sources.

Bach soon acquired a reputation as an organist and at the age of 18 was offered a post in a church at Arnstadt. It was here that compositions of his had their first performances. He now became familiar with the works of the leading organist of North Germany, Dietrich Buxtehude. Bach was granted a four weeks leave for the express purpose of visiting Buxtehude in Lübeck. So fascinated was he by the cantatas and organ works of the northern master that he stayed four months. He was especially impressed by Buxtehude's cantatas which emphasized melodic richness and simplicity of structure.

At Weimar, where Bach took a position in 1714, he became friendly with his talented relative, Johann Gottfried Walther, who later became author of the first musical dictionary of biography, bibliography, and terms (1732). Walther had a tremendous contrapuntal facility and Bach's work at this time showed the influence of his canons. At the same time Italian concertos were being circulated with great enthusiasm among musicians throughout Europe, and both Bach and Walther made many transcriptions of concerti by Vivaldi.

By his contemporaries Bach was known chiefly as a fabulous organ virtuoso. And indeed records of his instructions for rebuilding an organ at Mühlhausen show how early in his career his grasp of organ construction was already unsurpassable. A description of his conducting at Leipzig attests to the facility with which he played and directed while singing whatever part needed his support at the moment. A notable instance of recognition during his lifetime came from Frederick the Great, an accomplished musician in his own right. This ruler invited Bach as an old man to come and play for him and improvise on a theme provided by him. On his return to Leipzig where he was then employed, Bach wrote *The Musical Offering* (*Das musikalisches Opfer*, 1747) dedicated to Frederick the Great, which included a setting of the royal theme.

Bach's compositions received little recognition from his immediate successors who favored the lighter, rococo style. Haydn and Mozart became familiar with his works in their later period. Wider public recognition dates from the performance of the *St. Matthew Passion* under the direction of Felix Mendelssohn at the *Singakademie* in Berlin on March 11, 1829. This was the first performance of the work since Bach's death in 1750.

Bach achieved a universality of expression while devoting himself within the narrow confines of his own church and meeting the demands of his own immediate surroundings without consciously aiming at the larger public.

BACH'S WORKS

First Period, Arnstadt and Mühlhausen

It is customary to consider Bach's works in terms of five periods. In the first, he was a church organist at Arnstadt (1703-7) and Mühlhausen (1707-8) - both cities in Thuringia. The works of this period show influences of various composers such as Pachelbel, Buxtehude, and Kuhnau. The most mature of these works is the cantata *Actus tragicus* or *Gottes Zeit* (*God's Time is Best*), a funeral cantata. Like the concertato it is continuous in structure without recitatives and without the contrast that the division into recitative and aria gave to the later cantata. In it death is presented not as cause for grief, but as an occasion for renewal of faith in God and submission to His will. To set off this concept more effectively, it is contrasted with a quotation from *Ecclesiasticus* (by Jesus ben Sirach - <u>not</u> *Ecclesiastes* and not part of the Lutheran Scriptures)-: "It is the ancient law, all men must die". The inexorable character of the text is illustrated musically by its being treated in strict contrapuntal structure, and the text is set to a fugue subject with a precipitous descent outlining a diminished 7th. Against this fugue a chorale enters representing Christianity, first sounded by recorders and then sung by the soprano to the words "O come Lord Jesus". Then follows a duet framed between two choral numbers entrusting to the Lord the spirit of the departed, first in the words of the Old Testament (Ps. 31) and then using Luther's version of the *Nunc dimittis*. Though lacking the structural organization of his later cantatas, this work is full of youthful spirit and beauty.

Early Maturity - Weimar

Bach's second period coincides with his service as court organist and later concert-master of the orchestra in the petty principality of Weimar (1708-1717). At that court French and Italian influences reached him. He now applied the German contrapuntal skill he had already acquired to themes which, in their concise structure and strong tonality, showed the stamp of Italian influence. He copied Frescobaldi's *Fiori musicali* here and wrote a Variation-Canzona in D-minor on a theme derived from this work. This period sets Bach forth primarily as the great organist - a virtuoso and composer for his favorite instrument. Many of his great organ works stem from this period of his early maturity, especially those not dependent on chorale melodies. He also began to write cantatas using Neumeister's texts - cantatas in which he followed that writer's precepts. Among the organ works dating from this period are the D-minor Toccata and Fugue and the C-minor Passacaglia. The D-minor Toccata and Fugue is one of Bach's most popular organ works. In its passion and exuberance as in its rather loosely organized form it is characteristic of his earlier work. The toccata blends into the fugue without articulation and the fugue dissolves in turn into toccata-like figurations. The C-minor Passacaglia is one of his great organ works.

The Duke of Weimar was a deeply religious man of ascetic character, and the court atmosphere was one which Bach found sympathetic to his own aspirations. It was here that he became intimately associated with his relative Johann Gottfried Walther. Involvement in family quarrels between the reigning Duke and his nephew and heir who was Bach's pupil finally resulted in Bach's seeking a new position. His being in official disfavor in Weimar seems to have been the cause of the very superficial treatment he received in Walther's Lexicon.

Third Period - Cöthen, Secular Music

Bach's third period coincides with his next position as court conductor to the Prince of Anhalt-Cöthen, another tiny principality. Since the state religion here was reformed, or Calvinistic, church music was of the simplest kind; and Bach was now to be concerned with secular music for the next six years (1717-1723). He was not called upon to perform on the organ or to produce church cantatas here, and thus he produced much chamber music, orchestral music, and music for stringed keyboard instruments. Much of this keyboard music was intended for teaching purposes. It was while he was negotiating for his departure from Weimar - a negotiation which resulted in much bitterness and even led to a month's sojourn in jail - that Bach went to Dresden to hear the famous French organist, Louis Marchand, whose compositions he had long admired. There is an unsubstantiated story that when it became known that Bach was in Dresden, a competition on the clavier was arranged between him and Marchand, a competition at which Marchand failed to appear because he was overawed by Bach's reputation as a performer. The story, true or not, is evidence of Bach's reputation as a virtuoso.

At Cöthen Bach was held in high esteem by a patron who was an accomplished musician and one of deep understanding. His position here afforded him the highest social standing he ever achieved. It was here that he wrote the great secular instrumental works, such as the *Brandenburg Concerti* (a set of six concerti grossi, dedicated to Duke Christian Ludwig of Brandenburg); violin sonatas; and two orchestral suites. One of the most famous compositions of this period is "The Great" G-minor Fantasy and Fugue for organ which Bach composed for an audition in Hamburg where he was competing for a church post. Most important to him were his compositions written for teaching purposes - a side of his work which lay in the family tradition. He had sons of genius whose education was of great importance to him. These teaching pieces were, of course, music of the highest calibre and were intended, not merely as exercises to train performing skill, but to teach the principles of composition as well - a fact which Bach mentioned specifically in the introduction to his Two- and Three- Part Inventions. The origin of the term is rather obscure as is the form itself which is based on invertible counterpoint. These

Inventions were written at Cöthen as was Book I of his collection of preludes and fugues known as *Das Wohltemperiertes Clavier* (The Well-Tempered Clavier). The *Orgelbüchlein* (Little Organ Book) contained settings of chorales with the melody almost always in the soprano and with three obbligato voices in strict counterpoint. The obbligato voices used figures independent of the chorale melody, but they were unified by the consistent use of the chosen figure. The choice of accompaniment figure was frequently dictated by the affection of the text. For example, in the chorale prelude *Durch Adams Fall* (By Adam's Fall) the fall is represented by the descent of a diminished fifth, and a chromatically winding inner voice represents the snake. The *Clavierbüchlein* (Little Clavier Book) for Wilhelm Friedemann Bach (his eldest son) was also written at Cöthen.

The Inventions and especially The Well-Tempered Clavier are the major didactic works. The latter collection was designed to illustrate the practicability of writing in the twelve major and twelve minor keys - a feat made possible by the scale of equal temperament as set forth by Werckmeister. The Well-Tempered Clavier presents a great variety of forms and styles; yet each prelude is unified within itself by the consistent employment of a chosen figure; and each fugue is unified by its subject. The term *clavier* is a general term for any keyboard instrument, and though the influence of various instrumental styles is to be found, such as organ, stringed keyboard, etc., no attempt is made to specify which instrument is meant.

Concerti and Sonatas

The *Brandenburg Concerti*, six in number, represent artistic climaxes in the form evolved by Vivaldi. In his violin and cello sonatas Bach dispensed with the keyboard accompaniment and figured bass which served only to fill out the harmony. The arpeggio (broken chord) technique was used here to construct true contrapuntal pieces for solo instrument - pieces in which both harmony and counterpoint are clearly delineated. It was the kind of challenge that called forth the highest creative powers of the master. Among the forms represented in these sonatas are the sonata da chiesa (sonatas for solo violin); dance suite (six Cello Suites) in which the traditional form found in the keyboard works is strictly maintained; and the partitas for Solo Violin which are rather free collections of dances. The Second Partita contains the famous Chaconne in D-minor, a set of continuous variations whose theme is a set of harmonies.

Fantasy and Fugue in G-minor

The Fantasy and Fugue in G-minor was one of the few organ works of the period. After the death of his first wife, Maria Barbara, Bach felt the need of returning to church music, and this composition was written for the audition at Hamburg. The Fantasy is a rhapsodic toccata in the North German style, but organized in the form established by Merulo, that is, an alternation between free passages (based on chords and scales) and contrapuntal passages. Bach further unified the Fantasy by having the contrapuntal passages based on the same musical material. The Fantasy, passionate and dramatic in utterance, is still bound together by a sense of construction that never fails. The fugue theme is striking in character and joyful in feeling; the theme is long but unified by a recurrent motive; and the fugue itself is extended but well organized.

Dance Suites

Bach's best known set of keyboard suites, the French Suites, also date from the Cöthen period. They represent the purest examples of the keyboard dance suite. The orchestral suites of the period are also typical of the form beginning with a French overture and continuing with a set of contemporary dances, *"galanteries"*. Bach, in the German tradition, developed the contrapuntal section of the overture into a full-blown fugue. One of the orchestral suites, written at a later period, (The Suite in D-major, No. 4) contains the celebrated air known in transcription as the "Air for the G-string". Such transcriptions are relics of a time when it was felt necessary to "improve" the works of such masters as Bach by transcribing them - an attitude now happily replaced by desire for more authenticity of sound.

The marriage of Bach's patron to a woman who did not share her husband's interest in music, in addition to Bach's grief at the death of his own wife, finally led to Bach's departure from Cöthen. As was customary, Bach soon remarried. His new wife was Anna Magdalena, daughter of a court trumpeter. She was an excellent soprano singer and likewise an excellent wife for Bach.

Fourth Period - Leipzig

Bach's musical output in Leipzig was dominated by his cantatas of which he had to supply one for each week of the church year. The chorale cantata became his chief vehicle. It was a form which grew out of the chorale concertato of the 17th century, but differed from it in the fact that it used recitatives and arias and that the texts of these operatic forms paraphrased the chorale texts instead of using them literally. A transitional work is the well-known Easter cantata, *Christ lag in Todesbanden* (Christ Lay in the Bonds of Death, No. 4), probably begun in Weimar and revised in Leipzig. The text uses Luther's words unchanged, and each number is a variation of the chorale melody. Likewise, there are no recitatives. However, the organization shows the over-all grasp of structure characteristic of Bach's mature work. Choral numbers come at the beginning, middle, and end; duets just after the beginning and just before the end; and solos before and after the middle chorus. Thus, the whole structure is in the shape of an arch dominated by the central chorus. Each number is based on a single affection. The repetition of the opening motive of the chorale (a descending minor second) gives poignancy to the words "O'er death no man could prevail" because it is coincident with the "sigh" motive of Late Baroque affective representation. The whole atmosphere of the cantata is one of deep seriousness and profundity.

Wachet auf *(No. 140)*

The cantata *Wachet auf* is in a different mood and is also more typical of the mature chorale cantata since (1) it makes use of the contrast between recitative and aria, and (2) its text is a paraphrase of the original chorale text. Typically, also, it opens with a complex setting of the chorale melody and closes with a simple four-part setting of the same melody. In its central number the chorale melody is sung by the tenors in unison to the text "Zion hears the watchmen's voices" (in Troutbeck's translation) while the violins have a caressing feminine melody representing the procession of virgins going to meet the bridegroom. The subject of the text is the New Testament parable of the Ten Virgins as told in Nicolai's hymn. The text also borrows many figures and images from the Song of Songs whose tender vernal aura is evoked by Bach's music. The three choruses use the words of three verses of the chorale while the recitatives and arias borrow material from the other verses. It should be understood that Bach. himself did not compose chorales. The chorale to him was what Gregorian chant was to Catholic music - a body of traditional melodies of sacred character.

Secular Cantatas

During his lifetime Bach wrote five sets of compositions for every day of the church year. Many are lost, but some 190 sacred cantatas are extant. In addition, there are some two dozen secular cantatas known. Though they are by no means inferior works, they have received comparatively little attention except for one or two selections, such as the lovely aria mentioned above known in English as "Sheep May Safely Graze". Because of their folk-song character, one or two of the pieces from the "Peasant Cantata" (*Mer hahn ein neue Oberkeet)* have appeared in children's song books. The secular cantatas are Bach's closest approach to opera, and they include both humorous and dramatic works several of which are masterpieces. In *Der Streit zwischen Phoebus und Pan* (The Contest between Phoebus and Pan, No. 201) he equates the judge of the contest (who with ill-conceived judgement preferred Pan's playing and was given donkey's ears as a result) with the critic Scheibe who thought Bach's music was too old-fashioned.

Larger Choral Works

Four great choral works crown Bach's output of vocal music in Leipzig: the *St. John Passion*; the *Magnificat* (1723); the *St. Matthew Passion* (1729); and the *Mass in B-Minor* (1733-38). Of these the last two are the most famous of his large choral works.

St Matthew Passion

The *St. Matthew Passion* was conceived on a larger scale than any of Bach's other works, and the composer attached great importance to it. It requires the largest number of performers of any of Bach's works: two mixed choruses; two orchestras; a choir of boy singers for the chorale sung in the

Since Augustus III was Catholic, Bach conceived the idea of writing a complete setting of the Mass - a setting which was not completed until much later and probably never performed in its entirety during Bach's lifetime. Its vast dimensions - it requires some two hours to perform - makes it unsuitable for liturgical purposes. The *B-minor Mass* was the only one of Bach's religious works that ventured beyond the confines of a specific church service and sought to transcend denominational limitations. There are many notable features which might be mentioned. The striking contrast which presents itself so vividly between the two movements of the *Crucifixus* and the *Resurrexit* is breathtaking in its impact and derives its power from the unity of affection which characterizes each of the movements. A mysticism with ancient roots reveals itself in the use of number symbolism. Bach used the system of numbering the letters of the alphabet and using the sum thus obtained to represent a given word. By applying this system to the word *credo* we get the number 43, and the word *credo* appears 43 times in Bach's *credo* movement. The thirteen appearances of the ground bass in the *Crucifixus* represent the perverse fate associated with the number thirteen. Though this movement was adapted from Cantata No. 12 (*Weinen, Klagen*), the sudden modulation to a major key at the end (signifying redemption) was an inspiration which occurred to Bach in applying the movement to this Mass. The *Dona nobis pacem* (Grant us peace) and the *Gratias agimus tibi* (We thank Thee) use the same music; thus Bach thanks the Almighty for peace which, he has faith, will be granted. The *Dona nobis pacem* is the central movement of the Mass. In two parts of the *Credo* (the opening *Credo in unum Deum* and the *Confiteor*) Bach introduces Gregorian canti fermi to underline the significance of the texts and emphasize the unity of Christian tradition which they represent.

The Clavierübung

The *Clavierübung* (lit, "Keyboard Exercise"), published in four parts from 1731-1739, includes harpsichord and organ music as follows:

Part I: Six *Partitas* (dance suites) for harpsichord.

Part II: The *Italian Concerto* (a composition in the Baroque concerto form) and the *French Overture* (in form similar to the orchestral dance suite), both for harpsichord.

Part III: A group of organ chorales introduced by the Prelude in E-flat and ending with the Fugue in E-flat ("St. Anne") also for organ, and four duets for harpsichord or clavichord.

Part IV: The *Goldberg Variations*, an extended set of variations for harpsichord with two manuals.

The dance movements of the compositions in the *Clavierübung* are the ultimate in stylization and are far removed from actual dances. The *Partitas* are among the most modern sounding of Bach's works with their more regular phrasing; idiomatic harpsichord style; and hints of thematic contrast. In the *Italian Concerto* the concerto form is transferred to the harpsichord and uses the two manuals to reproduce the contrasts called for by the juxtaposition of tutti and concertino. The *Goldberg Variations* were a set of 30 variations on a sarabande and were written for Bach's pupil, the harpsichordist Johann Gottlieb Goldberg. These variations, as well as the *Italian Concerto* and the *Partitas,* illustrate how the comparatively undifferentiated instrumental style of Bach's earlier keyboard music gave way to a more idiomatic harpsichord style which took full advantage of the two manuals; used crossed hand techniques; and used

Reliqua Canonica Arte Resoluta (By Order of the King, the Theme and Other Material Realized in a Canonic Style) appears on the King's copy. It is an acrostic on the word RICERCAR. Bach's last composition, *The Art of Fugue* left unfinished at his death, was another of his didactic works in which he set out to exploit to the fullest the possibilities of fugal composition on a single theme. At the end of the unfinished last fugue the name B-A-C-H is spelled out in music by the notes B-flat (B in German), A, C, and H (B-natural in German terminology). The whole work has been compared to a gigantic variation ricercar in which each section is expanded to the dimensions of a complete fugue. It is thus a series of fugues on a single subject in which the subject is varied from fugue to fugue, and the fugues themselves become increasingly more complex.

Bach wrote great music within the framework of his duties as church composer and composer of didactic works. With his passing an era came to a close. The succeeding generation sought music of a light entertaining character and, like the critic Scheibe, found Bach's music old-fashioned in its heaviness and complexity. Bach drew on the whole of the Baroque period for his background; and among copies found in his own handwriting for his own studies are included works of such an Early Baroque composer as Girolamo Frescobaldi, as well as works of his own contemporaries and those of the preceding generation. His greatness lies in the intrinsic value of his music. He absorbed the French and Italian styles as well as the style of his own countrymen. His craftsmanship in contrapuntal technique was unapproachable and based upon a solid harmonic foundation.

While his music was neglected by his immediate successors, some 30 years after the death of the master, Mozart became familiar with the music of J. S. Bach at the Sunday morning musicales at the home of the cultured Baron van Swieten in Vienna. Its influence can most clearly be seen in Mozart's C-minor Mass, K. 427. The first important public revival of Bach's music took place 80 years after his death with a performance of the St. Matthew Passion in 1829 under the direction of the famous composer Felix Mendelssohn. Since then, throughout the first half of the 20th century, Bach's music has remained a vital influence on the music of each succeeding generation of composers. The neo-classic movement of the first half of the 20th century was largely a neo-Bachian movement. Witness such compositions as Piston's Chromatic Study on the Name of Bach; Villa-Lobos' *Bachianas Brasilieras* (Bach-like Music in the Brazilian Manner); Stravinsky's *Dumbarton Oaks* Concerto (a composition in concerto grosso form); and works by Paul Hindemith, such as *Ludus tonalis* (a collection of preludes and fugues for pianoforte). The continuing presence of his works on concert programs attest to his present significance on the broader cultural scene.

SUMMARY

The periods into which Bach's works are customarily divided are identified by the positions which he held:

1. <u>Arnstadt</u> <u>and</u> <u>Mühlhausen</u> (1703-1708) two towns where Bach was employed as a church organist. At this time his music showed influences of Pachelbel, Buxtehude, and Kuhnau. The most mature work of this period was the funeral cantata *Gottes Zeit (Actus tragicus)*. This work was continuous in structure, without division into recitative and aria, and was reminiscent of the concertato.

2. <u>Weimar</u> (1708-1717) where Bach was court organist and concert master of the orchestra. This was the period of his early maturity. French and Italian influences reached him here

Der Streit zwischen Phoebus Und Pan (*The Contest between Phoebus and Pan*, secular cantata)

galanteries	Georg Böhm
chorale cantata	Johann Adam Reinken
Missa brevis	Francois Couperin
concerto-allegro	Johann Gottfried Walther
trio sonata	Louis Marchand
ricercar	Christoph Graupner
longer and shorter catechism	C. P. E. Bach
dance suite	Franz Joseph Haydn
Wolfgang Amadeus Mozart	Felix Mendelssohn

Piston, *Chromatic Study on the Name of Bach*

Villa-Lobos, *Bachianas brasilieras*
Stravinsky, *Dumbarton Oaks* Concerto

Hans Bach	Frederick the Great
Veit Bach	Prince Leopold of Anhalt Cöthen
Maria Barbara Bach	Augustus the Strong, King of
Anna Magdalena Bach	Poland and Elector of Saxony
Baron van Swieten	

Eisenach	Mühlhausen
St. Michael's at Lüneburg	Weimar
Arnstadt	Cöthen
Lübeck	St. Thomas in Leipzig

LIST OF SCORES

(Note: Bach's works are widely available. The works listed below are those which are included in the same anthologies which contain the other works noted at the end of each chapter.)

From Cantata No. 4: chorale, *Christ lag in Todesbanden*, MM 46; chorus, *"Es war ein wunderlicher Krieg"*, MM 48

Chorale prelude, *"Christ lag in Todesbanden"*, MM 47

From the oratorio, *St. Matthew Passion*, arioso for alto solo, *"Ach Golgotha"* , MM 49

From *Die Kunst der Fuge*, *"Contrapunctus III"* , fugue, MM 50

Cantata: *Nun komm, der Heiden Heiland*, NAWM1,90

From *Mass in B-minor:* *"Credo"* (Nicene Creed), NAWM1,91; *"Et in Spiritum sanctum Dominum"*,NAWM1, 91a; *"Confiteor"*,NAWM1, 91b; *"Et expecto resurrectionem"*, NAWM1,91c

Chorale melody, *Durch Adams Fall*, BWV637, NAWM1 99a ; Chorale prelude, NAWM1 99b

Music	Political History	Intellectual History	Art
1723 Bach, *St. John Passion* **1724** Handel, *Giulio Cesare*, opera **1725** *Concerts spirituel*, Paris Fux, *Gradus ad Parnassum*, species counterpoint **1726** Vivaldi, *The Seasons* Rameau, *Nouveau système de musique théorique*, treatise on harmony **1727** Handel, *Coronation Anthem* **1728** Gay and Pepusch, *Beggar's Opera* Bach, cantata, *Ein feste Burg* **1729** Bach, *St. Matthew Passion*; **1730** Bach, cantata, *Ein feste Burg* Hasse, opera, *Artaserse* **1731** Bach, *Clavierübung* Part I **1733** Giovanni Pergolesi, *La Serva padrona*	**1724** Paris Bourse opens **1727-60** George II King of England **1731** Treaty of Vienna between England, Holland Spain, & the Empire **1733** Founding of Georgia War of the Polish Succession	**1723** Voltaire, *La Henriade*, epic poem on Henry IV **1726** Jonathan Swift, *Gulliver's Travels* **1731** Abbé Prévost, *Manon Lescaut* **1732** Voltaire, *Zaïre*	**1724** Figueroa, West entrance, St. Telmo Palace, Seville, Spain **1726-28** Tiepolo, frescoes in the Palace, Udine **1728** Chardin, *Rain* **1731** Hogarth, *Harlot's Progress*

Music	Political History	Intellectual History	Art
1734 Bach, *Christmas Oratorio* Tartini, Sonatas Op. 1 for violin			**1734** Boucher, *Rinaldo and Armida*
1735 Rameau, *Les Indes galantes*, opera-ballet	**1735** W. Pitt elected to Parliament	**1735** Linnaeus, *Systema naturae*, origin of the modern system of classifying plants and animals	**1735** Hogarth, *A Rake's Progress*
1736 Handel, *Alexander's Feast*, secular oratorio	**1736-39** Russo-Turkish war		
1737 Rameau, *Castor et Pollux*, opera Domenico Scarlatti, first published sonatas San Carlo Opera opens, Naples		**1737** First lodge of Masons in Germany	**1737** Boucher, designs for Beauvais tapestries Chardin, *La Gouvernante*
1738 D. Scarlatti, *Essercizi*, sonatas Bach, B-minor Mass Handel, oratorios: *Saul, Israel in Egypt, Serse*		**1738** Methodist Church founded by Wesley & Whitefield	
1739 Handel, *Concerti grossi* Mattheson, *Der vollkommene Kapellmeister*	**1739** Turks threaten Belgrade, Emperor Charles VI signs treaty	**1739** David Hume, *A Treatise of Human Nature*	
	1740-46 War of the Austrian Succession **1740-86** Frederick the Great, King of Prussia **1740-96** Age of Enlightened Despotism	**1740** Richardson, *Pamela*, first novel	**1740** Giovanni Tiepolo, *Triumph of Amphitrite*
1741 Gluck, *Artaserse*, opera		**1741** Voltaire, *Mahomet*, tragedy	**1741** Boucher, *Autumn*

h
Bach,
Var
Hand
, or
for
C.P.E
Prus
tas
Hand
son,
C.P.E
Wür
Son
Gluck
Engl
Johan
at M
Hande
Mac
orat
Bach,
Off
Fred
Grea
Hand
Bach,
Fug
Rame
ast
Quar
Con

ixty
ndel
side
heres
ance,
usic
ang,
The
for
del's
into
ment
dy of
nters
sses
ese
itled
Bach
nost
very

recently, Handel's operas met the same fate as the rest of the immense production of Baroque opera.

Handel, unlike Bach, came from a non-musical family but showed musical talent early and received thorough instruction from Zachow, a Halle organist. After a year at the University of Halle, he resigned to go to the brilliant cultural center of Hamburg not, like Bach, to listen to the organ playing of Reinken, but to become familiar with opera. In Hamburg he was influenced chiefly by Reinhard Keiser. The secular music there was influenced more by French and Italian practices than was the church music which retained its German character. At one point Handel presented himself as a candidate for a position as church organist, but secular music finally won out. After leaving Hamburg, he went to Italy in 1706 to visit the important musical centers there. In Venice he was influenced by Caldara, Legrenzi, and Lotti. He also visited Florence, Rome, and Naples. The influence of the Italian *bel canto* provided the finishing touches to the development of his style. He had previously mastered counterpoint and harmony and even absorbed some Italian influence through his training and experience at Hamburg. By the end of his three years in Italy Handel was already famous; one of his operas (*Agrippina*) having been performed 27 times.

England

Between the time he left Italy and the time he took up residence in England where his work attained the peak of maturity, he spent a short time at the court of the Elector of Hanover where he was appointed court conductor in 1710. From this position he took leave and returned to it only very briefly. In 1712 he went to England, ostensibly for a short visit. He overstayed his leave, and in the meantime his master, the Elector of Hanover, came to England as King

George I in 1714. This circumstance caused Handel some embarrassment, but evidence shows that the King was a great admirer of Handel's music. Handel is known to have composed and conducted a suite for wind instruments to be played on a barge on the Thames in honor of the King. A selection of these pieces consisting of a French overture and a group of dances was published as the *Water Music* (composed in 1715).

When Handel first went to England, Italian opera was thriving there under the patronage of the nobility. His first operas there were influenced by Alessandro Scarlatti and Steffani. His early opera *Rinaldo*, based on Tasso's epic of the First Crusade, scored a great success in 1711. Two arias from it are especially famous: the *"Lascia ch'io pianga"* (Let me Weep) and *"Cara sposa"* (Dear Wife). Stylized dance rhythms characterize these two arias. A joint stock company was formed by a group of nobles for the purpose of presenting Italian operas; and Handel and Bononcini, who became arch rivals, were its chief composers. Rivalry between leading sopranos also added to the difficulties though, nonetheless, Handel wrote some of his most important operas for this company- operas, such as *Giulio Cesare* (Julius Caesar, 1724) and *Rodelinda* (1725).

Decline of Opera in England

The power of the English nobility, however, was declining before the rising wealth and power of the middle class. The nobility were the only group with which opera in a foreign language could flourish. Their decline was hastened by the disastrous machinations of the South Seas Company, authorized by the government in 1711 to finance the War of the Spanish Succession. This company was authorized to assume the national debt in return for being allowed a monopoly on British trade with islands of the South Seas and

Arias are usually based on a single affection and are influenced by stylized dance rhythms and the concerto type of vocal technique. They are generally in *da capo* (A B A) form but also include influences of the concerto form. Stylized dance rhythms include the siciliano, bourrée, allemande, gavotte, courante, and minuet. The siciliano is used to represent idyllic affections, but is also used to represent inner conflicts. Rhythms of the bourree, allemande, and gavotte are found in allegro arias based on repeated rhythmic patterns to represent the affections of triumph or agitation. Rhythms of the courante and minuet are found in simple ariettas in popular melodic style which come closer to the *style galant* than his other aria types. Other arias consist of slowly flowing bel canto cantilena, through-composed, usually in triple meter, and with densely textured accompaniment (*Ombra mai fu*). Arias related to the concerto are in unison or have obbligato accompaniment. The ground-bass aria of the 17th century is little used; instead are found patterned basses. In its relation to the flow of the plot the aria is reflective, while the action is advanced through the medium of recitative which plays a vital and expressive role, or the continuous scene (grand *scena*).

The chorus plays a much less important role in the opera than it does in the oratorio. Handel's opera choruses are homophonic in texture. Instrumental music in the operas consists of processional and dance music as well as overtures and the concerto-grosso sections of arias. In his overtures he is fond of the French overture form but also uses overtures consisting of several dance movements.

Sources of Handel's dramatic material include the Renaissance poets Ariosto, Guarini, and Tasso, whose poetry had been set by the madrigalists; the 18th century opera librettists Zeno and Metastasio; and his own favorite librettists Nicola Haym and Paolo Rolli, (in addition to Metastasio). As to subject matter, historical subjects, such as *Guilio Cesare* (Julius Caesar) and *Riccardo primo* (Richard I); classical mythology, such as *Admeto* (Admetus was a friend of Hercules) and *Arianna* (Ariadne*); and romantic legend, such as *Orlando* (a story which stemmed from the time of Charlemagne) are found among his opera plots. The libretto of *Rinaldo* is by Paolo Rolli based on Torquato Tasso's epic. *Il pastor fido* is also by Rolli based on Guarini's pastoral play with its nymphs and shepherds. *Orlando* is by Braccioli, based on Ariosto's *Orlando furioso*.

Oratorios

Musically, the oratorios used the same resources as the opera: aria, arioso, and recitative; but in their emphasis on the chorus they reflected the English rather than the Italian tradition. They are influenced by Purcell but are stamped with the grand and monumental style that is Handel's own. The chorus assumed increasing importance in the later oratorios. It frequently represented the children of Israel in the dramatic action, as it does in *Israel in Egypt.* Thus, allegorically, the chorus became identified with the British people and with the hopes and aspirations of the rising British Empire based on the strength of its middle class.

The Messiah

The most famous of Handel's oratorios is the *Messiah,* not necessarily because of any greater musical value, but rather because of the appeal of its subject matter. It is not typical of Handel's oratorios since it lacks any dramatic, narrative action and is of a purely devotional nature. As with all oratorios the work is non-liturgical. The text, taken entirely from scriptures, was compiled by a literary dilettante, Charles Jennens. It covers all phases of the life of Christ in three sections beginning with the Christmas section.

predecessors of the oratorios. They also were the source of much material that recurs in Handel's later works. Other choral works of note include the celebrated *Coronation Anthem* (1727) for King George II and the *Dettingen Te Deum* (1734), a composition on a grand scale written to celebrate the victory over the French in the War of the Austrian Succession.

Instrumental Works

The improvisational background of Handel's music is particularly notable in his instrumental works. He himself was famous for his improvisations, and the improvisational quality carries over into his written works.

Solo Keyboard and Orchestral Works

Among his keyboard works can be found a great variety of styles and forms. The best known work for clavier is a set of variations from his Suite no. 5 in E named (though not by Handel) "*The Harmonious Blacksmith*". His most significant instrumental works are his concertos. The most famous of his orchestral works are a set of 12 concerti grossi (Grand Concertos) for strings alone (opus 6) written in 1739. His concertos are conservative in their ordering of movements which shows Corelli's influence and follows the scheme of the church sonata. In the internal form of the movements, however, influences of Vivaldi's concerto form can be found. There is also a set of concertos for woodwinds and strings (op. 3) and a set for organ. The opus 3 concertos are generally considered oboe concertos. The organ concertos were intended chiefly for Handel's improvisation. Handel's organ music made little use of the pedal. Perhaps his most famous orchestral composition is the *Water Music* in the form of an orchestral suite and written for wind instruments. An air and a hornpipe are particularly attractive.

Evaluation

Handel is indubitably one of the great masters and one of the most accessible in the directness and simplicity of his expression. His music has grandeur and breadth, and a sustained flow. Power and triumph echo from his massive choruses. Though conservative in some of his instrumental forms, he was progressive in his response to the changing social conditions of England. It was that which led him to the oratorio. In his continual striving to reach the large public audiences, he was led to a more homophonic style than his great contemporary, J. S. Bach. And this greater stress on homophony looked to the future.

Bach and Handel

The careers and music of the two great masters of the Late Baroque invite comparison. Bach and Handel were born in the same year and in the same part of Germany, but their careers were in sharp contrast. Bach's creative years were passed as a cantor in a succession of local churches not far from his birthplace, while Handel sought international centers from which he could reach the widest public. Handel spoke in broad sweeping gestures while Bach was complex and intricate. Handel's style was more improvisational than Bach's and less personal and individual. Bach's melodies are subtle and full of implied polyphony; Handel sweeps the listener away with the powerful and immediate appeal of his melodic flow. He uses counterpoint only as a means to a dramatic end. With Bach counterpoint is of the essence. Handel's music is characterized by a free flow of creativity, a continual outpouring of new ideas; Bach is involved in a searching

ela
wr
inst
his
of
cor
wri
de
sa
cha
on
eac
eac
pe
occ

1.
nev
2.
faile
inte
fina
3.
ma
em
the
for
the
the
tes
to

(

Beggars' Opera   Greensleeves   Baroque

Giulio Cesare   *Agrippina*   *Rodelinda*
Serse   *Samson*   *Saul*
Semele   *Rinaldo*

Israel in Egypt:	The *Messiah:*
"He sent a Thick Darkness"	"Why do the Nations"
"They Loathed to Drink of the River"	"But as for his People"
"But the Waters Overwhelmed Their Enemies"	"I Know that My Redeemer Liveth"
"All We Like Sheep"	"Hallelujah" Chorus
Judas Maccabaeus:	"Egypt was Glad when they Departed"
"Hallelujah Amen"	*Chandos* Anthems
"Harmonious Blacksmith" variations	Coronation Anthem
Grand Concertos op. 6	Dettingen Te Deum
oboe concertos, op.3	*Water Music*

LIST OF SCORES

(Note: Handel's works are widely available. The works listed below are those which are included in the same anthologies which contain the other works noted at the end of each chapter.)

       Concerto grosso in C-major, for oboes and strings (first movement), MM 43

       "Cara sposa" from opera *Rinaldo*, recitative, sinfonia & aria, MM, 44

       "How dark, O Lord, are Thy decrees" from oratorio *Jephtha*, chorus, NAWM1,89

       "Draw the Tear from Hopeless Love", chorus from oratorio *Solomon*, MM, 45

Music	Political History	Intellectual History	Art
1700 Bach at Lüneberg **1701** Muffat, *12 Concerti grossi* **1703** Handel at Hamburg **1704** Handel, *St. John Passion* first Bach cantatas Telemann founds Collegium musicum at Leipzig **1705** Handel's first opera **1706** Rameau, 1st book of clavecin pieces **1706-10** Handel in Italy **1707** Alessandro Scarlatti, *Mitridate eupatore*, opera **1708-17** Bach at Weimar–organ works **1709** 1st pianoforte built *opera buffa* in Italy **1710** Campra, *Fêtes venitiennes* Handel appointed in Hanover visits England **1710-12** Handel returns to England	**1700-1746** Philip V, King of Spain **1701-13** Frederick I, King of Prussia **1703** St. Petersburg founded **1702-14** Queen Anne, queen of England War of the Spanish Succession, efforts of Louis XIV to extend French power **1706** Charles XII of Sweden defeats Russians and Saxons at Franstadt	**1700** Congreve, *The Way of the World*, comedy **1701** Yale College founded **1704** Daniel Defoe, in prison, begins *The Review*, weekly newspaper **1709** *The Tatler* & *The Spectator* founded **1710** George Berkeley, *The Principles of Human Understanding*	**1702** Watteau in Paris **1703** Work begun on Buckingham Palace, London **1707** Fischer von Erlach, Kollegen-Kirche in Salzburg completed **1710** Sir Christopher Wren, St.Paul's Cathedral, London, completed

Music	Political History	Intellectual History	Art
1711 Keiser, *Croesus*, Handel,*Rinaldo*, operas	1711-1740 Charles VI, Holy Roman Emperor	1711 Pope, *Essay on Criticism*	1711 Kneller founds London Academy of Arts
1713 F. Couperin, *Pièces de Clavecin I*	1713 Peace of Utrecht	1712 Pope, *Rape of the Lock*	1713 Watteau, *L'Indifférent*
1714 Bach, cantata, *Ich hatte viel Bekümmernis*	1714-27 George I, Handel's patron in Hanover, King of England	1714 Leibniz, *Monadologie*	
1714-59 Handel in England			
1715 Founding of *opéra comique* A.Scarlatti, *Tigrane*	1715 Death of Louis XIV	1715 Alain Lesage, *Gil Blas*	1715 Beginning of Rococo
1716 Handel, *Water Music* Couperin, *L'Art de toucher clavecin*	1718 Quadruple Alliance, England, France,the Empire,& Holland	1719 Rediscovery of Pompeii & Herculaneum Daniel Defoe, *Robinson Crusoe*	1717 Watteau, *Embarkation for Cytherea*, major Rococo art work
1717-23 Bach at Cöthen, chamber music			
1717-18 Handel Duke of Chandos's chapel master			
1720 Marcello, *Il teatro alla modo*	1720 Collapse of the South Seas Company		
1721 Bach, *Brandenburg Concertos; French & English Suites*		1721 Montesquieu, *Lettres Persanes*	
1722 Bach,*Well-Tempered Clavier I* Rameau, *Traité de l'harmonie*			
1723-50 Bach at Leipzig- cantatas			

Music	Political History	Intellectual History	Art
1723 Bach, *St. John Passion* **1724** Handel, *Giulio Cesare*, opera **1725** *Concerts spirituel*, Paris Johann Fux, *Gradus ad Parnassum* **1726** Vivaldi, *The Seasons* Rameau, *Nouveau système de musique théorique* **1727** Handel, *Coronation Anthem* **1728** Gay and Pepusch, *Beggar's Opera* **1729** Bach, *St. Matthew Passion* **1730** Bach, cantata, *Ein feste Burg* Hasse, opera, *Artaserse*	**1724** Paris Bourse opens **1727-60** George II of England reigns	**1723** Voltaire, *La Henriade*, epic poem on Henry IV **1726** Jonathan Swift, *Gulliver's Travels*	**1724** Figueroa, West entrance, St. Telmo Palace, Seville, Spain **1726-28** Tiepolo, frescoes in the Palace, Udine **1728** Chardin, *Rain*
1731 Bach, *Clavierübung* Part I **1733** Giovanni Pergolesi, *La Serva padrona*, intermezzi	**1731** Treaty of Vienna between England, Holland Spain, & the Empire **1733** Founding of Georgia War of the Polish Succession	**1731** Abbé Prévost, *Manon Lescaut* **1732** Voltaire, *Zaïre*	**1731** Hogarth, *Harlot's Progress*

Music	Political History	Intellectual History	Art
1734 Bach, *Christmas Oratorio* Tartini, Sonatas Op. 1 for violin			1734 Boucher, *Rinaldo and Armida*
1735 Rameau, *Les Indes galantes*, opera-ballet	1735 W. Pitt elected to Parliament	1735 Linnaeus, *Systema naturae*, origin of the modern system of classifying plants and animals	1735 Hogarth, *A Rake's Progress*
1736 Handel, *Alexander's Feast*, secular oratorio	1736-39 Russo-Turkish war		
1737 Rameau, *Castor et Pollux*, opera Domenico Scarlatti, first published sonatas San Carlo Opera opens in Naples		1737 First lodge of Masons in Germany	1737 Boucher, designs for Beauvais tapestries Chardin, *La Gouvernante*
1738 D. Scarlatti, *Esercizi*, sonatas Bach, B-minor Mass Handel, oratorios: *Saul, Israel in Egypt, Serse*		1738 Methodist Church founded by Wesley & Whitefield	
1739 Handel, *Concerti grossi* Mattheson, *Der vollkommene Kapellmeister*	1739 Turks threaten Belgrade, Emperor Charles VI signs treaty	1739 David Hume, *A Treatise of Human Nature*	
	1740-46 War of the Austrian Succession	1740 Samuel Richardson, *Pamela*, first novel	1740 Giovanni Tiepolo, *Triumph of Amphitrite*
	1740-86 Frederick the Great, King of Prussia		
1741 Gluck, *Artaserse*, opera	1740-96 Age of Enlightened Despotism	1741 Voltaire, *Mahomet*, tragedy	1741 Boucher, *Autumn*

Music	Political History	Intellectual History	Art
1742 Bach, *Goldberg Variations* Handel,*Messiah,* oratorio, per-formed, Dublin C.P.E. Bach, *Prussian Sona-tas* for piano 1743 Handel. *Sam-son,*oratorio 1744 C.P.E. Bach, *Württemberg Sonatas,* piano 1745 Gluck in England Johann Stamitz at Mannheim 1746 Handel, *Judas Maccabaeus,* oratorio 1747 Bach, *Musical Offering,* to Frederick the Great Handel, *Joshua,* 1749 Bach, *Art of Fugue* Rameau, *Zoro-astre, opera* 1750 Quantz, Flute Concertos	1742-45 Charles VII, Holy Roman Emperor 1746-1759 Ferdinand I of Spain	1743 Voltaire, *Mérope* 1748 Montesquieu, *The Spirit of Law* Voltaire, *Zadoc* Klopstock, *Der Messias* 1750 Fielding, *Tom Jones* Buffon, *Histoire naturelle*	1746 Boucher, *Toilet of Venus* 1747 Fredrick the Great's castle at Potsdam, *Sans souci*

LE DEVIN
DU VILLAGE

INTERMÉDE

RÉPRÉSENTÉ A FONTAINEBLEAU

Devant leurs Majestés

les 18. et 24. Octobre 1752.

ET A PARIS PAR

l'Académie Royale de Musique

le 1.er Mars 1753.

PAR

J. J. ROUSSEAU.

Prix 10.th 4.f

Avec l'ariette ajoutée par M.r Philidor, chantée par M.r Caillot

A PARIS

Chez LeClerc, Rue S.t Honoré aux la Rue des Prouvaires, et
la rue Dufour à Sainte Cecile.

Et Aux Libraires Ordinaires.

AVEC PRIVILLEGE DU ROY.   Imprimé par C

CHAPTER XIII

NEW DIRECTIONS 1700-1750

THE ENLIGHTENMENT

While the great monuments of the Late Baroque were still being created, the roots were being laid for a new musical style which would reach fruition in the last quarter of the 18th century; i.e. the Viennese Classical style. The masters of the new style were Haydn and Mozart, and Beethoven in his early period.

The social background against which the new artistic atmosphere developed was once again focused on man's life on earth. Men became more tolerant of each other's ideas and religious practices. The Deists reacted against all kinds of formal religion, but granted to each man the right to his own form of observance.. The concept of progress evolved and subservient respect for the Ancients was dispelled. The divine right of kings was questioned and the concepts of constitutional monarchy, enlightened despotism, and democracy appeared. A love of nature and of the natural man and his rights became current. The idea of entertainment in the arts superseded the heavy emotionalism of the Baroque.

Historical Background

With the death of Louis XIV in 1715, the foremost exponent of absolutism left the scene. His successor, Louis

371

XV, lacked the force of character and the gift for organization of his predecessor and was far more interested in exploiting the privileges of his position than in governing France.

The importance of careful observation of a sufficient body of facts before drawing conclusions had first been set forth by Francis Bacon, but it now reached implementation in social thought. There was also an appreciation of how ideas had changed in the past. Thus a spirit of tolerance came about. Men recognized their own frailties and thus forbore from treating the ideas of others with disdain. Though Calvin was nothing if not autocratic in Geneva, when the Calvinists came to Catholic France, they became proponents of religious tolerance; and the idea took on a life of its own.   Religious tolerance and the idea of religious freedom were among the great products of this age. The principle that a man's worth was independent of his religion or racial background was expressed in literature in Lessing's *Nathan the Wise*.   This portrayal of a Jew as a wise and noble person grew out of Lessing's friendship with the Jewish philosopher, Moses Mendelssohn. Mozart's operas the *Abduction from the Seraglio* and *The Magic Flute* portrayed a Turkish Pasha and an Egyptian high priest in sympathetic terms for their human values. Lessing and Mozart, of course, belong to the second half of the century.

Deism

The Reformation, the Counter-Reformation (Catholic Reformation) and the bloody religious wars of the 17th century now led to a reaction against all kinds of religious dogma and ceremony. Deism was a belief in a Supreme Being without reference to any established church or religion. The Deists retained their belief in God but rejected orthodox Christianity. The movement had its origins in England; spread to the continent where it had such adherents as J. J. Rousseau and Voltaire; and then came to the United States with Thomas Paine, Benjamin Franklin, and Thomas Jefferson. The spirit of religious tolerance is also reflected in Paine, even though he rejected formal religious practice for himself.

Progress

The idea of progress, of the advance of civilization, and of the achievement of happiness on earth, developed through the 18th and 19th centuries. In the late 17th century the French philosopher Fontenelle (1657-1757) rejected the idea that the ancients and pagans were more advanced than the men of his own age. The concept that human knowledge is cumulative evolved throughout the 18th century after having been set forth in the writings of Fontenelle. Fontenelle distinguished between the cumulative nature of scientific and industrial knowledge and the non-cumulative nature of artistic achievement. He maintained, however, that even in modern art man was fully capable of achievements equal to those of the past. The most elaborate statement of the idea of progress was contained in the work of Condorcet (1743-1794) who divided the evolution of human civilization into ten stages from its beginnings in a society of hunters and fishers to the French Republic (the ninth stage) and the future (the tenth stage).

The Enlightenment rejected the concept that kings ruled by divine right, a doctrine promulgated by such absolutist rulers as Louis XIV. Rousseau (1712-78) set forth the idea of the social contract, the idea that men surrendered certain freedoms to a central authority in order to gain the protection that could be had through large-scale coöperation. Spinoza and John Locke also contributed to the theory of the social contract. From it developed theories of government, such as constitutional monarchy, enlightened despotism, and democracy. The growth of a strong merchant class contributed to the spread of these doctrines, especially in regard to the duty of the government to protect the "natural " rights of private property. Refusal of rulers to recognize these rights led, in the 18th century, to the American and French revolutions - revolutions that were called for by the writers who promulgated the idea of the social contract.

Nature

The concept of natural rights and of the natural man untainted by civilization was current during the mid-18th century, prominently in Rousseau. Love of nature, of scenery, and of natural landscapes runs through his work and had a profound influence on artistic productions of the time. The rigid organization of the gardens of Versailles under Louis XIV was altered around the middle of the century in accordance with the more informal and natural appearance of English gardens. It is interesting to note that when the critic Adolf Scheibe attacked the music of J. S. Bach, he took it to task for being "unnatural".

Speculation concerning human nature led to the "nature-nurture" controversy begun by Locke and Rousseau. Locke felt that the infant was a *tabula rasa,* a blank slate on which experience and environment wrote, while Rousseau believed in the natural goodness of man which made training and bringing-up only minimally important.

The Rococo

The Rococo was the art of the French aristocracy in the period following the death of Louis XIV. The social life of the nobility became decentralized and reverted from Versailles to the individual dwellings of the nobles. The emphasis in artistic decoration moved from the court to the boudoir. Louis XV was noteworthy for his succession of mistresses, of whom the most famous were Mme. Pompadour and Mme. du Barry. The people starved; the church was divided by feuds; and the middle class strove for recognition while Rococo art remained gallant, light-hearted, and immoral with its pastorals, its hunts, its amours, and its pleasures. It sought freedom from the "rules" of the Baroque in a "back-to-nature" movement. But the Rococo only created its own nature world in which the nobility played at being country folk. Under the Rococo the decorative minor arts flourished; the designing of furniture, for example, reached a high state of perfection. While the Baroque had dramatic intensity, grandiose rhetoric, pathos, broad sweeping gestures, and unified structures of architectural scope, the Rococo was intimate; stressed interior decoration; had wit, grace, and polish; was entertaining; sought variety; and was preoccupied with love-play in its subject matter.

The visual arts under the Rococo, had a repertoire of shepherdesses, goddesses, nymphs, rosy clouds, and delicate boudoirs. Its subject matter portrayed the secret rendezvous, the bathing beauty, or the secret love discovered. The most famous artist of the Rococo was Antoine Watteau (1684-1721) whose *Embarkation for Cytherea* (Cytherea was an island sacred to Venus) is a representation of the refined and delicate love-theme characteristic of the Rococo with its wistful air of unreality.

In this atmosphere, indeed, the nobility were playing at a game in which they scarcely believed themselves. Mme.

Pompadour, herself of middle-class origins, was a staunch supporter of Voltaire and the *Encyclopédie* .

MUSIC OF THE ROCOCO

Music for Stringed Keyboard Instruments

The most characteristic musical sound of the Rococo was the plucked-string sound of the clavecin (harpsichord). While the greatest masters of the Baroque were creating their monumental works, the great French court clavecinist, François Couperin (1688-1733, known as le Grand) was composing ornamented keyboard miniatures that were the essence of Rococo. Though he wrote a significant body of chamber music that shows Baroque characteristics, his miniature keyboard pieces issued in four books from 1713-1730 during the Regency and reign of Louis XV are examples of early Rococo style. In contrast to the generalized instrumental style of the Baroque they are idiomatic specifically for harpsichord; use short repetitive phrases instead of the long spun-out Baroque sequences; and use typical Rococo ornaments whose execution is carefully set forth in a table by the composer. There is little real counterpoint, and although the pieces have fanciful titles (*La Galante* is a typical Rococo title), they can usually be related to one of the standard dance types of the suite. The keyboard music of Jean-Philippe Rameau (1683-1764), greatest French composer of his day, is also in the Rococo vein, e.g. his well-known keyboard piece *La Poule* (The Hen). We will have occasion to return to him in the discussion of opera.

Domenico Scarlatti

Among keyboard composers the outstanding master was Domenico Scarlatti (1685-1757). Born in the same year as Bach and Handel, his music is of the Rococo, rather than of the Baroque. Son of the famous opera composer Alessandro Scarlatti, he was born in Naples. Around 1720 at the age of 35 he went to Lisbon, Portugal, as maestro of the royal chapel and teacher of the Princess Maria Barbara who was later to become queen of Spain. She married the heir to the Spanish throne in 1729, and Scarlatti accompanied her to Madrid where he was to spend the rest of his life. It was for her that he wrote his harpsichord sonatas which he modestly called *esercizi* (exercises). It is on these sonatas of which some 600 survive that his fame rests. Though he had written operas earlier in his career, he appears to have devoted himself exclusively to the composition of keyboard works after he came to Madrid.

The court of Spain was at this time dominated by French influences. Philip V, king when Scarlatti came to Madrid, was the grandson of Louis XIV of France; and Philip's successors were also Bourbons including Ferdinand VI, the husband of Maria Barbara. Thus, the influences that reached Scarlatti in Madrid must have included those of the French Rococo.

The term *sonata* as applied to Scarlatti's keyboard compositions had no connection with either the Baroque or Classical sonatas. They are all one-movement compositions in bipartite (two-part) form. As was typical of the Rococo style, he had little interest in the severe contrapuntal writing of which Bach was master. Like Couperin his approach to harpsichord writing was progressive. Scarlatti, in fact, advanced the technique of keyboard performance to new heights. His music was specifically devised for the sound and technique of the harpsichord. Such devices as crossing of the hands (which suggests a harpsichord with two manuals); repeated notes; rapid alternation of the hands in measured tremolo; and Alberti basses (broken chords) point to the harpsichord. Contrast of melodic material, foreign to the internal structure of Late Baroque movements, made its appearance in his pieces. Contrast between melodic ideas in the internal structure of a movement was to play an important role in the Viennese Classical style, as was the Alberti bass. Scarlatti's harmonic style with its use of unresolved dissonances was meant specifically for the plucked string sound of the harpsichord. Influences of the Spanish guitar may have played some part in the moulding of Scarlatti's style. Some of Bach's last keyboard works seem to show influences of Scarlatti's harpsichord writing. We have seen how Bach's Italian Concerto and *Goldberg* Variations were intended specifically for a harpsichord with two manuals. An important pupil of Scarlatti was Padre Antonio Soler.

ROCOCO OPERA

Campra

The most important composer in France between Couperin and Rameau was André Campra (1660-1744). In his music Rococo elements entered into opera. He created the ballet opera, a type in which the various scenes have different plots designed around the element of ballet and chorus spectacles. The whole is loosely unified by its relationship to a given subject. The first ballet opera (Fr. *opéra-ballet*) was entitled *l'Europe galante* (1697). The ballet opera was an outgrowth of the emphasis on ballet which was characteristic of French opera. Lully's opera contained many scenes (called *entrées*) whose purpose was merely to furnish the opera with ballet spectacles and which had little dramatic significance. These *entrées* combined with the standard operatic forms of recitative, aria, and chorus, made up the separate scenes of the ballet opera. In Campra's *Fêtes vénitiennes* (Carnival Time in

Venice) the separate scenes deal with love affairs taking place at the carnivals in Venice. The love affairs are treated in the delicate, artificial, charming way that is characteristic of the Rococo. Campra's music is characterized by a predilection for graceful tunes in a quasi-folksong manner which reflects the philosophy of the "back-to-nature" movement.

Rameau

The operas of Rameau constitute a high point in the history of French music. His earliest opera was written when he was 50 years old and thus represents him in his maturity. This opera, *Hyppolite et Aricie* (1733) constituted an advance over the operas of Lully and touched off a typically French journalistic controversy between the *Lullistes* and the *Ramistes*. Rameau himself abjured this controversy, and in the introduction to his successful ballet opera *Les Indes galantes* (The Gallant Indies, 1735) declared that he, like Lully, "sought his models in nature". His style was characterized by harmonic richness and homophonic texture, the result of his preoccupation with harmonic theory. He considered harmony to be of first importance, and to him melody was nothing but the surface of chords. In his operas he abandoned the traditional French overture and wrote descriptive pieces that led directly into the opera. His orchestration techniques were very progressive, taking into account the characteristics of the individual instruments in regard to tone color and performance capabilities. He even used clarinets which were very new at the time. But the growing Rococo influence made him unresponsive to the demands of dramatic continuity. He felt that any kind of words could be set to music and was quite oblivious to the quality of his libretti. This attitude towards the sonority of words is perhaps reflected in the 20th century French composer Darius Milhaud's setting of a catalogue of agricultural machinery to music in a pastoral style (*Machines agricoles,* for voice and 7 instruments, 1919). Rameau's preoccupation with sonorous material itself resulted in his formulation of the first treatise on harmony. His major contribution was the discovery that a chord could be inverted without losing its identity, and he also brought out the importance of the chords on the first, fourth, and fifth degrees of the scale. In working out his harmonic theories Rameau felt that he was expounding the principles of nature (viz. his comment on Lully) and that, philosophically, he was part of the "back-to-nature" movement.

In 1737 Rameau's masterpiece, *Castor et Pollux,* was produced, and with it Rameau achieved recognition and financial success. In 1745 he received an appointment to the court of Louis XV as royal chamber music composer, and after this time he turned to the Rococo style that was demanded for court performance. His works before 1745 are of greater significance, works where the Baroque influence is more pronounced.

Rameau's great contributions were in the harmonic richness of his music, his skill at orchestration, and the undisputed power of his portrayal of scene and mood. His neglect, however, of the dramatic importance of the libretto, and thus of dramatic continuity of his works, has militated against their survival on the stage. The Rococo influence led to too great an emphasis on individual spectacles, dances, and processions.

The Comic Opera

The comic opera unlike the Rococo art stemmed from the middle class rather than from the aristocracy. As early as 1728 (the *Beggar's Opera*) the English had poked fun at the upper classes and at the serious opera's predilection for contriving a happy ending through a *deus ex machina* to avoid displeasing the nobles who were being portrayed as the protagonists in the plot. The *Beggar's Opera,* an example of the ballad opera, was in English. It included spoken dialogue and used borrowed musical material consisting of folk songs like *Greensleeves* and simplified versions of tunes from Purcell and even Handel, himself. It was written by John Gay with the musical assistance of Christopher Pepusch. The ballad opera, somewhat comparable to our musical comedy, was a musical satire on conventional opera and included political satire directed against the upper classes. It was modeled after the French *vaudeville* or *Théâtre de la foire* and sparked a flood of imitations leading to the birth of the German *Singspiel.* A modern adaptation of the *Beggar's Opera* by Brecht with music by Weill was entitled *Dreigroschen Oper* (Threepenny Opera).

Pergolesi- The "Buffoon War"

Pergolesi's *La Serva padrona* (The Servant Become Mistress) likewise showed the upper classes at a disadvantage. *La Serva padrona* was originally a series of small scenes (*intermezzi*) with their own plot to be played between the acts of a serious opera. The practice of having intermezzi of light character with their own plot interpolated between the acts of serious opera dates from the first quarter of the 17th century, while musical interludes introduced into plays were found as early as the 15th century. The 20th century composer Richard Strauss adapted the idea in his opera *Ariadne auf Naxos* (1912). In the plot of this opera the ruler commands the composer to combine the serious opera and the intermezzi into one work. Thus, *commedia del arte* figures come into the fabric of the story about the Minoan princess deserted by Theseus and wander in and out of the action, now commenting, now participating. In Pergolesi's *intermezzi* a servant girl orders her master around unmercifully and finally tricks him into marrying her. The music is delightful in its simplicity and humor and includes an amusing passage which pokes fun at Handel's *Hallelujah* chorus. Here, the comic opera overshadowed the serious opera into which it was interpolated and gained an independent life of its own. It played to great acclaim in Paris in 1752, touching off the journalistic "buffoon war" in which the *encyclopédistes* and especially Rousseau praised Pergolesi and attacked Rameau for the complexities of his music. Rameau, while not unsympathetic to the new movement, defended himself ably. Rousseau, though a musical amateur - or perhaps because of it - illustrated his theories by writing a comic opera with simple folk song-like tunes and a rustic setting. Called *Le Devin du village* (The Village Soothsayer), it parodied the use of the supernatural in serious opera and achieved considerable success. A one-act opera, it was, like the comic operas of Pergolesi, intended to be performed between the acts of a serious opera and was subtitled *Interméde*.

Germany - Georg Philipp Telemann

When J. S. Bach was hired in Leipzig, he was second choice. The composer whom the town fathers really wanted was Georg Phillip Telemann (1691-1767). Famous in his own day - he ranked with Hasse and Graun - his music fell into oblivion after his death. In an unprecedented phenomenon, however, his music was rediscovered in recent years, not by the concert-halls but by the record-buying public; and his music now has a very respectable representation in modern record catalogues. Telemann represents the Hamburg school of the second half of the 18th century. A highly prolific composer and skilled contrapuntist of unquestioned technical mastery, he wrote operas, instrumental music, and a vast quantity of church music. His output includes Passions, oratorios, cantatas, and psalms. Among his instrumental works are French overtures (orchestral suites), concertos, and table music (chamber music). His music shows familiarity with the important national styles of the day and exhibits French, Italian, and German influences. The weighty and serious Baroque had subsided from his music which is light, pleasant, and witty and has an easy flow. A gift for the comic prevails in his operas which lean strongly toward the buffa and include *intermezzi*. He was a progressive composer and his music looks toward the *style galant* (gallant style) rather than backwards to the Baroque. Cantatas, however, being liturgical, represent the more conservative side of the religious music of the day.

SENTIMENTALITY

The Berlin School

The Prussian court under Frederick the Great (r. 1740-1786) was completely under the influence of French culture. He wrote and spoke French and numbered Voltaire among his intimates. Politically, he was an enlightened despot, the form of government which Voltaire himself favored. He instituted legal reforms, promoted education, and aided industry. He was also an accomplished musician though uncompromising and conservative in his musical tastes. Among the musicians at his court were J. J. Quantz who did much to advance the playing of the transverse (modern) flute and Karl Philipp Emanuel Bach who was chamber musician and clavecinist there from 1740-1787. Emanuel Bach was J. S. Bach's second oldest son, a great composer in his own right and one who played a highly significant role in the emergence of the Viennese Classical style. His music was highly esteemed by Haydn (who acknowledged his debt to him) and also by Mozart. His influence extended to Beethoven.

While influences of the French Rococo, and the Italian *opera buffa* as well, played an important role in eliminating the

Baroque from the music of the Berlin school, another trend, that of sentimentality (*Empfindsamkeit*) gave the German music a distinctive stamp. Sentimentality was part of the reaction against dominance by the aristocracy since it was marked by the arousing of pity for the poor, the defenceless, and the downtrodden. It became fashionable to "wear one's feelings on one's sleeve". Sentimentality was to be found in what is generally considered to be the first English novel, *Pamela* (1740) by Samuel Richardson, in which a poor but virtuous serving-girl resists the attempts of a gentleman to seduce her. Lawrence Sterne and the poet Thomas Gray (*Elegy in a Country Churchyard*) and in Germany Klopstock, also gave expression to this concept. Germany, in the music of Emanuel Bach, gave musical expression to the movement of sentimentality.

In German music the *Empfindsamkeit* sought delicate nuances in performance and turned to the intimate clavichord, of all keyboard instruments the most immediately responsive to the player's touch. It used the fragmented melodic structure of the Rococo, but it related these changes in melodic material to the expression of feeling, to constantly changing affections. Let us recall that the doctrine of affections in the Late Baroque period established the underlying affection of a given movement and then represented it with a given rhythmic or melodic figure that lasted throughout the movement.

The Sonata for Stringed Keyboard - Emanuel Bach

Emanuel Bach wrote keyboard sonatas of three movements in which the second, an adagio, frequently used elements taken from the opera: recitative and arioso. The fast-slow-fast scheme of the sonatas was taken over from the Italian overture. But the new element was the musical language. The rhythmic discontinuity of the Rococo became a means of constructing themes whose character made thematic development possible. This new type of melodic language was combined with a seriousness of feeling and a daring harmonic vocabulary that set forth definitively the style of the Classical period. Sets of keyboard sonatas by Emanuel Bach appeared as early as 1740 ("Prussian") and 1742 ("Württemburg").

ORCHESTRAL MUSIC

The new direction in the orchestral music of the period 1700-1750 points to the Classical symphony. The origins of the symphony lay completely shrouded in mystery for over 100 years, and much investigation still remains to be done. The "modernists" who were composing while J. S. Bach was still alive, and whose music overshadowed his in the following generation, were themselves overshadowed by Haydn and Mozart and by the Bach revival. It remained for Hugo Riemann (1849-1919) to unearth the music of Johann Stamitz and the Mannheim school. He believed that he had uncovered the origins of the symphony, and his work stands as a landmark of musicological investigation; but since then other important contributions to the Classical style have been uncovered.

An important precursor of the Classical symphony was the Italian opera overture as found in the works of Alessandro Scarlatti, founder of the Neapolitan school of opera. His overtures consisted of three movements, fast-slow-fast, with a finale in dance form. The finale was sometimes a minuet, sometimes a march, often a gigue of the idealized type found in the Baroque dance suite. Other sources were the Baroque concerto and trio sonata. All these forms had a common ancestor in the canzona for instrumental ensembles.

Among the earliest composers to write independent symphonies unconnected with opera was G. B. Sammartini

(1698-1775). He developed a homophonic style, and a classical melodic approach begins to appear in his works written in the 1730's and 1740's. His symphonies were in three movements, some with minuet and some with presto finales. One symphony is in four movements with a very brief slow movement. His works became very popular in Vienna and influenced composers there. Other Italian composers important to the new style were Niccolo Jommelli (1714-1774) who worked in Stuttgart, near Mannheim for 15 years, and Rinaldo di Capua (c. 1710-c. 1780). England, though a leader in the social revolution, remained somewhat conservative musically and was represented by the works of William Boyce (1710-1779). Boyce's music was Baroque in style though written with a freshness of invention and a lightness of manner.

The Mannheim School

The city of Mannheim in western Germany, located on the right bank of the Rhine and at the mouth of the Neckar river, became the seat of the Elector Palatine in 1720. A large palace was built there in the Louis XIV tradition, and a brilliant court was held. Under the Elector Karl Theodore an opera house was completed in 1742, and Mannheim became one of the great musical and theatrical centers of Europe. The Mannheim orchestra became world-famous. Mozart was to live there in 1777-78, and Schiller was to begin his career at the theatre there.

The orchestra was particularly famous for the way it could perform a crescendo (a gradual increase in volume), at that time a new device. The dynamics (changes in volume) of the Baroque were characteristically terraced; that is, they were at one level loud or soft for a relatively long time and then changed to another level without an intermediate increase or decrease. Terraced dynamics are implicit in the sound of the two-manual harpsichord which is incapable of dynamic changes other than the change between manuals, or the combination of both manuals. The effect of the crescendo on the mid-18th century audience was something quite startling. It also became the custom here to direct the orchestra from the concert master's (the leading violinist's) chair instead of from the harpsichord. The orchestra was also distinguished by its large woodwind section which was used to good advantage by Mannheim composers.

The golden age of the Mannheim school continued through two generations of composers spanned by the following names: Johann Stamitz (1717-1757), Franz Xavier Richter (1709-1780), Ignaz Holzbauer (1711-1783), Anton Filz (1730-1760), Guiseppe Toëschi (1724-1788) and Christian Cannabich (1731-1798). These men came from Austria, Bohemia, and Italy, and many of them joined the Mannheim orchestra in their mature years, bringing with them influences from their homelands.

The Mannheimers wrote four-movement symphonies which stemmed from the Italian overture. Their themes exhibit the variety of rhythmic structures that were to reach perfection in the Viennese Classical school. Stamitz established the existence of an unequivocally independent second theme and thus introduced one of the main components of the Classical sonata form. He made full use of dynamic contrasts and crescendi, and his musical style has a symphonic breadth, power, and drive which anticipates Beethoven. Some stereotyped effects of the Mannheimers were the "rocket" theme which consisted of rising arpeggio figures ascending over a wide range and the "Steamroller" effect in which a phrase was repeated with the addition of various instruments at each repetition. Important features of the Mannheim style were (1) its homophonic character, which gave prominence to the violins, and (2) the abandonment of the thoroughbass in favor of written-out accompaniment figures for the orchestra.

The Viennese School

The four-movement symphony in its Classical manifestation included both the minuet and the final allegro . In this form it seems to have appeared first in Vienna where the proponents of the new style were Georg Matthias Monn (1717-1750) and Georg Christoph Wagenseil (1715-1777). Monn had a predilection for experimenting with the order of movements, but a symphony in D-major dated May 24, 1740 had the order of movements which became standard in the Classical symphony and has been called the first complete symphony. Wagenseil's music is more significant and lies closer to the Classical style. Wagenseil, like Stamitz in Mannheim, created self-sufficient themes out of the rhythmic motives that came into being with the Rococo. On the whole, however, Viennese music stresses lyricism more than does the music of the Mannheim school and points to Haydn and Mozart rather than to Beethoven.

Berlin

The symphonies of the Berlin school were of a more conservative stamp. They cling to the older contrapuntal idiom, but in so doing, they evolved in the direction of thematic development. Johann Gottlieb Graun (1703-1771) was the chief symphonist of the Berlin school. Emanuel

Bach's interests, as we have seen, lay in the area of the sonata for stringed keyboard instruments.

Church Music

The liturgical church music of the post-Baroque took for its model the music of Georg Philipp Telemann rather than J. S. Bach. Bach's music in his own time was considered old-fashioned and "heavy" and his cantatas represented bastions of formal religious liturgical application. The tenets of Deism minimized the importance of formal religious ceremony. Though the Deist movement was limited in Germany to a comparatively small group of intellectuals, nevertheless, its influence could be seen in the fact that many of the most prominent religious compositions were non-liturgical. Bach's B-minor Mass by its very dimensions placed itself beyond the scope of liturgical use. And, of course, Bach was not Catholic. In England Handel's oratorios, though mostly religious in subject matter, were meant for the concert hall rather than the church. France, the center of Deistic thought under the influence of Voltaire, saw very little sacred music in the first half of the 18th century. Rameau's output of sacred music was very small. Gluck, very much the internationalist, also wrote very little sacred music. In Mannheim Johann Stamitz's output of instrumental music included some 70 symphonies but less than half a dozen sacred works. It is to be noted that in the second half of the 18th century the relationship between Mass composition and true liturgy was tenuous and problematical. Graun's *Tod Jesu* , the most famous Passion of the latter half of the century, was first performed in a theater and was likewise a non-liturgical work.

The sentimental aspect of religious expression outweighed the liturgical. As we have seen in reference to his intermezzi, Pergolesi was a prominent representative of the new style.

His *Stabat Mater* is frequently performed. It, as well as his other church music, tends to be sentimental in character.

SUMMARY

1. <u>The</u> <u>Enlightenment</u>. Its chief characteristics were (a) emphasis on life on earth and human experience, (b) tolerance, (c) Deism, the reaction against dogma, (d) the concept of progress, (e)love of nature and the concept of the "natural man", (f) rejection of the rule by "divine right" and emergence of the principles of the social contract, enlightened despotism, constitutional monarchy, and finally democracy.

2. <u>Classicism</u> <u>in</u> <u>Music.</u> Aspects of Classicism which emerged in the first half of the 18th century were (a) break-up of the rhythmic continuity of the Late Baroque concerto-allegro and introduction of contrasting themes within a movement, (b) homophony in place of counterpoint, (c) disappearance of the thoroughbass and use of written-out accompaniment figures, (d) crescendo and decrescendo instead of terraced dynamics, (e) idiomatic writing for specific instruments in place of a generalized instrumental style for both voices and instruments, and (f) the four-movement sonata: fast-slow-minuet-fast.

3. <u>The</u> <u>Rococo.</u> The Rococo was the first reaction against Baroque art and music. It followed the death of Louis XIV in France. An art of the nobility, it played at going "back to nature" in a genteel rusticity. Refined, intimate, and entertaining, it stressed the minor arts. Delicate love-themes run through the paintings of the period.

4. <u>Rococo</u> <u>Music.</u>

(a) Harpsichord music was highly characteristic of the style. (1) The pieces were idiomatic for harpsichord, (2) highly ornamented, (3) cast in short phrases,

(4) homophonic, (5) used descriptive titles, and (6) were brief. The chief composers were François Couperin and Rameau.

(b) Rococo Opera. The ballet opera was the operatic form of the Rococo. Its separate scenes have different plots designed around ballet and choral spectacles and are loosely related to a given subject. The chief composers were Campra and Rameau.

5. Comic Opera. This form, unlike the Rococo forms, stemmed from the bourgeoisie. It ridiculed the upper classes and the serious opera of the Baroque. An early model was the *Beggar's Opera*. Pergolesi's *La Serva padrona* was a landmark of the comic opera.

6. Sentimentality. This movement developed in Berlin at the court of Frederick the Great. The court was under French influence and Frederick espoused the concept of enlightened despotism. Sentimentality, as manifested in English literature, involved pity for the poor and downtrodden. In music it used (1) the clavichord, (2) rapidly changing affections. (3) The sonatas of Emanuel Bach contain thematic contrast, and are important forerunners of the Classical sonata.

7. Orchestral Music. Emergence of the symphony: (a) The chief precursor was the Italian opera overture of Alessandro Scarlatti. (b) G. B. Sammartini was one of the earliest to write independent symphonies. (c) There was a famous orchestra in Mannheim, and the Mannheim composers wrote music that exhibited all the characteristics of Classicism listed above. (d)) Karl Stamitz founded the school, and his music points to Beethoven. (d) The Viennese school (Monn and Wagenseil) was more lyrical and pointed to Haydn and Mozart .

CHECK LIST FOR REVIEW

Viennese Classical	minuet	"rocket" theme
Baroque	keyboard sonata	"steamroller"
Rococo	Mannheim school	ballet opera

sonata
Italian overture
Alberti bass
opera buffa
opera seria
"Lullistes" and "Ramistes"

Viennese school
Berlin school
dynamics
crescendo
decrescendo

entrées
Empfindsamkeit
(sentimentality)
harpsichord
clavichord

Haydn
Mozart
Beethoven
François Couperin
Domenico Scarlatti
J. S. Bach
Padre Antonio Soler
Lully

Campra
Pergolesi
C. P. E. Bach
J. J. Quantz
Jommelli
Di Capua
Boyce
Johann Stamitz

Richter
Holzbauer
Filtz
Cannabich
Monn
Wagenseil
Joh. Gottlieb Graun

Louis XIV
Louis XV
Diderot
Montesquieu
Voltaire

Benjamin Franklin
Thomas Jefferson
Fontenelle
Condorcet
Mme. Pompadour

John Locke
Hume
Lessing
Moses Mendelssohn
Schiller

J. J. Rousseau
Thomas Paine
Hugo Riemann

Mme. du Barry
DesCartes

Adolf Scheibe
Watteau

the *Magic Flute*
the *Abduction from the Seraglio*
La Poule
the *Beggar's Opera*
La Serva padrona
esercizi
Italian Concerto

L'Europe galante
Prussian sonatas
Württemburg sonatas
Fêtes vénitiennes
Hyppolyte et Aricie
Les Indes galantes
Castor et Pollux

Goldberg Variations

the *Embarkation for Cytherea*   *Nathan the Wise*

LIST OF SCORES

Stringed Keyboard

Rococo *(Style galant)*
Couperin, Francois (*le Grand*) (1668-1733), *Le Rossignol en amour,* piece for harpsichord, rococo, HAM2, 265a; *Soeur Monique* piece for harpsichord, rococo, HAM2, 265b; *La Galante, Pièce de clavecin,* gigue, (Piece for clavecin), MM, 40

Scarlatti, Domenico (1685-1757), Sonata in C-minor from *Essercizi per gravicembalo,* for harpsichord, MM, 42; Sonata in A-minor, HAM2, 274; Sonata in D-major, K. 119, NAWM2, 107

Muffat, Theophil (1690-1770), *Final,* from a suite for harpsichord, HAM2, 280

Platti, Giovanni (c. 1700-after 1740), Opus I, No 2, sonata, harpsichord, HAM2, 284

Rutini, Giovanni Maria Placido (c. 1730-1797), Opus VI, No 6, sonata, last movement, harpsichord or piano, rococo, HAM2, 302

Empfindsamkeit
Bach, Wilhelm Friedemann (1710-1784),*Polonaise II,* harpsichord or piano, HAM2, 288; *Fugue IV,* fugue, harpsichord or piano , HAM2, 289

Bach, Karl Philipp Emanuel (1714-1788), Fantasia, piano or clavichord, HAM2, 297; Sonata, 1st movement, piano or clavichord; Sonanta IV in A-major, 2nd movement, NAWM2, 108

Chamber Music

Telemann, Georg Philipp (1681-1767), *Fantasie* for violin solo, sonata, TEM, 48; Sonata, 1st mvt, for flute, violin, & harpsichord, HAM2, 271

Tartini, Guiseppe (1692-1770), Opus III, no 12, sonata for violin & continuo (style galant), HAM2, 275

Richter, Franz Xavier (1709-1789), String Quartet in B-flat major, Op. 5, No. 2, 3rd movement, NAWM2, 111

Orchestral Music

Italian:

Sammartini, Giovanni Battista (1701-1775), Symphony in D-major, HAM2, 283; Symphony in F-major, No 32, 1st movement, NAWM2, 113

The Mannheim School

Stamitz, Johann (1717-1757), Opus V, No 2, Symphony, HAM2, 294; Sinfonia in E-flat major, 1st movement, NAWM2, 113

Richter, Franz Xavier (1709-1789), Opus V, No 2, Symphony, HAM2, 294; Sinfonia in E-flat major, 1st movement, NAWM2, 114

The Viennese School:

Monn, Georg Matthias (1717-1750), Symphony in D-major, HAM2, 295

Vocal Music

Church Music

Couperin, François (*le Grand)* (1668-1733), *Qui dat nivem,* motet, solo voice, HAM2, 266

Telemann, Georg Philipp (1681-1767), *"Chor der seligen"* from *Tag des Gerichtes,* oratorio (Sturm und Drang), HAM2, 272

Terradellas, Domenico (1713-1751), *"in vasto mare infido",* motet, solo voice, HAM2, 298

Jommelli, Niccolo (1714-1744), *Mors et vita,* motet, solo voices, HAM2, 299

Comic Opera

Pergolesi, Giovanni Battista (1710-1736), *"Misero"* from *Liviett e Tracollo* , intermezzi, TEM, 50; *"Le virtuose"* from *Il maestro di musica,* opera, aria, HAM2, 286; *"Lo conosco",* duet from *La serva Padrona*, intermezzi, HAM2, 287; recitative and air from ibid., *Ah quanto mi sa male-Son imbrogliato io,* NAWM2, 121

Pepusch, John Christopher (1667--1752), "My love is all madness" from *Beggar's opera*, ballad opera, HAM2, 264a; "Hither, dear husband" fr *Beggar's opera,* HAM2, 264b; ibid. scenes 11-13, NAWM1, 81

Rousseau, Jean Jacques (1712-1778), *"Allons danser"*, air from *Le devin du village*, (intermède), HAM2, 291; Scene 1, air from ibid. *J'ai perdu tout mon bonheur,* NAWM2, 122

Hiller, Johann Adam (1728-1804), *"Bald die Blonde, bald die Braune* " from *Lisuart und Dariolette*, opera-Singspiel, pre-classical, HAM2, 301

Galuppi, Baldassare (1706-1785), *"Da me non speri"* from *Il filosofo di campagna,* HAM2, 285

Piccinni, Nicola (1728-1800), *"Achetez à ma boutique",* aria from *Le Faux Lord,* pre-classical, HAM2, 300

Opera-ballet

Campra, André (1660-1744), *Chaconne* from *Les Fêtes Vénitiennes*, TEM, 45

England

Arne, Thomas Augustine (1710-1778), "Come, O come my dearest" from *The Fall of Phaeton*, song (rococo), HAM2, 290

Watteau (1684-1721) was the leading painter of the Rococo. The period emphasized sentimental love scenes in bucolic settings with Lords and Ladies dressed in the highest fashion . Left is from a sketch for "The Embarkation for Cytherea", an island associated with the Goddess Venus. (After Pischel, A World History of Art)

Music	Political History	Intellectual History	Art
1697 Campra, *L'Europe galante, opéra ballet* **1700** Bach at Lüneberg			
	1700-1746 Philip V , King of Spain	**1700** Congreve, *The Way of the World,* comedy	
1701 Muffat, *12 Concerti grossi*	**1701-13** Frederick I , King of Prussia	**1701** Yale College founded	**1702** Watteau in Paris
1703 Handel at Hamburg **1704** Handel, *St. John Passion* 1st Bach cantatas Telemann founds Collegium musicum at Leipzig	**1703** St. Petersburg founded **1702-14** Anne, queen of England War of the Spanish Succession, efforts of Louis XIV to extend French power	**1704** Daniel Defoe, in prison, begins *The Review,* weekly newspaper	**1703** Work begun on Buckingham Palace, London
1706 Rameau, 1st book of clavecin pieces Handel in Italy **1707** Alessandro Scarlatti, *Mitridate eupatore,* opera **1708-17** Bach at Weimar-organ works	**1706** Charles XII of Sweden defeats Russians and Saxons at Franstadt		**1707** Fischer von Erlach, Kollegen-Kirche in Salzburg completed
1709 1st pianoforte *opera buffa* in Italy **1710** Campra, *Fêtes venitiennes* Handel in England		**1709** *The Tatler* & *The Spectator* founded **1710** George Berkeley, *The Principles of Human Understanding*	**1710** Sir Christopher Wren, St. Paul's Cathedral, London, completed

Music	Political History	Intellectual History	Art
1711 Keiser, *Croesus*, Handel, *Rinaldo*, opera	**1711-1740** Charles VI, Holy Roman Emperor	**1711** Pope, *Essay on Criticism* **1712** Pope, *Rape of the Lock*	**1711** Kneller founds London Academy of Arts
1713 F. Couperin, *Pièces de Clavecin I*	**1713** Peace of Utrecht		**1713** Watteau, *L'Indifférent*
1714 Bach, cantata, Ich hatte viel Bekümmernis,	**1714-27** George I, Handel's patron in Hanover, King of England	**1714** Leibniz, *Monadologie*	
1715 Founding of *opéra comique* A. Scarlatti, *Tigrane*	**1715** Death of Louis XIV	**1715** Alain Lesage, *Gil Blas*	**1715** Beginning of Rococo
1716 Handel, *Water Music* Couperin, *L'Art de toucher clavecin*			
1717-23 Bach at Cöthen, chamber music			**1717** Watteau, *Embarkation for Cytherea,* major Rococo art work
	1718 Quadruple Alliance, England, France, the Empire, & Holland	**1719** Rediscovery of Pompeii & Herculaneum Daniel Defoe, *Robinson Crusoe*	
1720 Marcello, *Il teatro alla modo*	**1720** Collapse of the South Seas Company		
1721 Bach, *Brandenburg Concertos; French & English Suites*		**1721** Montesquieu, *Lettres Persanes*	
1722 Bach, *Well-Tempered Clavier I* Rameau, *Traité de l'harmonie*			
1723-50 Bach at Leipzig- cantatas			

Music	Political History	Intellectual History	Art
1723 Bach, *St. John Passion* 1724 Handel, *Giulio Cesare*, opera 1725 *Concerts spirituel*, Paris J. Fux, *Gradus ad Parnassum* 1726 Vivaldi, *The Seasons* Rameau, *Nouveau système de musique théorique* 1727 Handel, *Coronation Anthem* 1728 Gay and Pepusch, *Beggar's Opera* Bach, cantata, *Ein feste Burg* 1729 Bach, *St. Matthew Passion;* 1730 Bach, cantata, *Ein feste Burg* Hasse, opera, *Artaserse* 1731 Bach, *Clavier-übung* Part I 1733 Giovanni Pergolesi, *La Serva padrona*	1724 Paris Bourse opens 1727-60 George II of England reigns 1731 Treaty of Vienna between England, Holland Spain, & the Empire 1733 Founding of Georgia War of the Polish Succession	1723 Voltaire, *La Henriade*, epic poem on Henry IV 1726 Jonathan Swift, *Gulliver's Travels* 1731 Abbé Prévost, *Manon Lescaut* 1732 Voltaire, *Zaïre*	1724 Figueroa, West entrance, St. Telmo Palace, Seville, Spain 1726-28 Tiepolo, frescoes in the Palace, Udine 1728 Chardin, *Rain* 1731 Hogarth, *Harlot's Progress*

Music	Political History	Intellectual History	Art
1734 Bach, *Christmas Oratorio* Tartini, Sonatas Op. 1 for violin Sammartini, 1st 4-mvt symphony			**1734** Boucher, *Rinaldo and Armida*
1735 Rameau, *Les Indes galantes*	**1735** W. Pitt elected to Parliament	**1735** Linnaeus, *Systema naturae*, origin of the modern system of classification of plants and animals	**1735** Hogarth, *A Rake's Progress*
1736 Handel, *Alexander's Feast*	**1736-39** Russo-Turkish war		
1737 Rameau, *Castor et Pollux*, opera Domenico Scarlatti, first published sonatas San Carlo Opera opens at Naples		**1737** First lodge of Masons in Germany	**1737** Boucher, designs for Beauvais tapestries Chardin, *La Gouvernante*
1738 D.Scarlatti, *Eser-cizi*, (sonatas) Bach, B-minor Mass Handel, oratorios: *Saul, Israel in Egypt*		**1738** Methodist Church founded by Wesley & Whitefield	
1739 Handel, *Concerti grossi* Mattheson, *Der vollkommene Kapellmeister*	**1739** Turks threaten Belgrade	**1739** Hume, *A Treatise of Human Nature*	
	1740 War of the Austrian Succession to1746 Frederick the Great of Prussia to 1786 Age of Enlightened Despots to 1796	**1740** Samuel Richardson, *Pamela*, first novel	**1740** Giovanni Tiepolo, *Triumph of Amphitrite*
1741 Gluck, *Artaserse*, opera		**1741** Voltaire, *Mahomet*, tragedy	

Music	Political History	Intellectual History	Art
1740-71 Graun at Berlin **1741-57** Joh. Stamitz at Mannheim **1742** Bach, *Goldberg Variations* Handel.*Messiah,* perf., Dublin C.P.E. Bach, *Prussian Sonatas* for piano **1743** Handel. *Samson,* oratorio **1744** C.P.E. Bach, *Württemberg Sonatas,* piano **1745** Gluck in England **1746** Handel,*Judas Maccabaeus ,* oratorio **1747** Bach, *Musical Offering* Handel, *Joshua,* **1749** Bach, *Art of Fugue* Rameau, *Zoroastre,* opera **1750** *Beggar's Opera* perf. in N.Y. **1752** *La Serva padrona* perf. in Paris War of the buffoons **1753** Rousseau, *Le devin du village*	**1742-45** Charles VII, Holy Roman Emperor **1746-1759** Ferdinand I of Spain	**1743** Voltaire, *Mérope* **1748** Montesquieu, *The Spirit of Law* Voltaire, *Zadoc* Klopstock, *Der Messias* **1750** Fielding, *Tom Jones* Buffon, *Histoire naturelle* Richardson,*Clar -issa* (senti- mentality)	**1741** Boucher, *Autumn* **1742** completion of opera house at Mannheim **1746** Boucher, *Toilet of Venus* **1747** Fredrick the Great's castle at Potsdam, *Sans souci*

BIBLIOGRAPHY

GENERAL REFERENCE AND ART HISTORY

Barnes, Harry Elmer, *An Intellectual & Cultural History of the Western World.* 3 vols. New York: Dover, 1965.

Bridgwater, W. and Seymour Kurtz, eds. *The Columbia Encyclopedia,* 3rd ed. New York: Columbia Univ. Press, 1967

Brinton, Crane, *Ideas and Men.* Englewood Cliffs: Prentice-Hall, 1950.

Bronowski, J. & Mazlish, Bruce, *The Western Intellectual Tradition.* New York: Harper, 1960.

Bronowski, J., *The Ascent of Man.* Boston: Little, Brown 1973.

Eisler, Colin, *Flemish & Dutch Drawings.* Boston: Little, Brown 1963.

Grun, Bernard, *The Timetables of History.* New York: Simon & Schuster, 1979.

Hamilton, Edith, *Mythology.* New York: Little, Brown, 1942.

Pike, E. Royston, *Encyclopedeia of Religion & Religions.* New York: Meridian, 1958.

Pischel, Gina, *A World History of Art.* New York: Newsweek, 1978.

Robb, David M. & Garrison, M. A., *Art in the Western World.* New York: Harper, 1953.

Russell, Bertrand, *A History of Western Philosophy.* New York: Simon & Schuster, 1945.

Sachs, Curt, *The Commonwealth of Art.* New York: Norton, 1946.

Winks, Robin, Crane Brinton, John B. Christopher, and Robert L. Wolff, *A History of Civilization,* Vol I: *Prehistory to 1750,* 7th ed. Englewood Cliffs: Prentice Hall, 1988

Wölfflin, Heinrich, *Principles of Art History*. Trans. M. D. Hottinger. New York: Dover, 1932.

GENERAL REFERENCE, MUSIC

Apel, Willi, *Harvard Dictionary of Music*. Cambridge: Harvard Univ. Press, 1969.

Grout, Donald J., *A History of Western Music*. New York: Norton, 1960.

Hindley, Geoffrey, ed., *The Larousse Encyclopedeia of Music*. London: Hamlyn, 1971.

Lang, Paul Henry, *Music in Western Civilization*. New York: Norton, 1941.

Sadie, Stanley, ed., *The New Grove dictionary of Music & Musicians*. London: Macmillan, 1982.

Slonimsky, Nicolas, *Baker's Biographical Dictionary of Musicians*. New York: G. Schirmer, 1958. (latest edition,1992)

Weiss, Piero and Richard Taruskin, *Music in the Western World. New York:* Schirmer, 1984. (a selection of documents)

ANTHOLOGIES OF MUSIC SCORES

Davison, Archibald T. & Apel, Willi, eds., *Historical Anthology of Music*. 2 vols. Cambridge: Harvard Univ. Press, 1950.

Geiringer, Karl, *Music of The Bach Family*. Cambridge: 1955

Palisca,Claude V., ed. *Norton Anthology of Western Music*. New York: Norton, 1988.

Parrish, Carl & Ohl, John F., *Masterpieces of Music Before 1750*. New York: Norton, 1951.

Parrish, Carl, ed., *A Treasury of Early Music*. New York: Norton, 1958.

Schering, Arnold, *Geschichte der Musik in Beispielen*. Leipzig: Breitkopf und Härtel, 1931.

MUSICAL INSTRUMENTS

Baines, Anthony, *Musical Instruments Through the Ages*
London: Penguin, 1969.

Carse, Adam, *The History of Orchestration* New York:
Dover, 1964.

ANCIENT HISTORY, GENERAL

Aristotle, *Politics & Poetics*. Trans. B. Jowett & T. Twining.
New York: World, 1952.

Leakey, L. S. B., *Adam's Ancestors*. New York: Harper,
1960.

Plato, *The Republic*. Trans by B. Jowett. Cleveland: World,
1946.

HISTORY OF ANCIENT MUSIC

Idelsohn, A. Z., *Jewish Music*. New York: Tudor, 1948.

Sendrey, Alfred, *Music in Ancient Israel*. New York:
Philosophical Library, 1969.

Wellesz, Egon, ed., *Ancient & Oriental Music*. London:
Oxford Univ. Press, 1957.

MEDIEVAL HISTORY, GENERAL

Duby, Georges, *The Age of the Cathedrals*. Trans E. Levieux
& B. Thompson. Chicago: Univ. of Chicago Press, 1981.

Heer, Friedrich, *The Medieval World*. Trans. J. Sondheimer.
New York: New American Library, 1962.

Huizinga, J., *The Waning of the Middle Ages*. New York:
Doubleday, 1954.

Waddell, Helen, *The Wandering Scholars*. New York:
Doubleday, 1955.

HISTORY OF MEDIEVAL MUSIC

Apel, Willi, *The Notation of Polyphonic Music 900-1600.* 5th
ed., rev. Cambridge: Medieval Academy of America, 1961.
Apel, Willi, *Gregorian Chant.* Bloomington: Indiana Univ.
Press, 1958.
Reese, Gustave, *Music in the Middle Ages.* New York:
Norton, 1940.

RENAISSANCE HISTORY, GENERAL

Burckhardt, Jacob, *The Civilization of the Renaissance in
Italy.* Trans. S. G. C. Middlemore & I. Gordon. New York:
New American Lib., 1960.

HISTORY OF RENAISSANCE MUSIC

Reese, Gustave, *Music in the Renaissance.* New York:
Norton, 1954.

HISTORY OF BAROQUE MUSIC

Bukofzer,Manfred F., *Music in the Baroque Era.* New York:
Norton, 1947.
Geiringer, Karl, *The Bach Family.* New York: Oxford
University Press: 1954

HISTORY OF PRE-CLASSIC MUSIC

Einstein, Alfred, *Gluck.* Trans. Eric Blom. New York: Collier,
1936.
Pauly, Reinhard G., *Music in the Classic Period.* Englewood
Cliffs: Prentice-Hall, 1965.
Rosen, Charles, *The Classic Style.* New York: Norton, 1972

LIST OF ABBREVIATIONS

GMB
Arnold Schering, ed., *Geschichte der musik in Beispielen,* [History of Music in Examples], Leipzig, 1931, reprint, New York, 1950, editing not always reliable by modern standards. Scores, notes [in German] .

HAM1
Archibald T. Davison and Willi Apel, eds., *Historical Anthology of Music*, Cambridge, 1950. Vol I: Oriental, Medieval, and Renaissance Music. Scores, notes and translations

HAM2
Archibald T. Davison and Willi Apel, eds., *Historical Anthology of Music*, Cambridge, 1950. Vol II: Baroque, Rococo and Pre-Classical Music. Scores, notes and translations.

MM
Carl Parrish and John F. Ohl, eds. Masterpieces of Music before 1750, New York, 1951. Scores, notes and translations. A most useful brief anthology for the student.

NAWM1
Claude V. Palisca, ed., *Norton Anthology of Western Music,* 2nd Ed., New York, 1980. Vol I, Medieval, Renaissance, and Baroque Music. Scores, notes and translations.

NAWM2
Claude V. Palisca, ed., *Norton Anthology of Western Music,* 2nd Ed., New York, 1980. Vol II, Classic, Romantic, and Modern Music. Scores, notes and translations.

TEM
Carl Parrish, ed., *A Treasury of Early Music,* New York, 1958. Scores, notes, and translations. Supplements MM

INDEX

a cappella, 196, 281
Academie de poesie et musique, 156
accentual verse, 60
accentualist school, 39
Ad organum faciendum, 73
Adam de la Halle, 65; *"Robin m'aime"* from *Le Jeu de Robin et Marian,* 65
Adonis, 9
Aeschylus, 4
affections, 194, 218, 302, 329, 356, 358
affective representation, 199, 283
Age of Reason, 269
Agnus dei, 37, 46
Ainsworth, 229
airs de cour, 225
alba, 65
Albert V of Bavaria, 165
Alberti bass, 377, 378
Albigenses, 64
Aldhelm, 71
Alexander the Great, 31
Alia musica, 40
Alkaios, 10
allegro finale, 388
alleluia, 30, 42, 44, 58
allemande, 251, 252, 286
Alma Redemptoris Mater, 40, 59
Alypios, 5, 12, 29
Amati, 162
Amati, Nicolo, 162, 200, 249
Ambrosian chant (chap. 1), 33
Anakreon, 10
anglaise, 286

Anglican Church, 229
anhemitone pentatonic scale, 1
anthem, 151, 169, 229f
antiphon, 38, 59, 207
Antiphonal singing, 15, 148
Antiphonary of Leon (1066), 34
antiphony, 29, 43
Apollo, 2, 6ff
Arabs, 13
Arcadelt, Jacob, 127, 152
Archilochus of Paros, 10
Archimedes, 190
Archipoeta, 60
aria, 199, 206, 209, 217, 218, 220, 227, 233, 326, 331, 333f, 341f, 355, 358, 378; cantabile, 295; da bravura, 295; da capo, 218, 231, 275, 277, 293, 301; di mezzo carattere, 295; strophic, 218, 231, 254
Arias, Bishop, 28
arioso, 217f, 227, 230, 355, 384
Ariosto, 152, 356, *Orlando furioso,* 355, 357
Aristophanes, 4, 11
Aristotle, 4f, 29
Aristoxenus, 4
Arnaut Daniel, 66
Ars Antiqua, 106
Ars Nova, 106, see also Philippe de Vitry
Athanasius, 28
Attaingnant, 156, 244
Attila, 28
aubade, 65